GLOBAL LIMITS

SUNY series in Global Politics
James N. Rosenau, Editor

GLOBAL LIMITS

Immanuel Kant, International Relations, and Critique of World Politics

Mark F. N. Franke

State University of New York Press

Cover art: Portrait of Immanuel Kant ca. 1790, artist unknown. Courtesy of Kant-Forschungsstelle der Universitat Mainz.

Published by
State University of New York Press, Albany

Printed in the United States of America

For information, address the State University of New York Press,
90 State Street, Suite 700, Albany, N.Y. 12207

Production by Diane Ganeles
Marketing by Patrick Durocher

Library of Congress Cataloging-in-Publication Data

Franke, Mark F. N., 1963–
Global limits : Immanuel Kant, international relations, and critique of world politics / Mark F. N. Franke.
p. cm. — (SUNY series in global politics)
Includes bibliographical references and index.
ISBN 0-7914-4987-4 (alk. paper) — ISBN 0-7914-4988-2 (pbk. : alk. paper)
1. International relations—Philosophy. 2. Political science—Philosophy. I. Title. II. Series.

JZ1242.F73 2001
327.1'01—dc21 00-061923

10 9 8 7 6 5 4 3 2 1

Dedicated in loving memory to my greatest of playmates,
Juergen "Paddy" Franke

Contents

Acknowledgments

As my research interests progressed from political philosophy toward international relations in the early 1990s, it was not my intention to write a book on Immanuel Kant. To be honest, my first encounters with *Critique of Pure Reason* left me ungratified. I was happy to leave such study in the awkward struggles of my undergraduate education. However, in 1991, Rob Walker quietly urged me to return to Kant, with a broader look into his writings on history, politics, and ethics. And it was through these initially reluctant re-readings of Kant that the study of international relations truly gained importance for me.

I am deeply grateful to Rob for having drawn me back to Kant. And I thank him for the many words of encouragement and criticism he has offered over the past years, as I have ultimately developed that early inquiry toward a larger study of both personal and academic significance.

The general lack of serious attention to political philosophy in international relations on the North American scene forced me to operate largely *in-between* these fields. As a result, much of the work in writing this book was conducted in relative solitude. And for this reason itself, I accept full responsibility for any errors and misreadings that may occur within the text. However, several mentors and colleagues have contributed richly to the successful development of this project.

David Campbell helped me considerably in the early years of my research on Kant to more fully appreciate the deep theoretical stakes within the discipline of international relations. In this way, David lead me to understand the larger consequences of taking on a critical reading of Kant in this field.

I am thankful to William E. Connolly, James Tully, and Daniel Weinstock for taking the time to read and comment on most or all of this manuscript in its rough forms. Each offered powerful points of insight and criticism on specific aspects of my arguments that ultimately lead me to write a much better book.

From his very rigorous, thorough, and attentive readings of each rough draft of this manuscript, Siba N. Grovogui also provided me with invaluable points of constructive criticism and advice. He helped me to correct and sharpen my arguments and gave me considerable help in constructing the final and overall vision of this book. Moreover, I am forever indebted to Sibagro for his unfailing support and care in this undertaking. Without his tremendous encouragement and advocacy this project never would have come to fruition.

Finally, I give great thanks to Norma and Paddy Franke, Brett Grubisic, Heidi and Andy Holota, Jill Rusin, Kara Shaw, and Bryan Young. Throughout the research and writing of this book, these dear friends and family members took me and my work seriously. Through many conversations and expressions of support, they each helped me to find purpose and happiness in my efforts. And, most important, they challenged me, in diverse respects, to try to write this book with social meaning and value.

Introduction: Kant in International Relations

On the surface, the flow of this book may appear divided in its attentions. In much of what follows, I aim to pose serious questions to the ways in which theories of international relations have been historically constructed in reference to the works of Immanuel Kant. To this end, I ultimately explore the potential for describing an approach to international politics that more appropriately corresponds to the heart of Kant's own project. However, I also submit his political philosophy itself to substantial critical evaluation. And, on this basis, I identify within the crux of Kant's concerns for international politics self-defeating flaws. Furthermore, I suggest enormous problems in developing a successful Kantian theory of international relations whatsoever. Thus, one may wonder whether the primary intent of this study is to scrutinize recent and contemporary modes of international relations theory or to engage the international thought of Kant.

My general point of departure in this book, however, is that there is no fundamental disconnect between these two concerns. On the contrary, I contend that modern studies of international relations are inextricably linked with Kant's political philosophy. Certainly, students of international relations typically learn the discipline without any direct reflection on his writings. And Kant's presence in studies of international relations is expressed mostly in terms of the authority he may lend to several influential trains of thought and analysis. But, the importance of his work to the discipline does not reside simply within scholarly reference or questions of analytical accuracy. To begin with, Kant's ideas provide much of the framework through which international relations is now regularly conceived. And, as I argue extensively in this book, the substantial ground that international relations theory draws from his thought also provokes difficult points of debate that remain uncomfortably alive and unresolved within the discipline. Moreover, the failures of Kant's own approach to international politics indicate specific weaknesses inherent to discourses of international relations themselves. Thus, scholars of international relations must inevitably engage his philosophy in a serious manner. Until they do so, the efficacy of their own work and that of the discipline itself are placed into considerable doubt.

Strong analysis of the deep connection between Kant and studies of international relations in general is extremely rare, though. And this is ironically the case. For, Kant's thought is seldom engaged in the development of international relations theory most probably because of the depth to which specific readings of his work and projects are already assumed within the discipline. The majority of international relations scholars neither directly subscribe to or even are particularly aware of Kant's political and international theory. Yet, one can see the broader aims of his philosophical project consistently affirmed across the discipline. Rather than respecting and responding in any substantial manner to the theoretical controversy his work introduces to the study of international politics, scholars of international relations regularly develop their work as if Kant's contributions to modern thought provide a completed platform from which one may build appropriate worldviews, theories, explanations, and perceptions with respect to the international. Consequently, while the significance of his philosophy to the discipline is largely neglected, Kant's work is rendered into at least one of its foundational points of departure. And, interestingly, the study of international relations takes up a philosophical challenge formally indistinguishable from that pursued by Kant. It is thus within critical evaluation of his international theory that highly effective assessment and judgment of the discipline may begin.

Assuming the completion or potential finality of the Kantian project is precisely where theories of international relations signal a great failing. It conjointly displays the folly of having taken and promoted cursory readings of a foundational figure where such readings have little basis and ignore the full challenge that his thought demands. For, as I further demonstrate in this book, by no means do the Kantian aims that are mimicked in the discipline offer lasting or complete grounds on which to build and develop a certain understanding of international relations and politics. Missed in both readings of Kant and the conventional understandings offered by international relations theorists of their own discipline is the fact that a unified vision and study of inter-communal relations pervading the politics of all human societies on a world-wide level is at the very least a highly questionable goal. Consideration of the Kantian project and its example in the discipline of international relations, rather, must ultimately discover the impossibility of ever producing such understanding. Tracing the intellectual embrace between Kant's philosophy and the discipline shows that international relations can never represent the universe of human social and political life but is itself an illusory concept, embedded always in local and particular interests and politics.

A serious reading of Kant in international relations does not explain a specific historical tradition to international thought that may or may not be adopted. Rather, it shows crucial points at which theories of international relations must fail on two counts. First, reading Kant in international relations exposes a series of false and unexamined impressions from which international relations theory has been either built or built against. And, second, it describes important challenges that the discipline has avoided through the accepted authority of Kant but for which it has yet to provide adequate answers. But, through the betrayal of faults in both Kant and theories of international relations, such a reading may also give rise to the very productive ground through which a more viable approach to international politics may be conceived. By taking up the challenge that Kant and the discipline themselves so far fail to meet and by learning from these failures, it is possible to begin the work of re-imagining what it would mean to approach politics on an international scale in appropriate and productive means.

Politics of Theory Confronts the World

Kant was the preeminent philosopher of the European Enlightenment, living, writing, and teaching in the distant East Prussian center of Königsberg. His academic achievements in anthropology, logic, epistemology, metaphysics, and ethics are generally recognized as belonging among the greatest and most influential moments within the chronicle of Western thought. It is even regularly suggested that the true shift toward modern thinking may be traced to Kant's "critical" turn. For, perhaps the most definitively modern feature of his philosophy, running through all his varied interests, is the attempt to establish the final limits under which human life may be appropriately studied, judged, and enjoyed.

Continuing early-modern attempts to break from the command of Christian moral dogma and eschatology, Kant sought, from the position of human thought and being itself, a manner by which legitimate bearings for knowledge, truth, ethics, and political policy may be established for humans in their social lives. While the Christian God remains an important figure for Kant personally and as an idea, he strove from a finite worldly perspective to describe with precision the experiential and rational limits with which humans must finally contend. From this position, he dares not only to suggest the knowability of such bearings to thought and action; he goes further to describe in some detail what must follow morally, socially, and politically from such knowledge.

Theories of international relations are similarly concerned with questions about limits. It is in this way that they reproduce, in allegedly more practical terms, Kant's search to know the world and his arrogance in making claims to knowing how to know it. The very *discipline* that the discipline of international relations offers consists, first, in a description of the ultimate boundaries to human life and, on that basis, the limits of practical reason within the modern state. Second, it expresses a set of rules regarding how one can expect human social and political life to develop in accordance with such bounds. While individual scholars in the discipline may focus on such matters as the formation of the European economic union, Indian/Pakistani conflict, fishing disputes between Canada and the United States on the open ocean, the proliferation of nuclear threats to international security, and the relative effectiveness of United Nations' peace-keeping efforts, the discipline as a whole seeks to establish the confines within which the study of such issues can justifiably take place. Moreover, it sets out to determine the limits in which the agents involved in specific practices of international relations must understand themselves to be acting.

Those working within the discipline may at times represent problems and events in the relations between states as confusing or ambiguous. However, such an admission cannot be made without simultaneously promoting the idea, as fact, that there exists a certain and potentially knowable dimension of politics, beyond the state, that rightfully contains all instances of the local and specific. As R. B. J. Walker observes:

> To ask how theories of international relations manage to constrain all intimations of a chronopolitics within the ontological determinations of a geopolitics, within the bounded geometric spaces of here and there, is to become increasingly clear about the rules under which it has been deemed possible to speak about politics at all.[1]

Without the concept of a final space, surrounding all other geopolitical divisions, in which non-domestic politics should be understood to occur, one could not meaningfully speak of politics in the international, the world, or the globe. And, it is the function of international relations theory to establish the viable borders of such cartography. Furthermore, without the universal limits provided by the idea of "the international," there can be no clear ground on which to study national, domestic, or local politics either.

In the course of Kant's lifetime (1724–1804), the modern nation-state was beginning to develop as a means through which certainty, peace, order, unity, and calculability could be established in social and political life. Along with this development came the lesson that, while danger, conflict, and disorder might be largely excluded from the confines of civil society, these anarchic forces inevitably still condition the ultimate viability of the state externally. Neither the nation-state nor any form of local politics can contain themselves. They remain subject to world-wide movements, interests, and disasters, the most dramatic of all being war. So, as Kant concludes, the good life of the polis is knowable and practicable in any final manner only insofar as it is cast within an international perspective and approach. The universe of human politics must itself be known and, from that point, secured in order for all particular forms of human political life, and human knowledge of these particular forms, to themselves be peaceful and without doubt. Consequently, and as Walker continues:

> As discourses about limits and dangers, about the presumed boundaries of political possibility in the space and time of

> the modern state, theories of international relations express and affirm the necessary horizons of the modern political imagination.[2]

For there must be some form of container to one's political vision if the things and events one hopes to include in that view are to make sense and truly make a world with respect to one another.

The fundamental philosophical challenge taken on by the discipline of international relations, however, is by no means easily met. Despite the variety of approaches that fall within the broad discourse that constitutes modern theories of international relations, they all ultimately reproduce ways of expressing the limits of human experience and reason as articulated by Kant.[3] Implicitly, if not explicitly, they all seek to establish the precise singularity of the world that demarcates international politics within a specific set of conceivable relations. And, in this manner, each particular theoretical tradition, approach, or form of analysis employed in the study of international politics is rooted within conditions similar to those of the modern nation-state.

Scholars who wish to secure the intellectual and methodological integrity of their projects, must establish and admit to a universal discipline for inquiry into the international. If any investigation into politics in the world is to succeed in facing up to its inescapable philosophical challenge, of asserting the final limits to social and political life, and if inquiries must be conditioned within that broadest of contexts themselves, the investigator must be willing to enter a community of general international scholarship. Posing as a universal body itself, as in the International Studies Association or the International Political Science Association, such a community may then at least give the semblance of a unity in vision and, therefore, execute a performance of self-legitimization. Under such literal discipline, scholars of international politics may suggest that interdisciplinary and democratic consensus is ultimately possible regarding what the world is and how to approach it. And from this dramatic point, the social sciences and humanities with more local or domestic orientation, in which the general study of international relations must itself gain legitimization, will in turn enjoy the apparently solid bearings of their own disciplinary sovereignty from which to proceed in their respective projects.

The study of international relations thus not only adopts and champions the philosophical concerns and goals of Kant, it is committed to his politics as well. The very idea of a singular discipline of inquiry and analysis known as "international relations" is a response to political conflict between instances and modes of inquiry themselves. Just as Kant seeks a universal guide, grounded in communal public debate, to settle conflict in the human faculties, the function of the discipline of international relations is ultimately to provide the idea of a singular world to which all inquiries and interest ought to submit. Thereby, competing scholarship in the study of international relations may also enjoy its debates in relative amity. With the presumption of a prior singular realm to which all objects of study may and ought to conform, the other human sciences may find their own place in the peaceful order of curiosity, research, and knowledge. Theorists and practitioners of state politics, in particular, may then collectively determine how inter-community relations are best or most effectively worked through.

The kind of disciplinary and intellectual consensus or community required by scholars of international relations and Kant, respectively, however, cannot be reached by simply asking all concerned to observe the universal frontiers to human life and thought that already manifestly exist. If these things could be detected by direct empirical means, there would be no substantial source of disagreement and conflict to begin with. Rather, along with Kant, those seeking to fulfill the promise of international relations as a discipline must and do deduce the boundaries they seek from the particulars within view that already appear to stand on their own. The point is to determine how the broadest limits must be, given reflection on how finite limits emerge within the human universe, whatever that is.

Here, both scholars of international relations and Kant focus primarily on the modern republic. The republic is of most interest, because it is taken to represent a state legitimately and justly formed by the people or nation subject to its laws and institutions. It is not the result of mere might or tyranny. In each case, republics therefore appear as somehow naturally forming sub-universes of human culture and behavior within the ultimate yet unseen world of humanity and nature. To begin with, the republic is a mode of the modern nation-state, which allegedly may house the largest forms of social, political, and intellectual unity within itself. Such a state is thus conventionally taken as the central and primary actor in world politics. Furthermore, it is a state that, ideally, gains its unity through the will of the people at large, not simply at the will or interest of a monarch, aristocracy, or majority. Hence, the republic is truly sovereign in itself and, thus, self-legitimizing. It is a solid feature, a keystone, from which ultimate limits supposedly may be reckoned.

Assuming the calm or potential calm represented politically in the sovereign republic, both Kant and scholars of international relations then are able to portray and project the theoretical sovereignty of their parallel projects. As Jens Bartelson puts it, "Sovereignty and knowledge implicate each other logically and produce each other historically."[4] The authorized closure of human life in a particular way provides the apparently definitive structure around which truths may be woven. Similarly, the weight of disciplined knowledge gives legitimacy to certain representations of the fabric of human life and condition. The idea of an international order of some sort is shown to be intellectually and politically important for the very safety and survival of the domestic communities that groups of humans create for themselves. In addition, it is then possible to describe how this international realm must be thought and realized in order to benefit republican life as it is seen to be in its various real examples. On this basis, peace of mind and body become at least thinkable.

Nicholas Onuf traces the philosophical and historical relationship between republicanism and the very notion of an international realm in his important recent text, *The Republican Legacy in International Thought*.[5] While mindful of the fact that republicanism and international thought result from apparently divergent concerns, the former being a resolution to the demands of political community and the latter addressing the needs of a society of communities, he provides detailed evidence to illustrate how one always requires the other. With a focus on Kant, along with Aristotle and Emmerich de Vattel, Onuf's concern is to show that international thought could not proceed as it does today without a view to republican concerns.[6] Yet he provides the room in which to push this point the other way as well, to argue that republican interests and theory do not enjoy philosophical and historical success until they themselves are cast with a view to the international.

Onuf constructs the important point that the discipline of international relations, along with other forms of inquiry, requires some kind of taxonomy of particulars to even represent and conceive the larger whole of humanity. In this regard, he is particularly interested in the function proposed by levels of analysis in theories of international relations, as popularised by Kenneth Waltz and David Singer. Onuf contends that employing such images as man, the state, and war is not a matter of mere methodological utility. Rather, this kind of sense of particular units and strata in human society are metaphors exemplary of the ancient conventions by which wholes not visible in themselves may be marked and extended.[7] For Onuf also, the very structure and motive of international thought is thus thoroughly Kantian. It complies with Kant's sense that all human thought proceeds in terms of wholes.[8] And since the whole is not itself in view, humans must project a whole over the particulars we feel we can secure intellectually from experience. But we are thus then driven to secure our understandings of particulars in such a way that a human universe may indeed be extended around them with actual unity. Just as international thought requires the apparently stable particular units of republics from which to build a truly applicable concept of the world, republics can only justifiably expect their respective orders to enjoy peace once they are together shaped in terms of a social and political universe applicable to all.

It is not clearly the case, however, that the Kantian view—given at least tacit support, if not dramatic substance, in the discipline of international relations—that rational beings automatically think in terms of wholes, must be accepted so boldly. And it is in this point that the impossibility of international relations is first established. Granted, the thought of anything in particular gains rational meaning insofar as the specific thing may be thought within a fuller context. To contemplate one thing is to conceptually set it apart from other things. It is to establish its meaning in reference to a world of other possible things. But the universal implied in any specific idea or vision need not serve as a final guide to how particulars are to be thought and examined. Even if it is the case that the analysis of communal relations finally presses one toward a conception of international relations, this does not show that there is an international domain that can and ought to accommodate all particular instances of politics and social life.

Acceptance of the notion that one's understandings of particulars must ultimately conform to the appropriate whole that could in fact account for each thing is neither necessary nor natural. It is simply conditioned on a prior sense that the certainty and peace that such a totally organized vision may avail is indeed possible and desirable. This certainty and peace, however, is not obviously within reach or in the least surely welcome. For example, if one is forced to temper one's view to the international by what one knows of the national politics of human communities, there is no reason to believe that any vision of the world would be legitimately defensible. The totality of particular human communities is no more observable than is the international totality that supposedly unites them.

As Bartelson points out:

> In political discourse, centrality and ambiguity usually condition each other over time. A concept becomes central to the extent that other concepts are defined in terms of it, or depend on it for their coherent meaning and use within discourse.[9]

The sovereign republic may accrue an apparently central presence in the conduct of human social life, given that its concept lends itself to such clarity with respect to the political movement and flux it is intended to control in certain respects and exclude in others. On this basis, the nation-state may eventually seem to be the obvious kernel from which the larger sphere of human movements and conflicts is to be inferred. But, this does not mean that the state is therefore any more real or self-explanatory than, for instance, cultural norms, class formation, bioregional spheres, or the pathways of investment capital. Rather, one must admit that any international whole projected as a world-vision is rooted even in one's specific vision of what must universally hold. An international concept is always contestable, based on the infinite possible readings of particulars. The political and intellectual calm that is promised in the ultimate unity of international and republican ideals is therefore not even politically desirable either. For the analytic and social certainty that such a resolution would proffer could only result from the hegemonic imperialist success of one vision of human particulars universalized over all.

Interestingly, though, scholars of international relations continually seek illusory resolutions by which they believe worldly calm may be benignly attained. Desperate to solve a puzzle that in itself cannot be seen, they hopelessly seek for a way in which both the complete picture and the pieces may be identified through each other. Perhaps the most impressive and alluring of recent statements in this fashion is to be found in Andrew Linklater's *The Transformation of Political Community*.[10] And the details of his position in this respect merit considerable attention.

Linklater's analysis and proposals are particularly compelling, because he valiantly tries to adequately address the relationship between universal and particulars in international politics in a manner sensitive to how each term is becoming so thoroughly confused in the contemporary world. In addition to appreciating the theoretical and historical threats that republics face in maintaining social peace and order, he goes one step further to consider more overtly the ways in which national communities today are not so easily distinguishable from one another let alone other particular forms of human social relations.

Linklater recognizes that the unity traditionally associated with states in republican theory is neither natural nor genuine. If such unity exists at all, he insists, it comes about through systematic processes of inclusion and exclusion, through which differences are suppressed both from within and without.[11] It is for this reason that particular communities are morally deficient for the purposes of providing a universal vision and analytic approach to understanding the larger human world around them.[12] However, the rise of ethnic, cultural, and civil fragmentation proliferating within nation-states conjoined with the increasing globalization of economic life, social identities, and cultural experiences, Linklater contends, is bringing about an opportunity in which such moral deficits may be overcome historically.[13] The legitimate sovereignty and singularity of states is being successfully challenged to the point where particular communities are finding themselves more exposed to one another. A universal community of communities is in many ways becoming an inescapable possibility. Still, Linklater realizes that such a prospect also brings with it the danger of broader and more entrenched social divisions on a global scale, as humans across the world are segregated from one another in terms of material inequalities.[14] The false ordering of communities into nation-states may be giving way to unacceptable world-wide divisions of people into economic classes, with the hierarchy of privilege that come with them.

Facing this moment of simultaneous opportunity and danger, Linklater seeks to outline a way in which the play between universality and particularity may find authentic order for contemporary human community. Linklater already agrees that "an elementary universalism underpins the society of states and contributes to the survival of international order."[15] This expresses the point that the logic of republicanism requires an international mind-set at the same time. But with the eroding of the Westphalian ideal, in which the world is divided into distinct autonomous sovereign units, he wishes to discover a more appropriate human particular to serve as the keystone from which the universal is to be deduced and secured. To this end, Linklater focuses on the concept of citizenship. He claims that "citizenship is important because it avails societies of the possibility of overcoming their internal moral deficits."[16] He reasons that attention to the individual rights and interests that humans have with respect to one another may bring about the debate necessary to establish a true level of unity in political community on both a particular and universal scale.

Linklater argues that privileging citizenship, as opposed to alleged national interests, encourages the sort of dialogue needed to effectively fulfill the republican ideal of a community grounded in some commonly held values. Moreover, he submits that placing such debate at the center of a given society must inevitably invite discussion with individuals from outside the borders of community. He presumes that bringing to active communal debate the grounds of exclusion/inclusion on which the particular community is thought is to also bring into question why others are excluded at all.[17] Linklater contends that "modern citizens learn the language of a transcendent moral code which makes the critique of abuses of national power or cultural arrogance and visions of a less hierarchical international society possible."[18] His point is that persons who understand themselves and are able to live their social and political lives as equal individuals first, and not simply members of a singular nation, are prone to see themselves as part of a universe of human beings to which they also have membership. In this way, citizens of any given state may prefer to examine and activate their community needs in terms of the international interests of an imagined humanity.

According to Linklater, the transformation of political community availed by fundamental attention to citizenship will consist in the creation of social relations that "are more universalistic, less unequal and more sensitive to cultural differences."[19] In essence, he imagines here the possibility of a transnational citizenry. And perhaps most crucial of all elements toward this purpose is the conceptual sensitivity to differences between humans as such.[20] Linklater proposes an approach to international politics that is grounded both in the idea as well as the activities of individual human beings not primarily identified with national communities but rather with the condition of being shared universally with others. This is the simple notion of existing as a culturally specific being who nevertheless exists in, among, and through a larger whole of human cultures which, as given, do not necessarily mesh well. From the point of view of global citizenship, wherein basic rights and privileges are distributed equally amongst all persons, regardless of national identity or cultural perspective, he suggests that it may then be possible for a cosmopolitan community of communication to arise.[21] A universe of humanity that is actually responsive to the totality of particular perspectives may then proceed; and the particular identities and behaviors of each person may be so guided as to allow for a peaceful and legitimate universe to unfold.

Put bluntly, Linklater's suggestion is to replace the troubled republic with the individual human as the appropriate particular from which the international can be deduced. And one can see that an analytic focus on the needs, inherent rights, and interests of the individual person may provide a global understanding of how humans should conduct society with one another so that the international does not face them with such threat and danger. However, Linklater does not in this way really offer an alternative to the failures or dangers of republican internationalism at all. For his argument here rests on the prior notion that there simply is a singular universe that does or can embrace the particulars of human life. Being no more able than other theorists of international relations before him to directly perceive this alleged whole, Linklater still develops his argument from the point of view that there must be an international sphere that does or could capture us all. And the task he sets for himself is to find a particular building block from which such a whole may be projected, one that is more sensitive to contemporary political conditions and ideals.

That the vision of a cosmopolitan citizenry engaged in public discourse with one another may seem appealing does not mean, though, that it is any more naturally grounded than the republican ideal. To contemplate a vision in which all particular humans may enjoy a universal community in which their equality and interests are protected by the same rights and privileges extended to all others is to already presuppose that there is a universe of humans in which all members inherently possess the same basic needs and rights. An imagined international sense is already employed to give shape to the particular which, in turn, is to allow for the analytically correct deduction of the international sphere in the end. Linklater's understanding of the transformation of political community is therefore no less oriented in a particular perspective than those working from a European sense of state sovereignty. A specific notion of individual sovereignty is projected onto each possible person prior to any investigation of what that particular being may actually be and how she or he really wishes to express that being.

In this form, Linklater reproduces the interests, methods, and traps of Kant once again. And, this should come as no surprise. Regardless of one's point of departure in the analysis of politics in the world, any attempt to consider how communities and political life of all sorts are to be understood in a general sense sets up a discursive dichotomy between universal and particular without real ground on which to give it global validity. To give in to one's intellectual thirst for wholes in one's thinking about particulars prior to any empirical universal experience of a whole is to privilege the specific as general. It is to engage in a political activity aimed to calm one's own thought irrespective of how the thought of others may be excluded from the international vision thereupon extended.

My effort to privilege and center the Kantian character in studies of international relations is in itself then, of course, also a disciplinary and, therefore, limiting move. I must acknowledge the fact that I myself am describing a specific perspective on international relations that does not necessarily embrace all views of the term either. Directing my focus on what I see as the inevitable Kantianism of any particular theory of international politics, I am giving light to a universal picture of international relations that surely must face its competitors. But it is not my motive here to build yet another whole and total sphere in which the study of international politics is to be considered possible. I do not aim to remap the limits to international relations theory and, hence, the possibility of geopolitical representation. Rather, I offer here a pointedly strategic intervention.

Given the fact that the ultimate limits to human social and political activity are not themselves available for review and because any attempt to infer such limits from particular structures is inherently vulnerable to perspective, I am committed to the importance of keeping these limits *open* to question. This is a point with dramatic political implications, both intellectually and practically. At stake is the possibility of political imagination as well as justification for activity in the world. And, in this regard, I am especially interested in bringing challenges to the Kantian and Kantian-like resolutions that proliferate studies of international relations in the modern era.

Over the past two centuries, privilege of and excitement over the modern individual and the nationally based republic have permitted the world of human life to be structured around two primary, parallel, and mutually supporting dichotomies: individual/cosmopolitan and republican/international. The individual citizen of the state is faced with its normative obligations as a member of the human cosmopolis; the unified spirit of the republic must confront the inescapable danger of the inter-state realm. And while the tensions surrounding the terms of these dichotomies have spawned a range of responses from idealism to realism, globalism to statism, and cosmopolitanism to communitarianism, these ranges of options remain rooted in and propelled by a Kantian view.

Despite the fact that the pull between republicanism and internationalism as well as citizenship and global civil society have produced a selection of highly disparate views, the options available remain framed within specifically Kantian understandings of how politics may ever make sense. Kantian resolutions of the meaning of politics in the world, as described above, are perpetually reproduced under the general rubric of "international relations." The fundamental aims of Kant's project persist as the central driving forces under which modern cultures come to shape their approaches to understanding the world. Regardless of what one thinks of Kant's theory or whether one contemplates his ideas at all, it is, therefore, absolutely crucial that the grounds of his thinking are evaluated in some depth.

In order to effectively bring to question the potential narrowing practices of the discipline of international relations, as it has arisen from its Kantian turn, one must first trace and examine how it is that Kant is able to give the above-mentioned dichotomies such apparent substance in the first place. Furthermore, one must give critical consideration to the precise intellectual and practical exclusions to which his own resolution on this accord give rise. For it is in the act of opening these points of analysis that it may then be possible to truly bring to bear the potential importance of nondisciplined approaches to politics in the world. Without showing that the disciplinary acts reproduced in studies of international relations are themselves authorised through a particular perspective and philosophical interest, the legitimacy of their own framings of political issues in the world goes easily unquestioned. And, as I contend here, at this point in the history of modern Western thought, an important key to such analysis rests in the critical evaluation of Kant's internationalism with respect to the studies that gain their discipline from it.

Interests, Arguments, and Chapters

As is the case with certain other exalted thinkers before and after him, texts written by Kant have been recorded as part of a series of landmarks in political philosophy that inform the study of contemporary international politics as well as the development of modern foreign policy. His texts on politics and history have enjoyed a constant role within discourses of international relations theory. And, throughout the development of the discipline, a small selection of Kant's texts have served as the prominent marker for so-called liberal perspectives on accounting for and predicting politics in the world. His work as well as Kant's very name are generally presented within international relations literature as signs for the pinnacle of an idealism against which a tradition of political realism entrenches itself. In this fashion, he is conventionally received within the discipline as the fundamental proponent of and anchor for a naïve spirit who proposes and predicts an eventual evolution of international relations toward a world-wide peaceful federation of states, wherein basic agreement and consensus may be achieved among all peoples.

In contrast, drawing on received readings of such thinkers as Thucydides, Niccolò Machiavelli, and Thomas Hobbes, various attempts to sustain a mainstream tradition pay attention to the apparently incessant selfish character of states and the recurrent problem of supposed irrational and warmongering state leaders, who pose obstacles to the formation of any formal planetary community. In addition, political realists have spilled much ink in describing and demonstrating the practical impossibility of ever legitimately enforcing truly global interests on an international scale. They note that any such institution of force is vulnerable to the aspirations of dictators of the grandest sort or to the interests of robust states, which realists allege are the ultimate power-brokers in any case. Hence, historically, Kant's efforts remain identified largely as offering an extreme pole to theories of international relations that may be approached as a model only out of hope. His thought offers evidence for the extreme internal opposition and fierce intellectual conflict that has characterized the discipline. In this manner, while providing substantial semblance to the limits of international relations theory itself, his writing has served primarily as a mere point of reference within the debates that have over the past century successively waxed and waned between the great variety of competing shades of realism and idealism. And, over the balance of these debates, with few exceptions,[22] his work itself has rarely been taken up by theorists of international relations for serious mainstream analysis and consideration.

In recent years, however, Kant's texts have gained progressively stronger currency among scholars of international politics. Specific interest in Kant has mushroomed with noteworthy impetus across the subfields of international law, peace studies, theories of war, and international ethics in particular. The concerns here are highly disparate. There are those, such as Andrew Hurrell and Michael C. Williams, who seek to show that the liberal pole of international relations theory is less well anchored in Kant's writings than normally thought. In this way, a renewed interest in Kant is both reflecting and, in part, fueling the more recent disciplinary crises regarding the use of realism and idealism and their relations to one another as theoretical models for international affairs. Moreover, in the context of these debates, scholars such as Richard K. Ashley, Jens Bartelson, W. B. Gallie, Kimberly Hutchings, and Cecilia Lynch, for their own particular reasons and interests, see both specific dangers and potential benefits in stirring and restoring central focus to Kant's ideas. Further, Kant's writings are becoming an exciting region of study with respect to the philosophical debates underlying international relations theory in general.

More distinctly and dramatically, though, one additionally finds writers such as Michael W. Doyle, Wade L. Huntley, and Georg Sørensen who find positively renewed inspiration in Kant's political analysis. For Doyle and his colleagues, Kant's work has begun to emerge less as a mere point of reference and more notably as a practical and revolutionary theoretical ground. Kant develops a sophisticated interest in the complex social and political relations that he believes to persist necessarily amongst people across state borders. And in this view, internationalists such as Doyle find in his writing a more or less appropriate account of and response toward a contemporary world whose social and political arrangement does not translate well into traditionally understood schemes of power- and geopolitics as well as the categories on which these schemes rest.

In this latter domain of research, a relationship is typically struck between Kant's writings and recent calls for a "new world order." As balance of power models and stark theories of anarchy fall into less favorable light, he is often associated with current focus on multilateral security arrangements, globalizing political economy, world-wide environmental concerns, and the proliferation and mobility of multiethnic strife. In this regard, and justifiably so, Lynch has felt impelled to write:

> Just as Niccolò Machiavelli and Thomas Hobbes became etched into the minds of international relations scholars as the oracles of realpolitik during the Cold War, Immanuel Kant appears to be well on his way to becoming the prophet of "progressive international reform" in the post-Cold War era.[23]

Kant is indeed in ascendance as the seer for many scholars predicting and theorizing the possibility of a multipolar liberal international peace. The practical impact of his work in this domain is intensifying at a substantial rate.

My initial aim in this book, then, is to evaluate and scrutinize the recent revival of Kant's theory in the study of international relations to which Lynch points. I am particularly concerned to reflect on the intra-disciplinary politics surrounding Kant's place in international relations theory. More precisely, I am drawn to consider the employment of his writings for the purpose of developing a picture of the problems and possibilities residing within politics between nations. In addition, I wish to examine the implications of taking Kant's thought seriously with respect to international relations. Acknowledging the elements of realpolitik in his thought, Kant's texts still seem to require extreme shifts in ideas away from the convictions traditionally attached to Thucydides, Machiavelli, and Hobbes. Consequently, I contemplate how attention to Kant may not only advance radically divergent views as to how one is to conceive international relations but how such a focus may also necessitate transformation in the configuration of the discipline.

Providing one of the most convincing of current theoretical alternatives in the discipline, debate surrounding the association of Kant's writings with and within international relations theory is of no slight portent. His texts and ideas are emerging as a composite site in which the very stakes of international relations are being located, deliberated, and further cultivated. Hence, my project here serves to open entry into problems concerning how scholars of international relations reconcile themselves with the theoretical demands of their own study. Moreover, it operates to provoke contention over the legitimacy of the categories and structures of thought in which such work is done.

With this in mind, I study how an appeal to Kant must ultimately affect international political practice. His theory is generally posited as a manner by which *international* relations may be understood as standing alongside *transnational* and *intranational* relations within a more general domain of world politics. It might therefore be taken to give license not only to a more liberally minded foreign policy. It is possible, for example, to understand a Kantian theory of politics to authorize activities of war and peace that fly in the face of traditional views respecting the autonomy of states and national communities.

In some cases, the revival of Kant vindicates such options as intervention into the sovereign territory of other states, where under different conditions such 'interference' may have been understood merely as part of the anarchic violence serving egotistic interests within inter-state clashes. In other cases, attention to Kant's analyses offers possible political justification for what may be labeled as "humanitarian projects," such as development work, aid missions, and the implementation of policies to conserve and protect natural resources and environments, where such efforts may otherwise be deemed truly utopian and inattentive to the unfortunate yet real demands of everyday life. It is thus worthwhile to consider *how* in fact the adoption of tenets to be found in Kant's writing may give reason and inspiration toward a whole new world of world politics. Furthermore, and perhaps most crucially, it is appropriate to investigate whether such reason and inspiration is truly justified in his thought.

To this end, in chapter 1, I examine how Kant's work has been read historically as constituting a theory of international relations. In particular, I focus on the writings of those scholars of international relations who find value in his comments and seek to promote what they take to be "Kantian" perspectives on international politics. In this fashion, my aim is to understand what it is that current appeals to Kant's writings sanction in the way of further development of the discipline. I am interested to discover how it is that his texts operate in the project of comprehending international relations and prescribing political action within that sphere. In addition, I ask whether or not the revival of Kant in the study of international relations warrants such development at all.

My general conclusion to these queries is that the current interest in Kant is almost exclusively conditioned on problematic readings of his work. The Kant that is taken up as an answer to what may be perceived by some as troublesome "new world orders" proves a convenient device through which to suggest a renewed disciplinary unity to studies in international relations. However, it is also a Kant whose theoretical legitimacy is at least doubtful. Specific comments and viewpoints from his works are paraded like political banners. But, how either Kant or scholars of international politics may justify support for such comments is ignored. Rather, the reasons for which his writing is employed as a supposedly improved analysis of international relations draw attention to profound inadequacies in the theory underlying support for Kant. Traditional readings of Kant in the discipline completely disregard the intellectual debt that its mainstream owes him. And those renewing Kant's place in the canon pay more attention to how segments of his thought may serve disciplinary needs than to how the breadth of his theory may challenge such disciplinary practices overall. I therefore recommend a deeper critical reading of Kant with respect to how international politics becomes a relevant aspect to his investigations. And, this is what I endeavor to accomplish in the following chapter.

In chapter 2, I support the notion that what is conventionally subscribed to as "the Kantian theory of international relations" cannot be interrogated properly without understanding it as situated well within the full course of thought present in Kant's much larger philosophical projects. I suggest that it is in neglecting this fact that the majority of scholarly projects in international relations theory that display particular interest and inspiration in his ideas come to failure. Underlying these derelictions is a lack of attention to the specific meanings which Kant attaches to relevant terms and notions in his own discussion of international politics. Moreover, at least in this respect, scholars of international relations display little to no sense of what is implied by their own invocation of the categories and concepts on which their studies rest. Thus, in most appeals, Kant serves more often to add legitimacy and a new face to well-worn theory than there appears to emerge a valid appreciation of his particular analysis of the international.

In this chapter, then, I assess the grounds on which Kant is understood to reside within the tradition of international relations theory. I consider his placement within the spectrum of ideology between realism and idealism from which the discipline operates. I examine the manner in which Kant arrives at the categories with which he comes to think his way through dimensions of international politics. And, most important, I show how Kant comes to consider international relations as an area of political interest. For, I argue, it is in these philosophical moves that the key to what international relations actually means to him may be found. And it is also in this regard that one may discover how little Kant has in common with the traditionally overt assumptions and aims of scholars within the discipline of international relations, regardless of perspective.

In reading Kant's so-called political writings back into what I see as their source in his *Critical* projects and additional works on anthropology, education, ethics, and religion, I determine that his basic thought is not only largely neglected throughout the discipline; Kant's ideas work against traditionally received notions of what is to be achieved in the study of politics between nations. His writings do allow for a theory of international politics of an intriguing sort. However, as I anticipate in the opening to this introduction, my final point is that Kant's work ultimately argues against the practicality and instructive quality of such a discipline, conceived as a social science.

The fundamental tenets of his political thought imply that the study of international relations, as conventionally instituted, defines an *impossible* enterprise. I contend that Kant's writings refuse to accept a description of or a prescription for political practice and conditions in the world as minimally adequate to the concerns of world politics. In addition, I conclude that what is typically understood as Kant's contribution to international relations theory is his response to this very problem.

From this point, however, I do not mean to suggest that there is no relationship at all between Kant's writing and the interests embraced by those seeking to maintain and build on a disciplinary study of international politics. My aim is not to show that Kant's ideas are simply irrelevant to the tradition and that one should be intellectually divorced from the other. On the contrary, I argue that Kant's projects have more to say to the study of international relations than even his current champions within the discipline understand. His political theory discloses far more about what it means to study and theorize the international than scholars in the field normally perceive.

In chapter 3 I show that, although he ought to be read in contradiction to those who posit world politics within categories and aims conventional to the discipline of international relations, Kant does offer highly germane theoretical challenges to how politics are to be negotiated as a world phenomenon. Inspecting with greater precision the philosophical commitments of his political thought identified in chapter 2, I argue that Kant makes great efforts to show how an international approach to the political is both fully possible and simply unavoidable. Attempting to remove himself from the spectrum of ideology that pervades political realism/idealism, Kant relies on what one might call a politics-as-ethics, in which international relations is taken up more as an invigorated practice or vocation than a study and applied social science. Hence, my interest in this chapter is to consider the extent to which Kant really does offer a viable alternative to traditions of realism/idealism in ameliorating one's understanding of politics in the world. I aim to examine the promise of this different understanding of the political in the international realm that, as I contend, he provides. And, in this regard, I seek to finally establish a very exact understanding of the sort of philosophical operations that are inherent to the possibility of generating modern theories of international relations.

The conclusion toward which I work in this chapter, however, is that Kant's approach retains an elementary flaw that draws his theory far closer than he would like to the camps of thought he initially sets out to eclipse. I submit that, despite the theoretical gains he makes in coming to understand what it means to engage in international political theory, Kant fails to advance an idea of human political reality that is in keeping with the requirements he places on his project. Upholding and indebted to insufficiently examined notions akin to those that gird studies of international politics more generally, he does not wholly live up to his own criticisms of the sorts of philosophical assumptions that underlie traditions of realism/idealism. As a result, Kant's theory of international politics becomes peculiarly attached to central aspects of those visions he seeks to overcome. Furthermore, he demonstrates through his own example how any approach to the international must encounter similar failures.

My broader point here is to show that taking Kant's thought seriously in the study of international relations does not provide one with a thoroughly new and improved approach to negotiating politics on a world scale. This investigation does not clear and prepare finer ground on which the discipline may be built. His work, rather, inspires its own traps and disappointments. And it displays the fundamental problems with which theories and analyses of international politics are necessarily saddled. But I also contend that it is through these specific failings that a more precise location of where a Kantian critique of the crises of international relations scholarship must reside is betrayed. Despite Kant's attempts to withdraw from an ideological approach to the political, his project is frustrated by the extent to which he allows his ethics to gain dogmatic grounding. Still, it is not clear that his ethical approach need become so fixed. There remains room to contemplate how this ethic might yet succeed.

In chapter 4, I therefore explore the extent to which Kant's intellectual revolution could indeed sustain an ethic that is both consistent with this turn of thought and, at the same time, absent of unfortunate ideological anchors. I seek to learn how the force of his theory regarding international politics may be re-invigorated and set free of its self-constructed obstacles. My aim is to consider whether or not there is finally promise for a Kantian approach to international relations theory at all. And, in this regard, I identify a manner in which both a radicalized Kant and a radicalized theory of international relations may indeed be thought. In conjunction, I argue that there is important work being conducted within the realm of contemporary international relations theory that is commensurate with such a revised Kant. However, I must also conclude that to take up such an approach to international relations is to also give up any focus that could be entertained within the discipline as it is presently constituted. To consider in earnest Kantian theory and the debt that studies of international politics have to it is to ultimately deny the practicability of attention to international politics from the start. Rather, the central impetus of his thought must recommend a return to politics and political theory, where international politics and theories of international relations may be understood to first emerge.

What is at stake in this conclusion are questions regarding the limits upon which theories of international relations are constituted and in which they constitute themselves. Again, all theories of international relations necessarily assume global limits as the very basis from which international politics arise, that there is a definitive place (world) in which all humans, communities, or states must in the end come to face one another. And it is the apparent finality and commonalty of this social experience that gives rise to the seeming necessity of international politics and, thus, ways to think such politics well. Yet, what Kant's theory implies, albeit against the grain of the positions he himself hopes to take, is a questioning of the presumed finality and commonalty of these limits. In response, it suggests *global limits* (read here as "universal") to ever adequately assessing and describing the context typically referred to as "the international" or "the world." Hence, a re-invigorated

Kantian theory of international relations propounds global limits to ever thinking or acting appropriately within the limits of a globe. It must suggest that "the international" can never provide an adequate point of departure from which to understand and respond to politics experienced in the world. The struggles of international politics and debates within international relations theory ought, rather, always to be recognized as limiting representations of politics. Hence "the globe" ought to be conceived primarily as a political device, through which human conflict and struggles may be conceptually and, thus, practically contained.

In the end, my conclusions might be taken more as a combined affront to the discipline of international relations than a helpful contribution to it. My purposes here are perhaps better understood, however, as an attempt to demonstrate, through the example of Kant, exceptional problems that underlie the work that is pursued in this field. And in this regard it is true that I seek to engage international relations theory in a constructive, as opposed to destructive, manner. With this in mind, it is worth noting that I do not strive in this book to necessarily provide *the* correct or *the* final reading of Kant in international relations. I do not wish to stop conversation. Rather, I wish to provoke considerably more debate on the problem of Kant in international relations. For, I find that it is through an examination of his constitutive role in the discipline that international relations theory may gain one of its strongest moments of critical self-reflection. Moreover, an interrogation of Kant and the place of his writings in the discipline provide a compelling opportunity through which the intertwined associations weaving across international relations theory and the practice of international relations may be observed.

1

The Rendering of Kant in International Relations Theory[1]

Kant's political writings range far beyond the mainstream concerns of international relations. Yet, through a long succession of attempts to situate international relations scholarship in terms of the provocative challenges his thought offers the field, Kant's works have been rendered with considerable impact into one of the central points of reference for the discipline. The conventions underlying the resulting "Kantian theory of international relations" are found most obviously within the liberal extremes of the discipline, where international peace and order is given considerable hope. And, interest in this point of view has peaked as the pursuit for universal ideals and global concerns has appeared more important than any primary dedication to regional self-protection and constant preparation for the threat of war. Conversely, interest has typically fallen as the value attributed to these optimistic strivings has been belittled in the face of recurrent violence across the globe. Thus support for Kant's work has generally followed the ebb and flow of the "great debates" across theories of international relations.

Currently, 'Kantianisms' are again achieving considerable currency within mainstream arms of the discipline. There are in fact several versions of Kantian thought that are now promoted with respect to politics, ranging across philosophical, literary, and economic interests as well as theories of the state. Most impressively, though, a broad range of scholars are again seeing within Kant's writings the basis of analysis from which true inter-state peace may finally be anticipated or sought. Thus it certainly appears that some form of liberalism is gaining serious momentum against the realist core of international relations once again. However, it is my initial contention here, that most present appeals to Kant in this regard ought not to be viewed simply as movements in still one more swing of the pendulum between realism and idealism. Utopianism is not now gaining fashion across the discipline of international relations. Rather, I argue that despite the undeniably liberal tone present in such concerns, recent invocations of Kant's writings attempt to finally overcome the old intellectual see-saw that has afflicted the discipline from its beginnings. These are efforts to describe ways in which one may address the facts of contemporary international politics without falling into an either/or trap of realism/idealism. And, Kant's texts *function* largely to provide the authoritative voice behind such disciplinary and theoretical progress or escape.

Crudely put, theories of international relations traditionally shuttle between two apparently reasonable claims that are taken as mutually exclusive or, at least, inimical to one another: that, on the one hand, states are ultimately autonomous actors and naturally in eternal competition with each other and that, on the other hand, all political communities of the modern era are inherently interrelated and united in their attentions by the fact that they ultimately and inescapably interact with each other as well as share a singular and finite environment or social space. However, an increasing body of scholarship, concerned especially with international organization, international law, transnational politics, and international political economy, is now re-introducing Kant's work as foundation for theory that may build positively from the back-and-forth struggle that debates of realism/idealism encourage. Kant's thought is supposed to break down the essential contradictions between realism and idealism. And his words are employed to project a worldview that affirms change in the conditions of international politics as opposed to the supposed immutable truths provided by either side of the traditional debate.

To demonstrate how this is the case, I will first present the Kant that is most often and almost exclusively taken to be *the* Kant of international relations. In conjunction I will trace the scattered range of traditional renditions of Kant as a theorist of international relations from which current readings in this vein may and do find their most immediate source. In doing so, I aim to establish how Kant's thought is received ultimately as both a problematic and potentially connecting force across the discipline, as opposed to merely an emblem for the one side. From this point, I will go on to examine how this sort of reading is actually deployed, particularly in recent literature to do with the role of democracy in promoting international peace and the structure of international law in world order. With this in mind, I will, in addition, explore how these invocations of Kant's writings give license to a very specific treatment of questions to do with ethics in international relations. For, it is ultimately in this area of concern that current appeals to the revolution in thought regarding the potential for peace that Kant supposedly offers achieve their greatest impact.

In the end, however, my more pressing interest here is to show that what is displayed throughout contemporary readings of Kant, insofar as his thought is viewed as a progressive ground for approaching a world politics for states, is less a forward-looking reform than what may at first appear. I argue that the resolution to the perpetual crisis among theories of international relations that the bulk of current revivals of Kant's texts apparently offer is in actual fact a highly conservative move. The recent re-introduction of Kant into the heart of international relations theory proves mostly to announce a potential end to the contest between the intellectual bookends of the discipline and not a true examination of the problems that may be inherent within those limits. In this instance, his words are used only to displace debate from the politics of states to the apparently less controversial ground of human needs and interests. Consequently, old and unresolved problems of theory are disguised in new categories. But no new way for the explanation of international politics is actually constructed. And international relations theory, as a project, is thus falsely secured.

Of even greater concern, what this critical analysis shows is that the place of Kantian thought in theories of international relations is itself erroneously obtained. Those calling for a return to Kant are quite right to suggest that his position is not legitimately mapped within the traditional spectrum of theoretical debate. And, they rightfully indicate the need to fully reconsider the conventions of Kantian theory in international relations. However, it is also the case that the current revival of Kant does not take up this work in any serious way. Rather it is based on mere reworkings of the poor readings already established within the tradition. Thus, the true significance of Kant's theory for the study of international relations remains an enormous question yet to be engaged. And one of the central theoretical pillars of the discipline is shown to be conspicuously hollow.

Readings of *Perpetual Peace*

Kant gains his reputation as the consummate idealist in international relations theory largely in direct opposition to selected readings of Thomas Hobbes' *Leviathan*.[2] As most new scholars to the discipline are soon taught, in chapter 13 of Part I, Hobbes testifies that human life is conditioned always by repetitive violence—a war of all against all—and that the pain of such existence can be minimized only where a group of persons submits to a singular sovereign, who consolidates and concentrates the force and authority of all into One. Consequently, each sovereign commonwealth of persons faces each other as a singular subject and body, protecting its component organs within. Isolated from the rest of this lengthy and complicated work of political theory, Hobbes' claim that human life is "solitary, poore, nasty, brutish, and short"[3] serves as a banner for realism and suggests an entire mainstream of pessimistic thinking that places states and their power interests at the focus of every analysis and laments the reputed invariable character of human interaction. It is then only fitting that the place of optimism reserved for Kant is similarly defined and reduced on the basis of a singular short text. Trimmed from a career of prolific thought and writing, spanning well over fifty years, Kant's short pamphlet *Perpetual Peace*[4] has functioned as almost the sole ground for his reputation as a theorist of international relations. Other of Kant's short writings have proved of general interest.[5] However, it is indeed treatments of *Perpetual Peace* that come to govern Kant's role in the discipline most directly.

A reading of *Perpetual Peace* at its face-value quite handily delivers the idealist caricature that presides under Kant's name. In the confines of this particular text, Kant appears to theorise that war between states may not only be brought to an absolute halt but, more to the point, that international conflict may be eliminated as a potentiality altogether. He displays great willingness to place stock in the capacity of states to gain true respect for one another's existence, rights, and interests. Kant seems to treat egoism and domineering instincts as elements that may be outgrown in international politics. Read in this manner, *Perpetual Peace* then provides the very foundation of utopian thought against which E. H. Carr protests so vehemently in his celebrated *The Twenty Years' Crisis*.[6] Thus, *Perpetual Peace* serves as a text underlying the greatest turn against idealism achieved within international relations theory in the past century.

These general sentiments are first exhibited in Kant's six Preliminary Articles of a Perpetual Peace Between States:

1. No conclusion of peace shall be considered valid as such if it was made with a secret reservation of the material for a future war.

2. No independently existing state, whether it be large or small, may be acquired by another state by inheritence, exchange, purchase or gift.

3. Standing armies (*miles perpetuus*) will gradually be abolished altogether.

4. No national debt shall be contracted in connection with the external affairs of the state.

5. No state shall forcibly interfere in the constitution and government of another state.

6. No state at war with another shall permit such acts of hostility as would make mutual confidence impossible during a future time of peace. Such acts would include the employment of *assassins* (*percussores*) *or poisoners* (*venfici*), *breach of agreements*, *the instigation of treason* (*perduellio*) within the enemy state, etc.[7]

In these articles, he offers a basic guide as to how an international peace may finally take form.

Articles 1 and 3 underline the primary understanding of peace under which Kant operates in this text. He emphatically states that by "peace" he means a thoroughly new condition and advancement in the processes of international politics. He rejects the notion that any treaty or agreement that leads to a cease in battle and competition between states, no matter how successful or lasting, may provide sufficient grounds for peace. Peace, Kant reasons, could only truly be such if there is no cause for political leaders to even entertain war as a means to state interests.[8] On the assumption that the maintenance of a corps of professional soldiers or the stockpiling of arms or the capital with which to fund a military machine in itself may pose a visible threat, he claims that even a defensive position threatens peace between states. Moreover, Kant holds that the attempts made by 'peace-loving' states, through the accumulation of troops and other forms of material prowess, to deter the potential aggression in their neighbors can in themselves instigate direct confrontation. For, the requirements of maintaining such a deterrent, in the name of peace, may prove far more of a financial and social drain on states than can war and domination. And war may, therefore and unfortunately, become a more astute political option.[9]

In recognition of this problem Article 4 is offered as a preventive measure that seeks to stave off temptation toward such buildup. Kant argues here that foreign financial aid used to maintain social infrastructure and food-stores is not threatening in itself. Yet, he warns that the modern structures of international commerce that allow for mass lending and borrowing of capital between states make possible the funding of war machines far in excess of what any one state could muster of its own accord.[10]

Articles 2, 5, and 6, on the other hand, betray a high moral tone lying behind Kant's interest in encouraging such a peace. In these instances, one can see a staunch belief in what may be understood as the inherent autonomy of each and every state. He argues for the internal integrity of states, suggesting that they are not things that can truly be owned or commodified in any manner. A state, Kant claims, is at root constituted on the basis of a social will of some form and gains its structure from the rights that the citizens of the society attribute to one another.[11] Thus, in this light, he cannot tolerate the notion that one state could possibly have any just claim in meddling with the affairs of another people. Moreover, he refuses the suggestion that there is any ground under which one state may deem another society as deserving of disruption or punishment. As separately founded communities, Kant understands that no state has true authority over another in any manner.[12] It therefore does indeed appear necessary that the materials and arts conducive to international domination be eliminated.

Understanding, along with realists, that there is no international authority to bring international relations into accord with such Articles, Kant goes on to claim that it must and will be the states themselves who will mold this final peace.[13] Agreeing implicitly with Jean-Jacques Rousseau,[14] he suggests that even if there ever was a natural state of humans in which peace and equality prevailed it is certainly not something to which civilized persons may return. Hence, Kant actually offers even more direct concurrence with Hobbes, in this respect, claiming that the predicament of human life outside of the protection of the sovereign is surely a state of war. Moreover, Kant recommends that peace is something which may only be "*formally instituted*" in a political manner.[15] And it is, therefore, here that one may first see the assimilation of Kant to idealism as perhaps overstated.

Kant goes on in *Perpetual Peace* to underline this point regarding the central importance of state politics to international peace with his three Definitive Articles of Perpetual Peace:

1. The civil constitution of every state shall be republican.

2. The right of nations shall be based on a federation of free states.

3. Cosmopolitan right shall be limited to conditions of universal hospitality.[16]

Here he describes how such a pacific condition in international politics could be attained. Additionally, Kant may be seen to display a strong faith in the rational will of human individuals and organizations as the mechanism through which such conditions may be organised.

He anticipates the transformation of modern states into true republics. And, by a republican constitution, Kant means a political community which is founded on principles of freedom for all people, dependence of all members on a singular rule, and equality for all citizens.[17] Furthermore, he understands a republic to gain its legitimacy from and standing on a constitution brought about by the rightful consent of the citizenry as a whole in its origin. Decisions regarding whether such a state will or will not engage in warfare is up to the people themselves. Kant therefore hypothesises that the public itself will reject war and the inherent disposition of states will be such that interstate conflict will be avoided at all costs:

> For [supporting such conflict] would mean calling down on themselves all the miseries of war, such as doing the fighting themselves, supplying the costs of the war from their own resources, painfully making good the ensuing devastation, and, as the crowning evil, having to take upon themselves a burden of debt which will embitter peace itself and which can never be paid off on account of the constant threat of new wars.[18]

Holding to this level of logic, he imagines that republican states will in turn seek peace with one another in the form of a federal union. Without the existence of a transnational authority to which states may mutually appeal, Kant submits that republics will have no better option than to diffuse all potential threat with one another.[19] Just as one might expect that a republic may be successfully constructed to serve the interests of the citizens and the citizens themselves aim to avoid the destructive depletion of resources and the social fabric caused by war, he foretells that an international contract of some sort between states is attainable.

Kant's emphasis here, though, is that republics around the world can and ought to construct this federation as free states. It must be a voluntary union, where no power is transferred above state sovereignty.[20] Equality is of primary import, so as to divert the possibility of distrust, envy, or conceit from inaugurating imbalances of any kind. Hence, it is that Kant insists in the third and final Definitive Article that a mark of true peace will be the case in which any traveler is treated with civility on the soil of any foreign land. For this will signal a circumstance in which it is universally recognized that the entire globe is a single community of human beings.[21] It just so happens that different groups of humans have banded together under different forms of legitimate rule, as they respectively see fit.

When taken as the foundation of Kant's thought on international relations, his Preliminary and Definitive Articles, then, display a singular optimism in the ability of humans to overcome differences. In admitting to the sensibility of perpetual peace and in joining into a world-wide federation of states, each separate community inherently recognizes and stands for inalienable human rights that apply universally, regardless of one's association. Kant shows a belief in the notion that the strife of politics may ultimately be torn away from state structures and social hierarchies and taken up by the interests of each individual. In the hands of individuals, politics may, on a global scale, be rethought in terms of what humans each share. *Perpetual Peace* offers the hope that cosmopolitan interests can channel selfish desires.

Elaborating on his second Definitive Article, Kant admits that his political ideal would consist in the formation of an international state.[22] However, he recognizes the fact that humans and the communities that they compose are disinclined to give themselves over to a singular political constitution from which the appropriate social conduct and mores for all persons will be determined. He thus states that "the positive idea of a *world republic* cannot be realised."[23] Yet, Kant continues to provide potential evidence for those who would receive him as the radical idealist he is so often thought to be. Even if he denies the possibility of a world state structure as such, Kant does urge that international conditions require that states unite with other republics, both near and far, so as to form at least "something analogous to a universal state."[24] He disavows the possibility of global sovereignty. Yet, he apparently leaves the door open for an actual dominant body constituted from members world-wide.

It is precisely this sort of statement that impels such later theorists as Hedley Bull to perceive Kant as a proponent of extremes and to treat him as one who does indeed advocate world government.[25] Dedication to this reading, however, also forces one to recognize a frustrating inconsistency between what Bull sees as Kant's simultaneous prescription for universal political rule and recognition of the anarchical condition underlying its possibility.[26] On this basis, Bull argues that the only force that could bring warring states together would be the force of one will over all others, leaving the whole idea of a global union thoroughly unattractive.[27]

On the other hand, accepting the tension between world government and the conditions of anarchy as merely the realistic challenge of international politics, Thomas L. Carson states that it is the prospect of such an overarching global force that indeed makes Kant's position particularly compelling in the modern world of nation-states.[28] And Carson complains that Kant does not admit to what Carson perceives as the true benefits of a global military. Consequently, he retheorizes the grounding of *Perpetual Peace* in such a manner as to allow for the unifying power that Bull either finds absent or fears.

For those who have essayed to move somewhat beyond a narrow literal reading of *Perpetual Peace*, however, the majority opinion prefers a Kant who does not hold out for a world government, as such. This case is established already with some strength in the texts of Carl Joachim Friedrich and F. H. Hinsley, which have served as the central foundations to understanding Kant within international relations theory. Friedrich acknowledges the sort of dilemma of interpretation that leads someone like Bull in the path that he takes. But he draws his readers' attention back to other elements of *Perpetual Peace*, where Kant himself suggests the contradictory quality that an achievement of a world state would pose in the face of the supposed freedom of individual states.[29] Hinsley insists that Kant's use of the Latin term *foedus pacificum* in identifying what he means by "something analogous to a universal state" must be understood in its specificity. He notes that *foedus* refers to a treaty and not a state. Thus, he announces that, of course, "Everyone knows that [Kant] did not advocate world government or the complete but less universal merger of states: he explicitly rejects this solution."[30]

As noted above, though, from reading Kant's first Preliminary Article and his second Definitive Article one knows that he does not accept treaties as offering sufficient grounds for the final peace he envisions. He writes: "a *peace treaty* may put an end to the current war, but not to that general warlike condition within which pretexts can always be found for a new war."[31] However, it is also important to note that Kant is careful to make a strict distinction between a *foedus pacificum* and a *pactim pacis*. He refers to the latter as the simple peace treaty which itself, in his opinion, does little honor to the idea of peace. And with the former he appeals more directly to the notion of a "pacific federation" of states.[32] Kant in fact pushes this notion in so many words, stating that:

> This federation does not aim to acquire any power like that of a state, but merely to preserve and secure the *freedom* of each state in itself, along with that of the other confederated states, although this does not mean that they need to submit to public laws and to a coercive power which enforces them, as do men in a state of nature.[33]

With this in mind, Hinsley even suggests that the very style which Kant employs to write *Perpetual Peace* indicates that a world-state is furthest from his thoughts. Hinsley reminds his readers that this text is constructed primarily in terms of prefatory articles and as a description of what Kant sees as the conditions for peace.[34] His point is that *Perpetual Peace* does not offer a constitution of any sort. Nor, does it outline the substance of an international legal structure. Rather, as a document, Kant's text offers a guide and potential framework on which, he believes, a peaceful global order of states may be begun.[35]

With the sort of caution that each employs, both Friedrich and Hinsley have ultimately indicated the relationship Kant makes between politics and morality as the key point of access for subsequent readings into his entire thinking on international politics. Together their analyses show that it is in the certain association he perceives between these things that supposedly allows Kant to propose a true federation of republics which avoids the rise of a global ruler. And it is thus in this relationship that the notion of universal governance may be and is seen to finally mesh with an acceptance of anarchy in the world.

Within both his second Definitive Article and the Appendix to *Perpetual Peace*, Kant makes the point that all political action and posturing pays homage to some form of legitimacy, of a rule based on *right*.[36] He holds the position that all political actors seek the semblance of justification in their actions, whether such behavior warrants the excuse or not. Kant claims that, regardless of how a politician or government may strategize to get around the limitations of a rightful position, such figures invariably seek the cloak of legitimacy so as to maintain the support of subjects and allies.[37] And the basis of this right in action and position is the assumption that politics is ordered with respect to moral sense.

Whereas he distinguishes politics as the applied aspect of right, he appoints morality as the theoretical component of right.[38] In addition, Kant understands that politics on an international scale will succeed only once these branches of right are appropriately brought into balance. And that which will bring about such equipoise will be the free willing of a politics that operates under a concept of right that has already been morally determined. The international federation that Kant hopes for will occur only insofar as a particular moral position comes to drive the political portion of right. And this moral impulse is what each republic will ultimately freely adopt.

Kant recognizes that any political actor can conjure a moral attitude to accommodate given political actions and interests.[39] He refers to such a person "who fashions his morality to suit his own advantage as a statesman" as a "political moralist."[40] However, Kant believes that the political moralist ultimately defeats the possibility of his own political aspirations. The political moralist is always incapable of providing the moral underpinnings of his claim to right in any way other than in retrospect.[41] Hence, the political moralist is never in a position to truly offer a rightful direction in politics. He can never make a successful claim to right without having perpetrated illegitimate acts. In contrast, however, Kant does declare a belief in the possibility of a "moral politician" who is able to determine principles of political propriety in accordance with morality.[42]

What this means is that he imagines political actors who, through reason or experience, are able to establish political duty as prescribed by the natural conditions faced by all human beings. These conditions include the facts that humans naturally form communities through necessity, that these communities inescapably come into contact with one another, and that the space available for national migration on this planet is finite.[43] So, the conditions are such that the respective social interests of each state, and, thus, the respective interests of each individual, depend on the protection that the arm of politics may achieve in the interstate sphere. The only guarantee to such safety, according to Kant, is a total peace among them. And this peace must indeed be extended globally to ensure the domestic interests of each and every state. Hence, the moral politician will seek an order in which a variety of states living under a diversity of respective rules may coexist without bringing harm to one another. This is the very guideline posed in Kant's Articles of *Perpetual Peace*. And he pronounces these as moral by the fact that, as he suggests, they represent a social/political structure that could be adopted by all persons without injury. He believes that it allows for the rights of all to be respected.

Kant goes so far as to say that "a true system of politics cannot therefore take a single step without first paying tribute to morality."[44] The significance of this statement is that he suggests here a manner by which the dilemma of international relations may be thought without framing politics purely in terms of power. Kant's point is that the notion of maintaining domestic interests simply through the wielding and accumulating of force is counterproductive in an age of truly international politics. Political expediency, he argues, is best served through attention to the moral requirements of modern life. And once politicians and governments are finally impressed with this idea, Kant trusts, a political resolution toward peace will arise. Most important, though, he imagines that this will indeed be a volition that may compose the basis for a form of 'world government' without a superior force or leader. For, the moral position is supposedly one that each state could and ought to establish independently of one another. It is a will that may emerge naturally in each context.

It is primarily this early focus on the links made between morality and politics in *Perpetual Peace* that has made way for the reception of Kant as a particularly *new* theorist of international relations. As one can see through an examination of the histories of international relations theory written, respectively, by Torbjörn Knutsen[45] and F. Parkinson,[46] Kant's writing is cultivated as a point of specifically *modern* awareness. Parkinson, in particular, notes how Kant's concentration rests on an idea of a modern state, as opposed to any given territorial political institution that one might care to pull from European history.[47] This is a state modeled most specifically on the republic envisioned in the French Revolution, which inspired Kant directly.[48] It is a nation-state in which a popular government is installed, supposedly resting on the general will of a population viewed indifferently throughout the territory.

In addition, Knutsen notes how *Perpetual Peace* "ushers in a new epoch in International Relations theory," wherein the power dynamics of international politics are thoroughly rethought.[49] He identifies Kant as the figure who initiates a negation of the idea that an equilibrium between states is something that states themselves can control through negotiations of the physical force each represent. In this rendition, rather, *Perpetual Peace* represents the notion that a model of balance between states is something by which each republic must allow itself to be claimed. Each republic must give itself over to the rule constituted through the relations circulating across the balance. Knutsen draws attention to the points at which Kant argues that no one or collection of states is anymore able to successfully force one particular order in the world. In this regard, he suggests that states are not sufficiently in control of the conditions that underlie international relations.

Perpetual Peace certainly does present an argument for the recognition of the intranational, transnational, and multinational forces and movements that have come to characterize much of the dilemma of modern international relations. Kant is particularly mindful of the force of international commerce in the formation of international political orders.[50] He makes the point, which is commonplace among contemporary political economists, that commercial links made between and across communities, internationally, score a level of relations to which the states in themselves are not fully adequate. And on this basis, Kant suggests that states will inevitably seek peaceful relations with one another, so as to in part facilitate the industry that has so quickly and successfully outgrown the aspirations of mercantilism. Consequently, Parkinson interprets Kant as having finally got beyond the realist dilemma most often identified with Hobbes, where the state of nature is simply understood as being at odds with civil society.[51] In Parkinson's eyes, Kant recognizes that the very changes in international conditions noted above render the traditionally viewed obstacle of nature quite differently.

In Hobbes' *Leviathan* one learns that violence is inherent to the supposedly natural competition for land and resources and forces individuals into the formation of separate and distinct commonwealths, which remain at war with one another on a larger scale. Yet Kant suggests that this same violence, in a world progressively surfaced with nation-states that are in inescapable contact with one another and have grown intractable bonds, will alternately necessitate movement toward peace.

Already in the Anglo-American world of the early twentieth century, this representation of Kant's view proved compelling. Foremost on the mark, A. C. Armstrong inaugurates in 1931 a tendency, seen in some later writers,[52] to treat Kant's *Perpetual Peace* as a kind of *prophecy*.[53] He attempts to defend Kant against the charges of utopianism prevalent at the time. And, the point of his writing involves the fact that *Perpetual Peace* was already being used as a basis for theorizing a practical peace in Europe since the Russian disarmament proposals of 1899 and the Peace Conferences at the Hague.[54] Despite finding Kant to be a man of his times,[55] Armstrong reads *Perpetual Peace* as containing the ideas most parallel to the developments that lead to and the plan that characterized the League of Nations that came about after the World War I.[56] He remains unsure of how Kant would react to the specific conditions of international relations 130 years after his death.[57] Yet, Armstrong is convinced that Kant would find some way of adjusting the generality of his proposals and throw his lot well within the camps of those seeking peaceful resolution through the League.[58]

Hinsley is less upfront in offering an actual evaluation of Kant's relevance to historical reality. In this regard, he merely submits that if Kant's Preliminary Articles were indeed ever accepted on a global level, peace would most surely be accomplished.[59] Alternatively, Friedrich is even more enthusiastic than Armstrong in his assessment of Kant's potential role in sketching the future of international relations. Anticipating sentiments found within recent attention to Kant, Friedrich is of the mind that the success of any world order depends on what he understands to be the capacity of all humans to develop universal moral standards of value, regardless of particular domestic values.[60] And he attributes the supposed foresight of his own comments directly to the work of Kant. Thinking at this point in terms of the birth of the United Nations, Friedrich proclaims:

> What is more, looking back from San Francisco in 1945, we can test [Kant's] ideas by the intervening century and a half, and we can say, 'He was right.' Or rather, that he was more nearly right than anyone else at that time or since.[61]

Such ebullience over Kant's alleged relation to the design of either major inter-state union has surely waned as the initial fervour surrounding the founding of each body has itself lapsed. Still, his successive interpreters maintain a strong association between the analysis present in *Perpetual Peace* and the qualitative changes to late-modern international order. As Patrick Riley comments, one of the most striking points that emerges from Kant's writing in this context is the idea that the stability of each sovereign state is fully dependent on the manifestation of some form of international federalism.[62] And this may be and is read forcefully with respect to the manners in which states are progressively finding it necessary to expand alliances such as the North Atlantic Treaty Organization and the European Union. In this light, Charles Beitz finds Kant's attention to the growing interdependence of nation-states, along economic, political, and cultural lines, to successfully anticipate practical principles of justice on a global scale. Beitz suggests that Kant could be quite correct in assuming that international links and cooperation might lead to such cosmopolitan moral-political structures in the same way that one may understand social cooperation to found distributive justice within states.[63]

Along the way, then, the Kant which is at first glance associated with proposals for an alternative international order is replaced by or at least supplemented with a Kant who is the watchful interpreter and tracker of the historical movement in political conditions.

Ian Clark, for example, puts forth a rendition of *Perpetual Peace* in which Kant appears most significantly as a simple voice for change.[64] He too rejects the notion that Kant somehow advocates a world-state. And from this point, Clark establishes Kant's project as one in which the futility of international war is revealed and altogether new forms of world-wide political negotiation is recognized.[65] This point is all the more underlined in Howard Williams' attempts to highlight the gradualism to be found in *Perpetual Peace*. Williams insists that Kant's message be taken only as a potential and approximate way in which, through experience and debate, a truly new world order may be achieved at some unknowable point in the future.[66] Similarly, Jürg Martin Gabriel prefers to emphasize the idea that Kant's broad outline for an international code of law is not meant as an ideal structure to be realised as such but, rather, as a temporary expedient through which unforeseen alternatives may arise.[67] Consistent with Clark, Gabriel offers Kant as one who recognizes the necessity of shifts in thinking. And, in this manner, Gabriel too appears to betray a willingness to view Kant as a prophet of late-modern developments in international politics. For, in the same breath, he suggests that Kant's proposals are of the same quality that have ultimately been adopted in the Conventions established both in The Hague and Geneva, where the rights of humanity supposedly override those of specific government interest.[68]

However, this Kant, who merely sets out sensible guidelines for an approach to shifts and evolution in international relations, turns out to be a source of trouble. Read in this series of manners, *Perpetual Peace* does not offer a convenient source from which a new international relations theory may be built. In fact, it is on the basis of this set of impressions that Kant comes to take on his "difficult" role in the discipline.[69] For the classification of his writing becomes more of a question than an accomplishment. This rendition displays a Kant who offers both a resignation to states, as the uppermost political actors, and hope for practical change in the very manner in which international politics is conducted. Hence, within the confines of his own text, Kant is seen to embody the very contradiction or paradox that has given rise to the back-and-forth debates that characterize the discipline in the first place. For instance, while Armstrong, Hinsley, Friedrich, and Beitz see a prediction for the liberal globalizing trends of the twentieth century with his writings, Charles Covell finds Kant to, rather, anticipate Margaret Thatcher's attitude toward the European Union, wherein federalism is viewed as viable and desirable only through the primary protection of state sovereignty.[70] And, as a result, Kant's work has at times been adopted as a signal of legitimacy for both sides.

As is pointed out by Michael C. Williams,[71] the contrary manners in which Kant is taken up within the discipline is perhaps seen best in a contrast of the respective readings given by Clark and Kenneth Waltz. As noted above, Clark focuses on Kant as a proponent of global optimism, where real change may be anticipated through a variety of new developments in the international sphere. Clark pits Kant against realists.[72] On the other hand, Waltz prefers to place greater emphasis on Kant's lack of faith in the ability of states to act peacefully on their own accords. He writes: "While Kant may be seen as a backsliding liberal, he may also be considered a theorist of power politics who hid his Machiavellian ideas by hanging 'round them the fashionable garments of liberalism."[73] Waltz clings to a reading of Kant in which selfish, autonomous units hold sway, as proof that the philosopher is ultimately as pessimistic as Waltz himself:

> Kant sees in combination of what others have often separated—the defects, or as he says, the evil of men and the possibility of their living good lives, the strength of the state and the liberty of its subjects, progress amidst ever greater difficulties, the approach to peace as wars become fiercer and more frequent. He has, as many liberals do not, an appreciation of politics as struggle, an idea of possible equilibrium not as simple and automatic harmony but always as something perilously achieved out of conflict.[74]

He suggests that Kant, despite his hopes, accepts people to be essentially self-interested and warring throughout time.

On balance, though, such efforts to claim Kant for one or another tradition of international relations theory has proved fruitless. It remains difficult to campaign for one received aspect of Kant without dredging up those others that cause the first to fray. As a result, attempts to situate Kant simply as an idealist or a realist, or as a reformer of either view, appear somewhat more as ideological positioning than portrayals of careful or thoughtful analysis.

W. B. Gallie, one of the most sophisticated interpreters of Kant's theory of international relations to date and certainly the most influential, exemplifies through his own ambivalence this need to resist a single-minded view.[75] Gallie basically praises what he sees as the 'undeniable truths' generated in Kant's astute observations of the practical function human reason plays in the formation of international problems and the eventual resolution of international conflict. He accepts the liberal aspect of Kant's proposals, suggesting that Kant is certainly prescient in his discussion of the conditions required for international peace.[76] In this regard, he applauds Kant for being "mankind's first naturally global thinker."[77] And Gallie shows appreciation for what he identifies as the mature and wise liberal tone that he perceives in Kant's work.[78] However, Gallie also argues that Kant is ultimately naïve in his cosmopolitanism to a wide variety of important political realities in the realm of international politics.[79] He chastises Kant for concentrating too much on what he takes as Kant's focus on the ideal of situations in international affairs and for not appreciating the particular contingencies of what actually occurs in the world. In this regard, Gallie accuses Kant of unjustifiably treating all international concerns as somehow reducible to one grand problem.[80] And he finally finds himself bridling his commendations in a rather confused fashion. Gallie writes:

> To be sure, Kant's contribution to political philosophy as a whole remains inspirational rather than substantial: certainly it does not supply easily digested fodder for those who want good stock answers to old stock questions. But it suggests a way of conceiving politics as part of the task of Reason, or of the calling of Man, which in its width, and in its balanced view of human capacities, seems to me unrivalled in the modern world.[81]

He thus leaves Kant in a conflicted condition, suggesting that Kant is directly stimulating to the interests of both realists and idealists, and yet, as such, is not of much concrete assistance in either regard.

The most recent and sustained endeavours to inquire into this dilemma have in fact found it unfeasible to establish Kant's pedigree whatsoever. After considering all possible sides of the debate with respect to *Perpetual Peace*, Andrew Hurrell finally decides that Kant's position as a theorist of international relations is at heart indeterminable:

> Whilst Kant is certainly much more of a statist than the characterization of the Kantian tradition would suggest,

> the continuing interest of his work is strengthened by the tension between the two sides of his writings. This tension remains unresolved and there are many difficulties with the answers that Kant gives and with his fascinating but frustrating combination of rigorous moralism and political realism.[82]

Moreover, Hurrell suggests that Kant pursues the assumptions held respectively by both idealists and realists, so as to ensure a total inquiry into the concerns of international politics.[83] He argues that within Kant's refusal to theorise a world-state lies an experiment in which Kant tries to understand the potential relation between state-order and cosmopolitan interests. On yet another level, Michael C. Williams sustains the notion that Kant ought to be seen as operating well within both paradigms. Williams remains suspicious of any either/or solution to the interpretation of Kant's politics. As a result, he too comes to the conclusion that irresolvable tension resides at the root of Kant's thought:

> Kant steadfastly refuses to fall into the fatalistic dualisms of *Realpolitik* which leave only an "ideal" world of tranquility or a "real" world of continual war, a domestic society of "justice" and an international order of "power." His thought lives in a continual state of dialectical tension, a refusal to flee from the realities of the present and an unwillingness to see that reality one-sidedly as objectively fixed, finite, hopeless, or devoid of possibility.[84]

Williams' point is that Kant must be understood as one who refuses to divorce morality from the realm of states and simply into a competing vision of an evolving globalism. Rather, he takes the Kantian theory of international relations to involve an ongoing process in which the state and the globe mutually shape and inform one another within an inescapable relationship between domestic and foreign.

It is perhaps because of this conflicted classification that Kant ultimately gains in international relations theory that so few have been attracted to explore deeply the source that Kant offers the discipline. For, to take this set of readings of *Perpetual Peace* seriously does not simply ask that one entertain a novel or even unpopular position in the field. Rather, the Kant that emerges from interpretation within international relations theory demands an attitude of which it is difficult to make sense. Effectively, this Kant does not even appear to volunteer an alternative approach to thinking international politics. Instead, he takes bits and pieces from traditional aspects and offers them in a supposedly complete form. There is no recognized attempt in *Perpetual Peace* to show how these fragments of theory may be reconciled with one another. The apparent paradox is simply allowed to persist.

It is therefore of considerable interest to consider whether it is Kant who is confused or whether there are essential weaknesses across the theories of international relations that make it impossible to develop a coherent picture of his work. Attempts to render Kant's position within any of meaningful aspect of the discipline serve only to highlight the exceptional difficulty scholars in the field have in cleanly establishing the limits and categories of their discourse. Attention to Kant serves rather to demonstrate how the poles of international relations theory stand less firmly on their own feet than they come to give each other muddied and mutable ground.

Requirements of a 'Kantian' Paradox

It is helpful to view recent and contemporary works in international relations that acknowledge intellectual debt to the writings of Kant as generally reflective of the turns of thought made available, for example, in the Grotian sentiments presented by Bull[85] as well as John Herz's musings surrounding the world-wide security atmosphere present after World War II.[86] In short, those in the study of international relations who draw from Kant tend to build not only on a perception of the world in which the relations between states are irreducible to notions of inter-state conflict; current appeals to Kant, in general, also work from an understanding that posits a distinct and intimate connection between a multiplicity of agents throughout and across what are traditionally taken as the international and the domestic realms.

The inspirational role that Kant's writings take on with respect to perceived relations between these networks of political actors and levels may be witnessed in a variety of subfields to the discipline. However the character of this position is certainly most manifest within the range of writing in peace studies which seeks to link *Perpetual Peace* to what is sometimes referred to as the "peace-loving democracies hypothesis."[87] Kant's writings are now most actively introduced as founding a set of contentions that aims to show that liberal democracies are less likely to be warmongering than other states. Taking a very broad interpretation of Kant's interest in the development of republican state-rule based on right, a significant collection of scholars popularize his work as providing an argument on which efforts to spread democracy throughout the globe may be justified.[88] The fundamental assertion of those who agree with this particular representation of Kant's theory is that genuinely peaceful rules within states will provide the conditions under which an international peace as imagined by Kant may be possible. It is proposed that the just, representative, and legitimate rule ideally characteristic of a democratic state will in itself inherently encourage like societies on an international register. In other words, peace within will foster peace without.

It must be understood, though, that the building of such a position has a much more powerful effect than simply bringing attention to lines of contact between international and domestic politics, as indicated in *Perpetual Peace*. It is important to note how the highly complex and essentially "difficult" position of Kant's texts in the study of international relations is manifest here and has its effect. I argue that the theoretical license that is taken in the name of Kant in this respect actually goes to suggest an entire metamorphosis in the very stuff from which international relations is conventionally thought to be made.

To begin with, the sense of irreconcilable distinction between states, which is maintained as the basis of readings of international relations attributed at root to Hobbes, is, of course, placed into serious doubt. This complex of Kantianisms points to deep interests and relations penetrating through and shared between states. More startling, though, the state, read here as primarily a democratic creature, is recognized not so much as the particular rule to which human subjects submit but, rather, as an institution available to the bidding of those who give it support. Thus, I contend, those who now argue for this particular Kantian approach to world politics effectively displace traditional interest in the role of national and community identity. Focus on the conflict between group interests and broad territorial claims are fundamentally replaced with a concentrated concern to do with the organization and, indeed, self-organization of individual human beings with respect to one another across the political spaces of the world.

Current readings of Kant do not diminish the state and state institutions. These remain as important and unavoidable structural requirements to the functioning of human societies. However, the purpose of states, as structures, is transformed from one in which national groups gain protection and advocacy to one in which the presumed individuality of human beings gains facilitation. As a result, Kantian international relations is produced as a study of rudimentary human needs and interests on a global scale and, in turn, produces a discourse of international relations in which "human-being" itself becomes the most important political classification.

The path of thinking that associates Kant's hope for peace with support for democratic rule is founded most evidently and importantly within a project initiated by Michael W. Doyle. There he aims to provide empirical evidence with which to substantiate the general thesis that a pacific world order is made possible with the spread of liberal political bodies.[89] Doyle interprets the development of the structures and ideals of twentieth-century democracies to have closely mirrored the very challenges first laid-out in Kant's Articles of *Perpetual Peace.* Taking the fundamental rights subscribed to by modern liberal states to consist in:

1. freedom from arbitrary authority,

2. equality of opportunity in education and rights to health care and employment,

3. and democratic participation or representation,[90]

and identifying the characteristic institutions desired by all liberals to recognize and foster:

1. juridical equality among citizens and other fundamental civic rights such as freedom of religion and press,

2. sovereign authority grounded in the legitimate consent of the electorate and employed free from all restraint apart from the requirement that basic civic rights be preserved,

3. an economy resting on a recognition of the rights of private property, including the ownership of means of production,

4. and the shaping of economic decisions by the forces of supply and demand, domestically and internationally, free from strict control by bureaucracies,[91]

Doyle seeks to identify *Perpetual Peace* as the very blueprint for the emerging trends of international relations in the late-modern world. He perceives it to be the case that, historically, liberal states are less likely to go to war. And Doyle believes that it is Kant that offers the best guidance in coming to an understanding of the reasons behind this phenomenon.[92] Furthermore, he seeks direction from Kant's text as to how a total peace between a world of democracies may finally be achieved.

In this regard, one should note that Doyle tends to avoid alignment between Kant's theory and "democracies" per se. Rather, he clings more faithfully to the broader category of "liberal states." Still, he effectively names democracies as the strongest example of the sort of republic to which he imagines Kant refers.[93] Moreover, the very rights and institutions he understands to be characteristic of liberal states are indeed synonymous with what would normally be understood as the ideals of contemporary Western democracies in most cases.

In any event, along with Armstrong, Beitz, Friedrich, and Gabriel, Doyle's fundamental point with respect to Kant is that he was simply ahead of his time. In this instance, Kant serves as the commanding voice of one who long ago saw the inevitable truth. Doyle's Kant offers reassurance that, with care and modern spirit, the battle lines of state borders must progressively fall and be replaced with signs of cooperation and mutual interest. He writes:

> Kant argued that the natural evolution of world politics and economics would drive mankind inexorably toward peace by means of a widening of the pacific union of liberal republican states. In 1795 this was a startling prediction. In 1981, almost two hundred years later, we can see that he appears to have been correct. The pacific union of liberal states has progressively widened. Liberal states have yet to become involved in a war with one another. International peace is not a utopian ideal to be reached, if at all, in the far future; it is a condition that liberal states have already experienced in their relations with each other.[94]

Doyle acknowledges that both Kant's theory and the broad range of human experience allow for failures and setbacks along the way to this proposed condition of total peace.[95] He is also aware that democratic states are not somehow naturally more "dovish" than nonliberal states.[96] However, Doyle tries to show that there does appear to be a relationship between motives of restraint and the adoption of liberal tenets within a state.[97] And, he notes that it is the historical pattern that, when compelled to take sides in actual or potential conflict, liberal states tend to pursue alliances with one another over nonliberal states.[98]

Doyle's argument is taken up with a considerable range of agreement and disagreement. David E. Spiro, for example, offers a spirited attack on Doyle's method of interpreting the numerical results of his historical data.[99] Christopher Layne, in another vein, questions what he understands as the causal logic inherent to the hypothesis advocated by Doyle.[100] However, the major bone of contention sustaining these debates is whether or not democracy or liberal institutions and customs can truly be seen as *sufficient* conditions for the supposed spread of peace in the world. As seems always the case in most questions of international relations, debate focuses on the extent to which one need give up or give in to specific elements of either realism or idealism in adopting this alleged Kantian perspective. For example, Charles W. Kegley, Jr., provokes a second look at a Wilsonian version of Kantian idealism on this accord.[101] Alternatively, Diana T. Meyers offers direct opposition to Doyle, arguing that he puts too much faith in Kantian morals and not enough in the forces of nationalism.[102]

There is also a swell of literature, authored by such scholars as William Antholis, Bruce Bueno de Mesquita, David Lalman, T. Clifton Morgan, Bruce Russett, Valerie L. Schwebach, and Erich Weede, which seeks to qualify Doyle's broad claims in such a way as to suggest that one can only truly predict that democracies will not fight one another.[103] These writers heed caution toward both poles of debate. While acknowledging the positive effects of liberal domestic order on international relations, they assert realist dictums warning that it is by no means clear that liberal states will not war any less against nonliberal states. At any rate, there seems to be general agreement that, if one is to accept the position advocated by Doyle, a global peace may be achieved only once all states are prone to democracy. Hence, the pervasive sense is that an international order composed completely of democratic/liberal states will at least provide conditions under which international peace, of the kind associated with Kant, may be possible.

Absent from Doyle's words and the debate surrounding his efforts in general, however, is much sense of what is at stake in the wavering between and around these poles of thought. These attempts to consider how changes in international relations may be thought beyond the intellectual commitments attributed to Hobbes largely ignore the very theoretical change that is therein required. Rather, this set of literature, which has indeed grown significantly since Doyle's first articles, has ultimately come to flounder within a duel over precision and problems in classification and categories. The three images of international relations identified by Waltz during the early years of the Cold War—man, the state, and war—[104] remain fully intact as the primary limits of analysis. And dispute arises simply in terms of how one ought to apply these images more appropriately or supply to them further subdivisions. As evidenced particularly well in Harvey Starr's work on theses put forward by Bueno de Mesquita and Lalman[105] as well as Layne's general critique of the peace-loving democracies hypothesis,[106] discussion remains well-ensconced within the abstract realm of experimentation with these 'variables'. Little attention is paid to how international relations, as a set of problems, is actually being negotiated anew with such questions. Man, the state, and war are not themselves reconsidered.

Yet, in debating Doyle's trust in the Kantian world he imagines, Doyle's critics and commentators effectively deny the utility of Waltz's categories of analysis in this regard. Despite sympathy for Doyle's general outlook, debate repeatedly demonstrates: (1) that there exists no sufficient evidence from which one may show that war is any less profitable or desirable as a political tool for democracies than for nonliberal states, (2) that democracies are not any more or less prone to peaceful relations than are nonliberal states, and (3) that a democratic people are not any more or less aggressive than those living in a nonliberal state. Instead, what this discussion of a potential democratic peace with respect to the writings of Kant produces is a definite shift of emphasis from the relevance of the character of traditional political agents to the effects of specific social conditions on individual human beings. The three images of international relations are progressively undermined with attention to a social and political situation in which people in fact ideally gain autonomy from international politics altogether.

In order to understand and appreciate this move, it is important to pay close attention to the characterisation of liberal rights and institutions that Doyle first offers, as listed above. For the exigent point of concern throughout this dialogue pivots on these items. Although what is of ultimate interest to these scholars is whether this type of Kantian perspective may or may not allow one to better predict the evolution of inter-state relations in the late-modern world, the fundamental question underlying all these studies is whether or not democratic principles themselves will have an effect on the course of international politics. And this question does not in itself provoke an analysis of the specific disposition of given men, states, or wars. Rather, it directs attention toward a consideration of what humans each ought to enjoy as beings within society. And what is inherently proposed in these liberal principles is an order in which human beings are not only able to gain distance and independence from one another but also from the state.

The conditions of peace that are debated by Doyle and his critics involve the extent to which the force of politics may be removed from peoples' lives within each state. Hence, this particular reading of the possibility of global peace through *Perpetual Peace* does not in fact lead one first and foremost to questions of the relations between states, nations, and national-citizens but, rather, to questions regarding the removal of conflict between individual people, regardless of political affiliation and station. It leads the most prominent scholars promoting Doyle's general vision directly to the position staked out by Linklater, as discussed in the Introduction.

For example, in his analysis of Kant's theory with regard to the potential success of a global collective security structure,[107] Gabriel L. Negretto suggests that the foreign policy of any given state ought to be directed away from the potential threats or alliances posed by other states and should, rather, be pointed toward the people within foreign political bodies. Citing the lack of stability achieved in the use of international force and sanctions against Iraq in the recent Persian Gulf War,[108] he champions Kant's stand against the legitimacy of war and the viability of an international executive.[109] Negretto calls on states instead to actively and with practical methods contribute to the material, legal, and political betterment of the people in other and all states. In this manner, he does happen to agree that the spread of democratic rules will only benefit the cause of peace.[110] However, Negretto's fundamental point is that Kant offers the key to achieving a peaceful world by bringing attention to the need to understand that whatever might occur in the arena of inter-state politics is radically conditioned by inter-human relations. And the former will result in global peace and prosperity only once states take up the latter as their leading interest.

Developing Negretto's sentiments a great deal further, Jack S. Levy focuses on Kant's claim that a republic which is truly representative of citizens' individual interests will be less likely to promote war as a political act.[111] He suggests that the manner in which democracy is actually lived by persons in respective states can more easily explain correlations between peace and the spread of democratic rule than analysis of any supposed structural influences of democracy itself.[112] At stake for Levy is the extent to which individuals within any given democratic state do indeed find satisfaction with the local interpretation of privacy. For it could well be said, in this way of thinking, that it is only when citizens of a democracy are not themselves able to freely avoid the competing interests and desires of other persons and groups that they will find reason to advocate undemocratic political means. Similarly, Russett notes that it is indeed the perception of personal autonomy which operates most fundamentally in this hypothesis.[113] Finding justification in Kant's analysis, he finds it reasonable to believe that those people who gain self-determination within an implementation of liberal principles will value these freedoms so greatly that they will tend to treat them as that to which all persons, either inside or outside the relevant state, have a right to appeal.

Echoing Russett's interpretation and adding his voice to those of Doyle[114] and Beitz,[115] Georg Sørensen extends this notion to the level of states themselves. He suggests that some form of complex relations must be at work between individual conviction and political machine in a truly liberal democracy so as to give rise to a phenomenon in which democratic states also grant the service of mutual respect of autonomy to one another.[116] Still the basis of Sørensen's claims rest at the level of what is possible in the lived experience of individuals. To begin with, he recalls the points made by Kant that conditions essential to an international peace will include increased and highly dynamic communication and trade between individuals world wide.[117] But, in order to fulfill the vision of international peace he admires and attributes to Kant, it is imperative for Sørensen that each person gain the same understanding that individual freedom and equality is something morally right and that this way of being is the politically legitimate manner of being for all persons. For, in this analysis, it is only when all human beings on this earth do indeed *act as* individuals and recognise others within their species *as* autonomous agents that a planet of democracies may be actualized.[118]

In this respect, Sørensen makes a particular effort to argue against John J. Mearsheimer's pessimistic views of the anarchical relations of states.[119] Sørensen tries to show that Kant's ideas are not as far removed from the assumptions inherent to neorealism and calls, instead, for a rethinking of anarchy wherein state sovereignty is still recognised but where cooperation is not only desirable but naturally unavoidable. And Sørensen has gained significant support on this point from Wade L. Huntley, who continues the argument that a Kantian understanding of anarchy in international politics is really the primary manner by which one can ever hope to explain, for example, the peace that is emerging between the former East-West divide.[120] Accepting Kant's theories to be most consistent with contemporary concerns for human rights,[121] Huntley re-introduces Kant's vision for Perpetual Peace as a "third way" between concerns over inter-state competition and hopes for global calm. He argues that Kant's theory explains how the anarchy of international relations may conjure civility on a world scale as it finally forces respect for a rule of law indebted to individual rights and freedoms in both domestic and international spheres.

Intended or not, then, the primary function that Kant's writing thus serves in the emergent analyses of international relations which seek both inspiration and justification from *Perpetual Peace* is to establish a theoretical ground where others have apparently failed. Debate continues with respect to the relations and order of states. Yet the resignation to power politics and the faith placed within the ability of human communities to overcome selfish interests, upheld respectively by realists and idealists, are effectively displaced as the fundamental determinants of how the dynamics of international relations are to be read. As interpretations of Kant within the field have made it all the more difficult to establish legitimacy in either realism or idealism, the axioms of each have proved far less useful to those who seek a theoretical source in Kant's work. Hence a new premise has necessarily emerged in light of which those of traditional international relations theory may be deemphasized or rendered secondary. Whereas *Perpetual Peace* was once a site in which battles over the convictions proper to realism and idealism were conducted, Kant's text increasingly serves international relations scholars as a source from which an apparently far less difficult commitment may be posited. Appeals made to Kant on the question of peace ultimately look for and find a new constant, where the respective character of international actors and political agents in general are progressively seen to display volatility, idiosyncrasies, and a penchant for change.

This is a commitment to what might be called the essential quality and needs of each human being. And this constant is thus the conditions that each human, in her or his supposed essential being, inherently requires and ideally strives for as a matter of politics. As such, the new premise that appears in this literature may be seen to provide the solidity required by the rigours of analysis, because it is a category to which all people could ultimately allegedly appeal. Unlike the social and historical structures of state institutions and offices and the socially conditioned character of individual men and women, human need and requirement, as defined within liberal ideals, offer a universal rule which is not subject to the throws of politics per se. Rather, such attention to human beings may be perceived to provide an incontestable foundation on which to build political structures.

The problem remaining in such a discourse, though, is to come to terms with how liberal principles are to be interpreted in detail. On its own accord, this trust in democracy and liberal institutions in general requires that this essence be determined in as precise terms as possible. For it is indeed the universalizable character of the limits of individuality that is of importance here. The hope for peace is fostered by a belief that there is a particular structure which could accommodate what is at heart the constitution of each person, regardless of other inclinations and interests that may pertain to the specific circumstances in which each individual may find her- or himself. The point is simply to determine what the limits of this structure should be and how they ought to be established. It should therefore come as no surprise that attempts to establish a Kantian analysis of international politics entices particular interest in ethics as logically prior to the formation of policy.

Masking International Relations in *Perpetual Peace*

That efforts in the discipline of international relations to employ *Perpetual Peace* in a positive manner should ultimately betray a prior dedication to the positions of individuals should indeed come as no great shock. This is particularly the case given the fact that a broader investigation of Kant's philosophy must undoubtedly uncover a fundamental interest in the rational autonomy of each and every human being.[122] What is of concern here, however, is what the result of such a commitment may be, as formed within studies of international relations indebted to readings of Kant.

As shown in the above discussion, the sense that underlies these allegedly Kantian analyses of international relations is that attention to the domestic and finally human component of international politics may offer a solution to the traditional bind that is seen to so often trouble foreign policy initiatives. The focus typically perceived in *Perpetual Peace* is taken to offer a "way out" of the continuing conflict that arises between the positions of realism and idealism. This line of thinking brings one to the individual as the ground for analysis, and thereby, theory emerges as an avenue through which *traditions* of debate may be diffused and resolved with respect to a moment of *lived* reality.

It is the case, however, that this supposed move from a competition in theory to an ostensibly universal empirical foundation for thought is at least as great an abstraction or miosis as ever may be found in either realism or idealism or any conversation between the two. The solution that scholars attribute to or claim to derive from Kant in a focus on the benefits of liberal tenets and democracy in international relations does not provide the grounds on which the traditional conflict between realism and idealism may be eliminated whatsoever. Rather, as with Linklater's privileging of cosmopolitan citizenship over republicanism, this particular set of interests in the study of international relations reproduces the same tensions. Moreover, in this appeal to a Kantian approach the traditional line of conflict and frustration are really only concealed in a different form.

Perhaps the most striking evidence of how the use of Kant's work in the discipline of international relations finally comes to rest on a particular image of human individuality is within the field of international law. It is here where problems of definition and the moral foundation of international conduct are developed with the greatest rigor and political import. Admittedly, the logic apparent in Sørensen's writing has certainly not always been received with interest among theories of international law. As with international relations theory in general, the historical convention in this regard persist quite to the contrary. Leslie A. Mulholland's consideration of Kant's theory of war, for example, takes the possibility of Kant's perpetual peace to rest on a mutually defined international code in which states agree to respect the rights of other states.[123] On this basis, Mulholland then chastises Kant and those who would follow his words for relying on the historical horrors of war alone to impel nations toward this respect and for not proposing concrete efforts by which to ensure that the rational course toward formalizing a binding international code will indeed take hold.[124] Recent efforts to theorize precisely how such work may promote a Kantian perpetual peace, however, produce a far different understanding of what is at stake in international law than Mulholland's work would allow.

In just such a manner, Daniele Archibugi contends that it is within Kant's cosmopolitanism, evidenced most significantly in the third Definitive Article of *Perpetual Peace*, that supporters of a perpetual peace may gain their greatest hope. According to Archibugi, this is due to the reason that the third Article does offer precise focus on all individual human beings as the aggregate ground for international law.[125] He believes that Kant's vision would allow for "the founding of a body within the international community to represent the peoples as citizens of the world."[126] Archibugi sees implied in *Perpetual Peace* the organization of an assembly, operating parallel to something like the United Nations, which would function to establish and uphold cosmopolitan law under the authority of world citizens for world citizens. Thereby, while realizing that Kant's vision itself still requires improvement,[127] he trusts that there is at least the possibility that threats of war may be diffused through a globally active recognition of human community and all the universal rights that may therein apply.

Fernando R. Tesón, who is perhaps now the most prominent and energetic of those attempting to rethink the importance of Kant's thought to international law, mirrors the intellectual shift of focus from states to individuals more strongly yet.[128] He is quite direct on this point, claiming that "respect for states is merely derivative of respect for persons."[129] Inspired by the language of *Perpetual Peace*, Tesón laments the conventional lack of attention paid to what he understands as "the important normative status of the individual."[130] He argues:

> Kant's originality stems not so much from having been the first to show the strong links between international peace and personal freedom, and between arbitrary government at home and aggressive behavior abroad. Not only did he have the vision to predict modern international organization for

> the maintenance of peace; he also explained, for the first time, the connection between domestic freedom and the foundations of international law. In essence, he foresaw the human rights revolution of the twentieth century.[131]

Finally, as if in direct critical response to Muholland's call, Tesón demands that the foundation of international law be restructured so that the conduct of international actors and the global institutions that may arise from their activities have as their primary interest the development of each human's potential toward freedom and autonomy.[132] He offers tacit agreement to Muholland's desire for greater activity in the institution of anything which may be called perpetual peace. However, the manner in which Tesón believes this is to take place requires that international law be removed from the rights of states altogether and, rather, be recoded as an inter-human law to which respective state laws ought to conform.

In this regard, Lynch sees serious problems in Tesón's interpretation of Kant. For, as she notes,[133] Tesón takes the tenets of *Perpetual Peace* as an excuse from which to legitimize the use of state intervention to ensure liberally defined human rights within those nonliberal states where such rights do not flourish.[134] And Lynch herself wishes to show that Kant's theory can in no way support an international legal structure in which state intervention, for any reason other than within the dynamics of civil war, is condoned. Yet her point does not stray at all far from the move displayed across the writings of Tesón, Sørensen, or Negretto.

Lynch insists that Kant's call for respect between states is a direct result of his prior interest that a broader sense of mutual respect is engendered among the people who constitute the states on this globe.[135] Hence, it is the case that Lynch also takes the requirements that Kant places on international law to revolve neither around the actions or character of states or citizens but rather around the principles under which each person ought to be understood and treated. Lynch implicitly maintains that what matters in the formation of a truly Kantian international law is not simply that individual interests be secured but, rather, that specific rights supposedly peculiar to each and every human being be upheld. From such a universal and universalising code as that, the vertical political structures, rules, and institutions may then arise accordingly.

Exactly how this seemingly novel approach to the ordering of world politics may take place, though, remains an open question.

Very little in the way of claims regarding how a Kantian world order is supposed to be structured has been offered within the community of international relations scholars. Most often one is left with comments which merely indicate a perceived brilliance in Kant's texts, which supposedly points one in the appropriate direction. For example, in the words of Chris Brown Kant is simply the "greatest of all theorists of international relations."[136] And this is, professedly, largely due to the fact that:

> Kant is . . . the first great thinker to realise the need for a full characterisation of political philosophy as not simply concerning the relations of human beings to their communities but as equally concerned with relations between these communities and between individuals and humanity taken as a whole.[137]

Or, in Linklater's analysis, Kant, along with Marx, develops the most persuasive defence for a fully international community composed not simply of citizens but of human beings.[138] Despite his complaints against what he sees to be Kant's neglect of historical situation, Linklater admires Kant for what he understands as Kant's foresight in identifying a political progression from smaller to larger communities to, finally, a transcendent sense of society.

At best, one may find recommendations with respect to the broad ethical requirements of this perspective. Stanley Hoffmann, for example, suggests that Kant's "moral politician" is faced with the task of developing policy that will move political communities toward a true world order, despite fragmentation and danger and with the help of those actors whose conduct is the basis for suffering, injustice, and repression both domestically and abroad.[139] With the United States foremost in his thoughts, he urges that:

> We need a statecraft that stresses long-term collective gains rather than short or long-term national advantages; that accepts the need for a large measure of institutionalization in international affairs, and for important commitments of resources to common enterprises; that shows great restraint in its use of means; and that goes, in its choice of ends, far beyond the realm of interstate relations.[140]

In facilitation of such aims, Hoffmann asks that intellectuals, media, and educators all work to provide others with the critical perspectives necessary in order to appreciate the circumstances and experiences of 'others' around the world.[141] His point is that all must learn to rise above a purely national and parochial vision of political context and consequences.[142] Hoffmann hopes that global-communal awareness may in itself bring about unity and mutual respect of some sort on political planes.

In addition, Tesón claims that, in accordance with Kant's Definitive Articles, the conditions of peace on earth require the institution of a series of global judicial bodies: an international court of human rights, an international court of justice, and an international court of trade.[143] He goes on to claim that the Charter of the United Nations ought to be amended so that only democratic states which hold respect for human rights are permitted to send representatives and so that states that are ruled by governments not enjoying the legitimate support of its citizens may be expelled from the organization altogether.[144] Tesón's hope is that the world is already so socially and politically interdependent that disciplinary action of this sort from international bodies will actually be viewed as significant. He places his faith in the political pressure of community values.

In this way, both Hoffmann and Tesón give a sense of what they each think it is going to take, on a global level, to arrive at the political structures under which peace may be possible. But neither of them provide an understanding of what sorts of local political progress will be necessary to allow for such global moves in the first place. The assumption here seems, rather, to simply be that 'we' have in fact mostly arrived at a set of local political institutions around the world from which a truly world-wide and permanent peace may be imagined and practically willed. And this, of course, fits in with Doyle's original comment that Kant's words have already been largely fulfilled. Democracy, including all of the latitude of freedom in activity and expression that are ideally constituted within such a liberal society, is still simply asserted as the condition under which peace is possible. Yet, the problem of democracy is not really brought into to question, as would be hoped by such people as Levy and Sørensen.

If one is to truly push the logic underlying the general sentiments that not simply democracy but the lived experience of people who enjoy democratic freedoms constitutes the path to possible perpetual peace, though, one must arrive at a very familiar picture. That is, one arrives not at a new set of principles from which to build the political all the way toward a successfully unified international order. Rather, one is forced to contract with assumptions thoroughly inherent to the conventional forms of international relations theory. Hence, one is faced with the traditional dynamics of conflict within one's analysis.

In attempting to define, with precision, what exactly it is about human being that may allow for universal norms in public and foreign policy and international law one must appeal to a particular finite *image* or *representation* of human being. A human model is required from which to determine the structural requirements of politics. However, it is practically impossible to determine the universal interests and inclinations of humans through an investigation of each and every one on the planet. Even if such a task could be accomplished, it is difficult to see how such data may be reduced to a set of sufficient common denominators. It is, furthermore, impossible to ever take into consideration the grand variety of nuance in goals and needs that proliferate across the myriad circumstances and challenges which face humans. Hence, one must theorise to the best of one's ability what sort of essential conditions would be satisfactory to all and what sort of fundamental political expression should be adequate to all. In this regard, one inevitably arrives at an ethical dictum—like the liberal tenets proposed by Doyle—in which a particular representation of human being is posited or implied.

The thesis that associates democracy or liberal tenets with the formation of global peace does in fact rest primarily on the notion that what *is* at heart the needs and wants of each human being *ought* to be reflected in the domestic and thus international political institutions that humans build. It is only through a final moral and universal position based on what humans supposedly *are* that the sort of legitimacy and, thus, effective force that, for example, Tesón's international structures require could be gained. And regardless of the specific essential content that is finally attributed to the category of human being, what is inevitably taken to be the condition of human being in the position delineated here is a matter of internal strife. At the very least, what must be assumed in order to hold to the sort of contention initially offered by Doyle is that each human is essentially *both* self-interested and, yet, desires that all others enjoy personal fulfillment in equal or better stance than her- or himself. Hence, the ground of this approach to international relations theory harbors within its essence the initial paradox that it is supposed to overcome.

The axiom from which this understanding of a Kantian peace may be developed remains fully embedded within the language of realism/idealism, when referring to the paradox regarding states. For, as is the case with the sort of state image derived from Hobbes, this vision of peace demands an individual who is both naturally autonomous but who is not naturally respectful of the autonomy of other individuals. Rather, this individual must be faced with the supposed dangers associated with not treating other individuals as deserving of autonomy. Hence, just as discourses of realism/idealism seek a mutual recognition of sovereignty in the pursuit of peace, the political dilemma of this brand of neo-Kantianism involves, first, finding manners in which individuality may be generally recognized as inarguably the condition of human-being. Second, just as statists place their hopes in military and economic alliances, the Kantian peace entails developing a combination of culture and institutions through which universal respect for the autonomy of each person will be ensured.

The ethical dictates that many would hope to find some way of impressing on the presumable anarchy of state relations are simply transferred by the supporters of Kant to the lives of human beings. And this is necessarily the case. For the 'facts' of human life are no less open to scientific interpretation than is the verity of sovereignty associated with geopolitical institutions. The 'reality' does not find automatic accord with the 'ideal' in this instance either.

The Need for Philosophical Reflection

In reading Hans Saner's detailed and efficacious examination of Kant's political thought,[145] one may be persuaded that Kant's work provides the grounds from which traditional contradictions and conflicts within international relations philosophy may be removed and overcome. Saner concludes that all of Kant's philosophy aims to displace such dichotomies and paralysing debate.[146] Similarly, in his investigations of possible reforms to internationalism with respect to world politics, Bartelson may convince one that the paradoxes of international relations theory "find resolution" within Kant's writings.[147] However, as things stand within the discipline at large, it would be essentially illegitimate for the vast majority of international relations scholars who draw from and/or debate the role of Kant in international relations theory to adopt the theses offered respectively by these two authors. For, Saner's analysis is founded on a highly rigorous and attentive reading of Kant's so-called political writings with respect to Kant's much larger and more sophisticated philosophical projects. And Bartelson's argument rests on his work to show how, in a broader theoretical context, Kant's writings can be seen to provide a complete reformulation of how *the international* is to be understood in the first place.[148] It is the case that the efforts of writers discussed in the above sections may demand, in a backhanded fashion, more radical critique and theorizing of the matters at issue. But this is not work which has been accomplished by those involved in the revival of Kant as a canonical figure in the discipline. There is, therefore, almost no basis in this literature from which to recommend or even appreciate the views of Saner or Bartelson.

Rather, it is the case throughout the literature discussing Kant as the ground from which the peace-loving democracies hypothesis springs that Kant's writing is rarely studied at all. Instead, the Articles proposed in *Perpetual Peace* are generally introduced as if they in themselves represented the full depth of his thought on the matter. Rigor of analysis is missing. Truisms abound. Hence, it is inevitable that the Kant that is typically found in *Perpetual Peace* should offer little more than what is already available in the conventions of international relations theory. In this manner, Kant appears to provide simply a 'novel' device through which old solutions may be considered. No substantial reason why one may care to actually take Kant seriously as a founding theorist of international relations is made evident.

What is perhaps of even greater concern is the fact that little in the way of serious self-reflection is manifest among those international relations scholars who draw on *Perpetual Peace*. As Kantian positions are assumed and often uncritically promoted within this literature, so is it the case that paltry attention is paid to the intellectual commitments underlying the various shades of international relations theory relevant here. Kant's thought goes uninvestigated, because the theories that seek to attach themselves to him are themselves left to operate unquestioned in any radical manner. Certainly, the peace-loving democracies hypothesis is hotly debated. But, again, this discussion remains at the level of interpreting statistics and the evaluation of how received modes of analysis are used. Reasons why it even may or may not be important to appeal to Kant's thought are not considered.

This general problem may be found only too well within the eventual privileging of individuality and human autonomy across these discussions. To begin with, Kant himself may have something quite different in mind in terms of the human condition than what is put forward by contemporary theorists of international relations. And, as noted above, it is likely impossible to find a true empirical referent for these terms in any event. However, even without taking these concerns into account, it remains unclear that such categories are of any use at all for understanding international politics. The requirements of human autonomy in the place of those proper to state sovereignty may provide solace to one trying to rethink the fundamental framework of international relations with respect to an age of increasing globalism. But, the adequacy of such axioms is not by any means certain either. Just as modern states must be understood as interrelated through commerce, communication, and even war, one ought to recognize the radical interrelation of human beings in achieving basic sustenance, in communicating, and competing. People do not live as atoms either. They engage in and are taken up by such multiplying and fragmenting positions as class agency, identity politics, social movements, environmental conditions, and societal responsibilities, to name just a few.

As may be seen in John M. Owen's defence of liberal theories of international peace and in Payne's rejection of the same,[149] the peace-loving democracies hypothesis attributed to Kant must rely on the power and projection of ideas and norms regarding human-being. But effective challenges to the viability of these very ideas are already brought forth by theorists who operate within this debate. Hoffmann, for example, warns that analyses of the role which globalized capital may have in promoting international peace, where political economy is understood primarily as a sphere emanating from individual activity, neglect how it is that global capital operates in public regimes far beyond interests or purposes applicable to individuals per se.[150] Thereby, Hoffmann brings the social/political context and location of individuality into question. Also, Ido Oren raises relevant queries regarding the source of the ideas required to substantiate the supposed fixed character of human-being proposed in liberal tenants.[151] He argues that the ideas typically generated and adopted in the development of liberal foreign policy really only represent a consensus opinion of what sort of democratic creature is acceptable to those political communities most interested in the spread of democracy in the first place.[152] Oren thus identifies the very subjectivity of what may be understood as a human individual as itself a problem in need of critical assessment.

These minor points of inquest suggested by Hoffmann, Oren, and myself, of course, do not necessarily lead to damning conclusions with respect to contemporary liberal theories of international relations and the interpretations of Kant on which they rely. But before they be found trivial, crucial, or otherwise, it is incumbent that the terms at issue here actually be considered with some degree of depth. Statements regarding whether or not liberal institutions and norms may promote international peace are of little significance until there is also an investigation of what theoretical commitments are inherently granted within these things. Furthermore, assertions apropos the causal force of respect for human autonomy in the overall cause of peace among all persons are trifling without an analysis of what might be understood by "an individual" and why.

This need for such primary work is perhaps best illustrated in Neta C. Crawford's identification of the ideas present in *Perpetual Peace* with the political arrangements made between Iroquois nations from about 1450 until 1777.[153] Crawford claims that "The Iroquois League anticipates Kant's thesis that republican states should not fight each other, resembling in practice Kant's theory of a league of peace."[154] Furthermore, he suggests that if international relations theorists had taken as seriously this history of international politics between the Iroquois as they have the record of wars between Western European nations, the paradigms under which international relations now operates and is understood may be one far more gracious toward the ideas of Kant, or even Grotius, than they are to a Hobbesian pessimism.[155] In the end, Crawford's point is that the history of the Iroquois League suggests that international peace may be best secured where democracies are present and a will toward inter-state agreements emerges in a general fashion.[156] Yet, nowhere in this analysis is there the slightest attention to how in fact the Iroquois' idea of individuality or autonomy may differ from those present in European traditions or, for that matter, in the thought of Kant.

Using the criteria of "degree of political participation,"[157] Crawford merely attempts to show that the political organisations within Iroquois nations of this period are analogous to democracies, as theorised by Europeans. But even in this regard, he gives substantial evidence that betrays the possibility that very significant differences—perhaps even contradictions—exist between the Iroquois experience and Western custom. In contrast to the traditionally male-centred, property-oriented, majority-ruling, and stratified political order on which Western democracy has been and is constructed, the Iroquois practiced universal suffrage, followed matrilineal orders, developed policy on a consensual basis, and pursued nonhierarchical organization.[158] Hence, as with almost all current attempts to invigorate a Kantian perspective in international relations, Crawford's position is in the end empty. He essentially asserts that one may trust that a Kantian democratic peace may function quite well, because a peace between nations that has succeeded in the past was a democratic peace of the kind envisioned by Kant. No analysis of democracy or Kant's theory, however, is offered by Crawford. They are both simply assumed as given and related entities. Therefore, the potential relevance that either democratic values or the Articles of *Perpetual Peace* may have to the prospect of peace between nations is here thoroughly lost. The point remains, rather, effectively a tautology: that a Kantian peace has been shown to function in practice, because a Kantian peace has been shown to function in practice.

At base, scholars of international relations engaged in the debates discussed here need to ask: *How* is it that liberal theory must ultimately privilege respect for individual rights? The conditions under which it is possible to do so must be traced. To be sure, there can be no easy or straightforward answer to such a problem. Unfortunately, though, the response made most readily available to this question amounts simply to pointing a finger back at the spines of dusty books sporting such names as Kant. A liberal *tradition* is appealed to as if it were a past realm in which debate had occurred and concluded and from which one may now take and leave ideas as it suits one. But whether liberal scholars of international relations find it convenient or not, they are involved in the same theoretical dilemmas in which Kant wrestled with others. The theories and positions taken with respect to the peace-loving democracies hypothesis are fully complicit with philosophical disputes that were and remain unresolved in any final sense. Hence, at the very least, if it becomes attractive, either positively or negatively, to refer and appeal to Kant's thought on matters of international relations and political issues facing human beings across the world, one ought to actually read Kant in a critical manner. One should develop a sense of how it is that Kant himself comes to maintain and privilege certain categories and not others in his own discussions of politics.

2

Kant and the (Im)Possibility of International Relations Theory

The foundation of analysis that Kant offers theories of international relations is quite peculiar with respect to other approaches recognized within the Western canon of political thought. Scholars of international relations may directly devise ways in which the writings of Machiavelli or Hobbes appear to simply mirror and provide historical pedigree to central categories of analysis traditionally assumed within the field. And, this is certainly the case with such levels of analysis as man, the state, and war. However, it is difficult to escape the fact that Kant aims much further, to reflect deeply on how such categories may justifiably take shape. Given his central concerns for morality and theories of knowledge, Kant's writing serve to describe and order debates about the appropriate form of the world in which international politics is perceived. It also establishes the limits to and conditions underlying the possibility

This chapter is a revised and extended version of Mark F. N. Franke, "Immanuel Kant and the (Im)Possibility of International Relations Theory," published in *Alternatives: Social Transformation and Humane Governance* 20, no. 3 (July–Sept., 1995): 279–322, Copyright ©1995 by Lynne Rienner Publishers, Inc.

of action in this world. Thus, insofar as Kant is taken seriously, the manner in which his work is rendered as a point of reference or an intellectual source within theories of international relations has a potentially large impact on how the very structure of international politics is produced as an object of study.

Unfortunately, though, as I begin to indicate in the previous chapter, Kant is repeatedly *underread* as a thinker of international relations. He does receive somewhat valuable attention, in this regard, across the more general province of political theory.[1] However, the broader intellectual commitments that inform Kant's writing are persistently ignored or oversimplified within discussions and disputes over international politics specifically. Subsequently, those international relations theorists who draw on or refer to Kant's writings in a constitutive manner necessarily also neglect to question their own grounding. Thus, as witnessed in chapter 1 and as is often the case with Machiavelli or Hobbes as well, Kant's writings ultimately serve simply to legitimize or authorize assumptions about international politics that are typically taken for granted. And the form and character of international politics is assumed where these things ought to stand out as serious problems for debate.

At best, Kant's discussions of international relations are conventionally treated within the discipline as if they were simply derived from his philosophical inquiries. His account of international politics is traditionally approached as a mere application of his struggles in philosophy to the interactions between actors in the world. Hence, the pervasive treatment of Kant in the discipline duplicates the relationship more generally expressed by international relations scholars to political philosophy. There persists the sense that one may simply draw on the work of good philosophy for the purposes of building good theories of international relations. The fact that ideas of the international themselves are integral to certain philosophical problems is ignored. And figures like Kant are allowed to appear in a divided light, where their philosophical works, on the one hand, inspire them toward certain conclusions regarding politics, on the other hand.

My contention in this chapter, however, is that there is not simply *a* Kantian politics that is drawn from Kantian philosophy. I submit that Kant does not simply implement a particular perspective in the arena of international politics. Rather, I argue that a critical reading of Kant's political writings with respect to his larger intellectual projects shows that what may appear as his theory of international relations arises necessarily *within* his philosophy.[2] International relations is not a set of problems that he merely addresses. Politics alone, for that matter, is not for him already given as such. Rather, the politics of civil society and the state are things that Kant finds he must construct and engage, given his specific struggles to practically orient himself as a thinking, free-willing being. Politics is not for him something that one may or may not choose to confront. Rather it is a set of conditions that emerge inescapably in the practical engagement of rational life. And it is a problem, according to Kant's analysis, that necessarily takes international form.

In this manner, he illustrates the fact that the very conception of international politics, along with the idea of politics itself, does not refer to objects available to analysis in their own terms. Rather, Kant, provides substantial evidence to show that both dimensions of politics arise, in tandem, as responses to specific problems in epistemology, reason, and ethics. And he thereby indicates that the crucial debates regarding international politics are not to be found in the tension between competing views *of* the same. Rather, the stakes of any study of international politics resides in how one chooses to understand the constitution of the international as a question in general. To and fro arguments between realism and idealism simply disregard the intellectual foundation that provide these poles of concern mutual grounding. And such debates are therefore inadequate to the politics of their own conditioning.

Investigating his thought in this vein, I ultimately argue that Kant's reasoning suggests the *impossibility* of a theory of international relations, as such. Hence, I propose that to take his ideas seriously is to place the traditional constitution of the discipline at considerable risk and question, rather than to conserve any particular canonical moment. Instead of suggesting a mere rethinking of international relations, as proposed by Huntley, Negretto, Sørensen, and Tesón, Kant's writings offer an opportunity to more fully reconsider what politics in the world could and can mean.

My approach in substantiating the above claims proceeds along a mostly expository route. In the previous chapter I followed the traditional reading practice, focusing exclusively on the expression of Kant's ideas through *Perpetual Peace*. Here, however, I build from that point and expand my reading widely, exploring his thoughts pertaining to politics that appear throughout his three *Critiques* as well as his numerous shorter writings on politics, history, ethics, and anthropology. I first argue that, despite the seemingly endless efforts to understand where it is that Kant is best located within the spectrum of international relations theory, his writings fit neither neatly nor awkwardly into the traditional debates. I show, to the contrary, that Kant argues strongly against the premises of either realism or idealism, as they jockey respectively for the legitimate hold of the mainstream. Second, I demonstrate that the similarities that international relations scholars often claim to detect between the discipline's conventional concerns and his attention to the course of history, requirements of nature, and individual autonomy is founded on a failure to consider precisely how he theorises such notions to begin with. Third, I trace how it is that Kant's account of international relations is a direct result of his inquiry into such fundamental philosophical problems as knowledge, ethics, and judgment. In this fashion, I aim to illustrate how his understanding of the components of international affairs is radically opposed to that customarily offered in the discipline. Lastly, I discuss what it might mean to understand him as a theorist of the impossibility of theorizing international relations. Supporting the notion that his political thought is continuous with his project of critique, I consider the implications of Kant's challenges to analyses of interstate politics and what his writings might ultimately offer as a theory in this respect, if anything at all. And from this point, I show how he demands a project of politics and analysis altogether different from that upheld within discourses of international relations.

Kant's Refusal of Traditional Debates

There are specific points in his writing where Kant appears to share the outlook fundamental to the entire mainstream of international relations theory. None are more startling than his now renown statement: "Nothing straight can be constructed from such warped wood as that which man is made of."[3] Here he shares the view that humans are inherently self-interested and indisposed toward pure deeds that could benefit the concerns of humanity at large. Realism affirms this point as an ahistorical truism leading humans always to war. Alternatively, idealism takes it as the historical condition from which humans are ultimately impelled toward peace. And Kant seems to reflect this hope as well, asking elsewhere: "How indeed can one expect something perfectly straight to be framed out of such crooked wood?"[4] He too sees that people[5] have great difficulty in willingly founding a just civil society. And Kant displays concern over the apparent inability or lack of natural interest in humans to work toward political relations with others based on respect for the needs and conditions of those others, let alone all. But, he is curious to wonder what good things could still be formed from such a lamentable starting point.

Recent deliberation on this point may not be as polarized as in the time of Carr and Alfred Zimmern, but realism and idealism remain the intellectual limits of international relations theory. Despite the rise of new *isms* in international relations theory, such as globalism, neorealism, internationalism, structuralism, transnationalism, and functionalism, the suppositions of realism and idealism still sustain the roots of its debates, great or otherwise. Theories of international relations stay committed to the questions of whether there are particular patterns of behavior (faults) that remain constant in human beings and/or society or whether the inclinations and tendencies of people and the communities they form are subject to progressive transformation. With regard to Kant, then, the primary question still largely continues to be whether or not his comment on the "warped" character of men is to be interpreted as realist, idealist, or somewhere in between. Scholars contest each other for the right to claim his intellectual heritage in these terms.

As demonstrated in the previous chapter, though, readings of Kant's thought may arise on either side and throughout the range of possibilities here. And this is legitimately the case. For, it is certainly true that Kant holds to the notion of a Hobbesian state of nature[6] and admits to an anarchic realm between states.[7] It is also the case that Kant keeps faith in the possibility of a universal cosmopolitan community of human beings.[8] But the question regarding which *ism* or *isms* in international relations theory most appropriately have the right to claim Kant as a predecessor is ill-posed from the start. For, despite the apparent affinities noted above, he flatly refuses the legitimacy of either realism or idealism or any possible combination of the two. The philosophical ground from which Kant's political theory arises denies the great debates of international relations theory and sheds a quite different light on what his apparently contradictory or paradoxical stance on international politics might imply. As a result, one must finally admit that Kant's approach to theorising international politics has much less to do with adopting the appropriate theoretical framework than it does in questioning the grounds on which one would choose to view politics through a specific framework at all.

Consider the case of realism alone. In spite of Kant's depiction of inter-state politics as anarchic and his constant rejection of the possibility of any world-wide government,[9] Kant's writings are generally and most immediately found to challenge the assumptions of realism. For those who appeal to realism in their analyses of international affairs, Kant is more often deployed as a foil than a comrade. It is only Waltz who puts forward an overt argument for reading Kant as any sort of true realist. However, there is some textual evidence beyond *Perpetual Peace* which may be seen on first glance to sustain Waltz's interests in some regards.

First, while not fully supporting the notion that humans are naturally and eternally in a state of war with one another, Kant does appear to admit to a natural plan in the human environment that foretells precise limits to what they, as a species, may set their hopes. If one downplays the final emphasis on the presumably good ends, Kant seems here to imbue the movement of humanity only with what a natural state permits, regardless of what individuals may will:

> Individual men and even entire nations little imagine that, while they are pursuing their own ends, each in his own way and often in opposition to others, they are unwittingly guided in their advance along a course intended by nature. They are unconsciously promoting an end which, even if they knew what it was, would scarcely arouse their interest.[10]

In addition, Kant points to seemingly ingrained traits in human behavior repeatedly borne out in society. He praises, most of all, the supposed self-interest in humans, which he believes compels them toward both individual excellence and social completeness:

> Nature should thus be thanked for fostering social incompatibility, enviously competitive vanity, and insatiable desires for possession or even power. Without these desires all man's excellent natural capacities would never be roused to develop.[11]

However, for Kant to sustain the realist theory that purports to *explain* why it is that humans have finally banded into supposedly sovereign and warring states, he, like Waltz, would have to accept that there is a nature in human beings that is given and knowable in itself. To be able to account for a particular state of affairs in inter-state politics on the basis of what one understands as the warped character of all persons is to admit that individuals and their societies, as objects of study, are already immediately accessible to scholars. To profess that one may know and predict the international conduct of humans on the basis of the selfishness they allegedly display repeatedly through time is to do more than offer a description of historical patterns. It is to claim that patterns in the history of humanity provides consistent evidence of the very constitution of all persons. Realism must, at heart, lay claim to direct knowledge of what humans at least in part are. But Kant holds nothing of the sort and, thus, actually counters any theoretical hold which Waltz and his colleagues may assume they enjoy.

It is the fundamental starting point of Kant's *Critique of Pure Reason*[12] that, through failure, centuries of inquiry have shown it impossible for one to perceive that which may reside within an object in itself. At the root of Kant's theory is his argument that one's mind gains a "relation" to objects in themselves only via the mediation of particular intuitions of the mind. Thus he surely does not offer grounds for the direct epistemological certainty that realists prefer and require in determining the reality of human relations in politics.

Rather, Kant explains that one's mind gains connection to external physical objects, including other persons, the world around, and the relations between these things first through the intuition of *space*. According to Kant, through the capacity to sense the world, a person's intuition is able to then *represent* the world to her or his understanding:

> Objects are *given* to us by means of sensibility, and it alone yields us *intuitions*; they are *thought* through the understanding, and from the understanding arise *concepts*. But all must, directly or indirectly, by way of certain characters relate ultimately to intuitions, and therefore, with us, to sensibility, because in no other way can an object be given to us.[13]

With the representations in one's understanding, one may then *conceive* of a world and the things in it. Thus, Kant terms this intuition *empirical* and he names that which it represents from sensibility *appearance*.[14] But Kant rejects that on this basis one's mind knows an empirical fact *in itself*. On the contrary:

> That in the appearance which corresponds to sensation I term its *matter*; but that which so determines the manifold of the appearance that it allows of being ordered in certain

> relations, I term the *form* of appearance. That in which alone the sensations can be posited and ordered in a certain form, cannot itself be sensation; and therefore, while the matter of all appearance is given to us *a posteriori* only, its form must lie ready for the sensations *a priori* in the mind, and so must allow of being considered apart from all sensation.[15]

Though the senses offer objects to one's mind for it to know, what is sensed, the appearance, is understood still only insofar as it is represented to one's mind by the a priori intuition of space. What is sensed is known by one's mind only inasmuch as these objects affect the senses. No absolute encounter with what an object may be in itself is possible.[16] According to Kant, the context, meaning, and figure that the experienced world may take on in knowing are not material in themselves but, rather, exceed experience. Thus the *real* design of humans and their relations toward one another in the world is not obtainable for him through observation alone.

Alternatively, Kant admits that the mind gains impressions via inner sense as well. These are matters of pure intuition, which he calls *time*.[17] It is an a priori intuition that he understands to underlie all intuitions, in that some form of sequence and consecution to what is known is always required for understanding to take place.[18] However, the representations of inner sense depict no object at all, not even a soul or thought. Only those representations that have their source outside of the mind via space can be perceived as otherwise from it and are, thus, objectifiable. Therefore, he claims, internal sense provokes, instead, representations of the processes of one's mind, of the ordering and schematizing of the representations of the outside world.[19] It has no actual or potential geography to it, but only a flux of impressions from which no point of observation is possible.[20]

Furthermore, Kant warns that time is itself not capable of producing any knowledge or objective-in-itself reality in one's mind either:

> If we abstract from *our* mode of inwardly intuiting ourselves—the mode of intuition in terms of which we likewise take up into our faculty of representation all outer intuitions—and so take objects as they may be in themselves, then time is nothing. It has objective validity only in respect to appearances, these being things which we take *as objects of our senses*.[21]

Although all appearances understood by one's mind are in relations of time—which is not to say that *all* things are in time but only those that appear to a given mind—the reality of time itself persists only insofar as outer or inner senses make available appearances to be represented in time. Further, Kant insists:

> On the other hand, we deny to time all claim to absolute reality; that is we deny that it belongs to things absolutely, as their condition or property, independently of any reference to the form of our sensible intuition; properties that belong to things in themselves can never be given to us through the senses.[22]

If time were a property of phenomena it could not be known in any immediate sense. It too would have to be represented to one's mind.

Kant must then acknowledge that, on the one hand, the representation one human being makes of another in time does not reach the observed person's actual self as that person experiences her- or himself. For example, the view of other humans that the realist holds is first constructed from what appears to his senses via space and time. This view is not a glimpse within the heart of any being. Thus, the realist has no actual grasp on the reality of humans, their conditions, or their relations between each other per se.

On the other hand, Kant must also even deny the availability of certain and complete self-knowledge through simple introspection. Noting that "I" is always the referent to which all determinations of one's experience are made, he admits that one may very well establish an identical self-consciousness through time. The self is taken to be numerically identical at each point in time.[23] But, Kant argues, this "I" is only a logical constant. Self-consciousness in all times does not in itself demonstrate an actual persisting self, knowable across all times.[24] He explains:

> The identity of the consciousness of myself at different times is therefore only a formal condition of my thoughts and their coherence, and in no way proves the numerical identity of my subject. Despite the logical identity of the 'I' such a change may have occurred in it as does not allow of the retention of its identity, and yet we may ascribe to it the same-sounding 'I,' which in every different state, even in one involving change of the [thinking] subject, might still

> retain the thought of the preceding subject and so hand it over to the subsequent subject.[25]

One's own nature, as a human being, if there is indeed such a thing to be found, is thus also at a distance. And the possibility of developing realist perception of actual human being and society is therefore further frustrated.

In his *Critique of Judgment*,[26] taking up a discussion of the general purposiveness in nature, Kant makes a stand against realism in a much shorter and more direct order. Here he is referring to philosophical realism and not specifically to the "realism" of international relations theory, fixed retrospectively to Hobbes. But, as intimated nearer the beginning of this section, the theoretical commitments of political realism slide directly back to philosophical realism in any event. Political realism must ultimately, in order to give confidence to the social/political laws of behavior it purports to describe, admit to an essential constitution driving the behavior of humans objectively observable in nature. Otherwise it could not pretend to truly explain or predict anything about the relations of and between human communities. It could offer only belief based on perceived social tendencies, a ground insufficiently rigorous or stable for the aims of social science. On this point Kant charges that the realist who not only proposes some design in human nature but also seeks to account for human activity on that basis—which is surely the whole point of realism in international relations theory—must logically believe in some form of practical causality in this design. However, Kant argues that the certainty and objective reality of such a physical design operating in human beings is inconceivable:[27]

> But the possibility of living matter cannot even be thought; its concept involves a contradiction because lifelessness, *inertia*, constitutes the essential character of matter. The possibility of matter endowed with life and of collective nature regarded as an animal can only be used in an inadequate way (in regard to the hypothesis of purposiveness in the whole of nature) so far as it is manifested by experience in the organization of nature on a small scale, but in no way can its possibility be comprehended *a priori*.[28]

Kant suggests that a realist position, given the fact that it claims to know something essential about the very core of human life, must finally beg questions about what might be the purpose described in elementary matter. Kant views such a position as requiring an almost complete metaphysics. And, he argues, the ground on which such *hylozoism* may be constructed is as beyond possible experience as is anything posited as in-itself.

Kant rejects idealist conclusions in no less certain terms. One may certainly also find textual evidence that appears to support the range of hope in international relations theory which projects international peace as a reasonable promise. But, any expression on Kant's part that humans may learn to live peacefully with one another and that a warped character is not a final fact of nature but something out of which humans may naturally grow is wrongly linked to conventional liberal analyses of international politics. While he may share hopes and ideals with this arm of the discipline, he offers not even the slightest proportion of agreement with the science on which it purports to rest.

On the one hand, Kant agrees that humans display a propensity toward evil behavior at all levels of politics. He takes the cruelty, deceitful, and selfish character of humans to be manifestly obvious both in whatever one might understand to be "Man's state of nature" or within the protective confines of civilized states.[29] Moreover, Kant suggests that it is within the international realm where the nastiness of people is evident most of all:

> But if we are not yet content [with this thesis], we need but contemplate a state which is compounded in strange fashion of both the others, that is, the international situation, where civilized nations stand towards each other in the relation obtaining in the barbarous state of nature (a state of continuous readiness for war), a state, moreover, from which they have taken fixedly into their heads never to depart. We then become aware of the fundamental principles of the great societies called *states*—principles which flatly contradict their public pronouncements but can never be laid aside, and which no philosopher has yet been able to bring into agreement with morality. Nor (sad to say) has any philosopher been able to propose better principles which at the same time can be brought into harmony with human nature. The result is that the *philosophical millenium*, which hopes for a state of perpetual peace based on a league of peoples, a world-republic, even as the *theological millenium*, which tarries for the completed moral improvement of the entire human race, is universally ridiculed as a wild fantasy.[30]

On the other hand, it must be kept in mind that Kant sees here only a *propensity* toward evil, which does not, in his estimation, betray the nature of human being either.[31] For by "propensity" Kant is referring to the subjective grounds from which persons may deviate from moral laws.[32] He is not suggesting that people cannot help but be evil. In fact, Kant goes on to argue that the notion that humans are necessarily corrupt makes no sense whatsoever.[33] The extent to which a person is good or evil, on his account, is a matter of what that person freely wills. An evil human being is one who freely subordinates sensuous incentives over those of moral law.[34] Therefore, it is Kant's position that a person may conversely will the moral law as the condition of sensuous incentives as well. And, thus, it follows that he maintains the idea that people may always alter their actions toward the formation of a good and peaceful life.

However, Kant does not then claim that this fact gives one grounds from which to determine whether the relations of human beings can or will ever improve. He does not predict that they certainly will establish a social order that is not subject to corruption. To begin with, Kant argues that no person has the capacity to assuredly know whether his maxims are directed toward the good or evil in any event. He claims, rather, that the inner principles of one's maxims ("the deeps of the heart") are simply unobservable.[35] In addition, returning to his *Critique of Judgment*, one may see that Kant rejects the explanatory force required by the commitments of idealism in general.

Taking idealism to offer a thesis in direct opposition to realism—that what naturally transpires is essentially undesigned, as opposed to essentially designed, and that human nature must allow for change through the course of time—Kant argues that idealism can offer no predictions of the sort that Doyle and others attribute to him:

> The systems which defend the idealism of final causes in nature grant, it is true, on the one hand, to their principle a causality in accordance that it designedly determines itself to this its purposive production; in other words, they deny that the cause is a purpose. . . . Thus nothing is explained, not even the illusion in our teleological judgments, and consequently the pretended idealism of these is in no way established.[36]

It is also the case here that Kant is referring to idealism as a problem in philosophy and not the specific definition given the term in international relations theory. However, political idealism must ultimately find its support in metaphysics no less so than political realism. For if a theorist of international relations actually expects to be able to confidently claim that international politics, historically stricken by conflict and violent fragmentation, may evolve toward a universal community of human beings, she or he must also be willing to claim that the apparent habits of humans, or even the very nature they share, can be changed in time and changed in a specific direction in unison. However, this is what troubles Kant. His point is that, even if one could determine that the nature of naturally occurring beings is without design, which is exactly what international relations scholars of the idealist persuasion must finally profess, on that very basis, nothing could be said about what is definitely possible in human beings or specific societies, let alone international relations. To suggest that there is no matrix to be found in human nature is also to admit that the consequence of events or actions is also without logically determinant end.

Furthermore, on the same grounds that realism is rejected in the *Critique of Pure Reason*, Kant must also deny the most elementary step of the idealism employed in theories of international relations. For, as he argues that what a thing in itself may be is not available to experience, he must also admit that what a thing in itself may not be is also beyond sensibility. For Kant, one can no more claim with direct certainty that the nature of humans is undesigned than one can assert that it is designed. It is certainly the case that, for Kant, one can make reflective judgments about such design, which do have their own grounds of justification.[37] And I will spend considerably more time on this point in the following chapter. However, for the present purposes, it is safe to say that Kant denies the empirically objective purchase that both realism and idealism require to make their respective cases in the realm of politics.

The contradiction of both realism and idealism in the writings of Kant should not, however, suggest that Kant denies the possibility of knowing and studying the politics of human beings whatsoever. He does not slump into a radical skepticism on this point. Kant does not resign his knowledge to a mere intellectual life. Rather, his project is largely to argue against what he sees as the dangers of the skepticism offered by David Hume and other empiricists. Kant is concerned, instead, with showing that the sort of assumptions that underlie both realist and idealist approaches of the sorts taken up in the study of international relations are dangerously deceptive and display an irresponsibility in any effort to discover how it is that human beings may know and conduct study appropriately.

For Kant, the conditions of knowledge are far more complicated and have implications for political wisdom far different than those assumed in either realism or idealism. As Henry E. Allison effectively argues, a grasp of neither logical, psychological, nor even ontological conditions of the apparent empirical world is sufficient for the production of true knowledge in this regard. Rather, as Allison insists, there are specific "epistemic conditions" that must first obtain for Kant in full.[38] Otherwise, one is dealing only with belief, opinion, or dogma.

Concluding that the a priori intuitions of space and time themselves do not provide knowledge, Kant determines that knowledge is also dependent on a priori concepts (categories).[39] He reasons that it is under these that one's understanding unifies various representations gained through experience together in general terms. One's mind then makes sense in this relation of appearance and category through a synthesis in one's imagination of the manifold that is made available through intuition. By synthesis, Kant means the schematizing of aspects of the manifold into particular relations within specific points and moments of space and time.[40] Thus, he defines the understanding as a faculty of judgment.[41] For, it is through understanding that particulars of the manifold are distributed under universals, namely, the categories.[42] However, this faculty of judgment is not in itself sound but requires reason to secure the rules of understanding under principles.[43] And it is in reason that the true challenge of Kant's theory begins.

Kant's claim that reason secures the rules of understanding through principles means that he believes reason to maintain a correct apprehension of particular things, such as human beings, in the broader scope of reality through concepts.[44] The role of reason in this regard is, thus, to guarantee unity of the judgments made through understanding, "just as the understanding brings the manifold of intuition under concepts and thereby connects the manifold."[45] Through logical discrimination, reason is to render consistent one's respective understandings of individual things in the world in terms of what must hold for the entire domain.[46]

For Kant, Nature's gift of insightful understanding can gain precision and accuracy only through respect of its own limits.[47] However, in order to deliver such respect, reason must also be sure that the domain by which it disciplines its discriminatory practices is already logically justified. And such justification is not easily obtained or recognized. For the conclusion by which reason seeks to guarantee unity itself ultimately rests on a universal rule open to the requirements of the unity reason functions to discover in understanding. Reason has no obviously manifest universe before it by whose limits it could automatically make sense of the endless judgments made available through understanding.

Kant's point is that, in evaluating the soundness of one's various understandings of the world around one, reason discovers that its grounds for doing so well are themselves in need of logical support. The understanding provides no certain metric in its own judgments. And human reason is not necessarily guided by the true limits in which the unity of these judgments is made possible. As Kant notes, human reason has a natural tendency to transgress the limits of experience.[48] As he shows in his discussion of "The Antinomies of Pure Reason,"[49] it is possible for reason to build strong and contradictory arguments—not at all unlike the universal contradictions made between realism and idealism—about the character and nature of the world, the beings within the world, the causal connections between them, and the being that may or may not be responsible for the whole series. But, as Kant argues, neither argument is necessarily sound, given the fact that reason has no direct contact with the things from which reason can successfully argue its point. Reason's objects are not formed from experience, as is the case with understanding, but only from the representations available in understanding. They are representations of representations.[50] Thus, reason can only identify its limits through the power of logic alone.

According to Kant, in determining a unity for understanding, reason must then pursue a very general task: "to find for the conditioned knowledge obtained through the understanding the unconditioned whereby its unity is brought to completion."[51] And, he argues, it does so by first persuading itself that there must exist a necessary ground (being), by which all other phenomena are conditioned. Second, reason seeks the concept of such an unconditioned entity and discovers it in the sufficient condition of all reality. Hence, third, reason must conclude that what it conceives, as an all-containing and limitless unity, must be a single and supreme existence (God).[52] However, this supreme being, as unconditioned, can only be a thing in itself. It is therefore beyond the possibility of experience and not knowable as such.[53] And the ultimate task of reason is thus to discover the limits imposed by the unconditioned condition on the world it seeks to know without having immediate perceptions of that ground.

In this manner, it is certainly possible to see a form of idealism at the heart of Kant's thinking. For it is clearly the case that he takes the objects of reason to exist only within one's mind. Given the fact that they are not things in themselves either but, rather, conditions underlying the possibility of things, the intuitions that give appearances over to the understanding and the categories in which appearances gain order each originate within the subject.[54] Hence, for Kant, there is an ideal quality to the character of phenomena. Yet, in addition, he soundly rejects the Cartesian notion that ideas can be generated independently within the mind. Kant's point is that the "I think" cannot and does not stand on its own but must always involve a thinking about a something external to the mind itself.[55] He holds that it is only through experience outside of one's mind that one may actually engage phenomena about which ideas may be formed.[56] Kant is thus also fastly committed to the limits of empirical reality.

As Paul Guyer argues, the process of self-knowledge also requires and identifies a fundamental realism in Kant's position.[57] But this "empirical realism" leads Kant, necessarily, to what he terms "transcendental idealism," wherein the grounding of both the idealism and realism of international relations theory are still refused. For, from this position, Kant cannot simply seek to anchor ideas to an objective reality given as such. Nor can he aim to force the empirical to fit the ideal. Rather, Kant may only search for the manner in which a subjectively grounded objective world must be arranged in space and time in order for him to reason as he does.

For this reason, Allison quite correctly maintains that the simultaneously intelligible and empirical character of Kant's rational agent does not mean that this subject suffers from a contradictory nature. Rather this dual character is what permits it the rational agency that Kant attributes to it. The agent's actions, goals, and ideas are never either merely determined by objects of sensation nor psychological state. Rather, it is faced with the challenge of justifying one in terms of the other.[58] What is thus implied here is the need for a highly rigorous and sophisticated rational project directed toward gaining a final definition of the human practical condition and the politics therein developed. Kant's position does not lend itself to any point of departure from which the true structure of the human condition may be initially assumed. The nature of human living is something only to be discovered at the end of inquiry.

Thus even those international relations theorists who have attempted to reconcile Kant with the discipline by showing that he somehow maintains a straddling position between realism and idealism, both conceived in the political sense, also fail to capture the movement of his thought. The efforts of Hurrell to describe Kant's writings as persisting in both camps and the interests of Huntley and Sørensen to read Kant within an optimistic neorealism are illusory on this account. Huntley, Hurrell, and Sørensen each disregard the fact that Kant does not merely view realism and idealism as somehow inadequate and in need of theoretical augmentation or revision. The grounds for the explanatory force required by each perspective are simply not obtainable for Kant, in part or in whole.

In Michael C. William's treatment of Kant, the sophisticated epistemological difficulties that Kant puts forth gain greater appreciation.[59] Yet, in agreement with Karl Jaspers,[60] Williams surmises that Kant maintains a dialectical relation between realism and idealism in his theory, wherein the two positions constantly undermine and support one another.[61] Kant's imagined and prescribed perpetual peace is therefore to be taken as the imminent possibility that may emerge from an unremitting trembling and shuttling between the constant faults of humans and the potential resulting from them. Hence, in maintaining the foundational quality of these terms, as do Huntley, Hurrell, and Sørensen, Williams suppresses the full protest that Kant offers to theories of international relations. He also clouds the fact that dialectic in general for Kant is at the root of the sort of illusions that Kant believes can persuade reason toward realism or idealism as viable approaches.[62]

Williams, however, does introduce the extremely important notion that Kant's political theory ultimately constitutes a *critique* of international relations. The study of international politics, as with the case of any form of inquiry, must, at bottom, be a critical enterprise for Kant. The lack of unconditioned ground in possible experience does not thwart his pursuit of the unity required for knowledge. Kant argues that this only shows that the supreme being must be *assumed* by reason. In doing so, the systematic unity is maintained.[63] He argues that it will allow for the three objects necessary for the regulation of reason: namely, an *I*, through which experience may be interrogated; the *world*, which provides the ground for possible experience; and *God*, the singular and sufficient antecedent to the cosmos.[64] Kant takes this assumption and the objects it allows not to transgress the limits of reason by the fact that these things are mere ideas that are not taken to possess corresponding objects that can in fact be given in one's sense experience.[65] As such, Kant warns that these ideas provide only a regulative principle to guide one in discovering final unity. That one can and must assume the unconditioned and the objects that follow from such unity does not give one the right to assume a completeness to what one may then rationally conclude. Rather, he claims that one is given only grounds on which to believe that one has approximated to completeness in a way that one may verify the supposed unity within empirical limits.[66] The completeness is never attainable. Hence inquiry is always required. Kant holds that without the submission to critique, reason becomes dictatorial and, thus, necessarily fails.[67] Inquiry, then, must be persistent, unending, and always welcome of further critique.

Kant's Challenge to Conventional Attitudes

The assumption that Kant's writings are part and parcel of traditional discourse in theories of international relations is bolstered by his keen attention to nature and history. In language not at all unfamiliar to realism or idealism, Kant continually couches his analysis of and prescriptions for international politics within an appreciation for the natural course of human affairs and their historical tendencies. In fact, key elements founding Kant's understandings of nature and history are what brings him to posit a Hobbesian-like resolution to the supposed anarchic state of nature, as perceptible in *Perpetual Peace*. However, it is certainly not the case that his theory with regard to these concepts supports the aims found within the conventional attitudes of international relations theory.

Whereas different aspects of the discipline seek, either positively or negatively, some sort of explicatory function in an initial determination of human nature and history, Kant demonstrates how the difficulties that demand a flat rejection of both realism and idealism also lead to the formation of nature and history as ideas required by reason. Nature and history for him have, of course, fundamental empirical referents, as they may both be understood to represent an aggregate of appearances through time. However, Kant cannot entertain them as offering from the start the determinate positive contexts from which theories of international relations may hope to offer objective accounts of human behavior. Nature and history are not, for him, simply things of study, as such. As concepts they may finally provide appropriate guides from which the practical conditions of human life may be known. And, thus, they are subjectively determined propositions that are, thus, necessary for inquiry to begin. However, the objective validity of any one concept of nature or history is something that must itself be worked out through the process of inquiry.

Exceptional to the norm across theories of international relations, Lynch makes the very important argument that Kant's attention to nature and history must be understood with respect to his focus on problems in ethics.[68] She offers a strong account of the association Kant's historical analysis of international politics has with the base of his moral philosophy. And, following the implications of this problem, Lynch therefore initiates a helpful critique of the ways in which Kant has been misread within international relations literature. Still, her commentary runs short of its potential impact. For Lynch founds her discussion only on what she sees as a *connection* between Kant's ethics and theory, suggesting simply that "Kant's understanding of historical development and change cannot be considered apart from his emphasis on ethical action and moral purpose."[69] Hence, the fact that Kant's respective theories of nature and history, as conceptual guides to inquiry, are at heart themselves matters of ethics and morality is potentially displaced. Furthermore, Lynch possibly misleads her readers into maintaining the illusion that Kant's theory regarding international politics is something simply subject to the problems in epistemology and ethics that he engages. I argue that it is from these very problems, rather, that the kernels of his political theory are brought about. For it is in fundamental questions of knowledge and morality, for Kant, that one may begin to establish nature and history as workable lenses through which to understand the natural and historical appearances of human behavior. Moreover, it is through these questions that his conceptions of nature and history first bring politics to bear as a central issue for human beings.

Unlike scholars of international relations who build their theories on stories of war and state-building through the centuries, Kant denies the possibility of factually determining any explanatory rationale for what one may know of the course of human life:

> Since men neither pursue their aims purely by instinct, as the animals do, nor act in accordance with any integral, prearranged plan like rational cosmopolitans, it would appear that no law-governed history of mankind is possible (as it would be, for example, with bees or beavers).[70]

He claims that extending a chain of events that lead from a past to present experience is possible. However, Kant insists that such a reconstruction may be developed only on the basis of possible experience, as determined by contemporary perception.[71] The past in itself is not available as an object. He suggests, rather, that any history offered as such can provide only a systemic report of events where no system as such prevails.[72] History may tie together some series of possible incidents, but it must surely also neglect and endure unending anomalies and deviations to the chronicle and the norm figured therein. Thus Kant continues:

> The only way out for the philosopher, since he cannot assume that mankind follows any rational *purpose of its own* in its collective actions, is for him to attempt to discover a *purpose in nature* behind this senseless course of human events, and decide whether it is after all possible to formulate in terms of a definite plan of nature a history of creatures who act without a plan of their own.[73]

In other words, before a sense of history is of any positive use, it must first be aligned with the appropriate conception of nature. But why should an investigation of natural purpose offer the appropriate solution? Furthermore, what is so important about this question in general that Kant should press himself to such lengths?

To begin with, Kant does not see history as something that one can know. He, of course admits that one can observe changes in time. But, he rejects the opinion that patterns in the course of society are available in any immediate sense. Rather, Kant is initially driven to questions of history by his realization that knowing can occur only in terms of producing a narrative of events. This point, one might say, is what provides the first glimpse of a natural plan insofar as it may be revealed through experience. He thus takes it to be a universal law that all events must have a cause.[74] To think one thing demands the thinking of a regress of relations between different things. Understanding something in isolation offers nothing meaningful with respect to anything else. He suggests, instead, that any appearance brought to the mind must be understood in terms of how it is experienced with other appearances within the same experience in order to imagine the present. Likewise, any such appearance must also be thought in terms of its relation to other past things and events within the realm of possible experience, as they could connect through a potential series of continuous experience.[75] And without some form of totality or all-determining ground (the unconditioned) presupposed in this series of relations, the unity required by reason is lost. More specifically, without a self-sufficient plan underlying nature, the necessity of what is known to be done and appear in the present must be given up; knowledge beyond the mechanics of everyday life is itself not feasible.

As noted above, though, in this point Kant does not wish to make the grandly fatalistic suggestion that there is no empirical composition to a "history proper."[76] Rather, he is making what he sees as the most practical conclusion available here, with respect to the distance between oneself and such a chronicle. This is the crux of his famous "Copernican" move. He writes:

> If the course of human affairs seems so senseless to us, perhaps it lies in a poor choice of position from which we regard it. Viewed from the earth, the planets sometimes move backwards, sometimes forward, and sometimes not at all. But if the standpoint selected is the sun, an act which only reason can perform, according to the Copernican hypothesis they move constantly in their regular course.[77]

Kant states that truth is possible only with the agreement between what one knows and the object of knowledge.[78] Therefore, he ventures to establish the objective validity of a narrative of humanity that may accord with natural causation and the requirements of human reason. He adds:

> We cannot actually observe such an agency in the artifices of nature, nor can we even infer its existence from them. But as with all relations between the form of things and

> their ultimate purposes we can and must *supply it mentally* in order to conceive of its possibility by analogy with human artifices.[79]

While not a matter simply to be recorded, then, history for Kant is fundamentally something that must be written. History is not in this case something by which experience is to be explained and narrated. Rather it must itself first be appropriately explained through attention to experience. History for Kant is a crucial form through which to develop one's understanding of causation and relations as experienced in practical life. But the accuracy of this history is initially dependent on its alignment with experience itself. And this must be accomplished through properly establishing the nature of the world of which experience speaks. An extremely important question, however, remains for Kant in this regard: How is this act to be best accomplished? More to the point, how can nature's plan be adequately thought, when such a thing in itself could never come to view?

In his *Conflict of the Faculties*, Kant poses the question: How can one know human history? In the stead of observation or abstraction, he claims that it may be divined as a narrative that points to things imminent in the future, "as a possible representation a priori of events which are supposed to happen then."[80] Briefly put, such knowledge is available "if the diviner himself creates and contrives the events which he announces in advance."[81] Again, Kant negates the legitimacy of introducing ideas of human history as a proper account of what has been. For him, such action is a matter of mere fiction and possesses little significance beyond that.[82] Yet, Kant does permit conjecture on the *beginning* of human history. He does so, because, in this case, the beginning of history is not the same as history itself. Such an origin is to be understood as the organising feature of human events—"a product of nature"[83]—and not a historical event itself. Kant's quest is therefore to determine how the beginning of human history—its *natural purpose*—ought to have been in order for a person, as she or he experiences her- or himself, to be the way she or he knows her- or himself to be (to be the way in which she or he reasons she or he ought to be). Put differently, the beginnings of human history may be properly deduced insofar as a natural origin is so conceived that it allows for and encourages what a person imagines her- or himself to experience in the present and what she or he may conceive as her or his possible experience in the future.

In this regard, Kant is compelled by the very processes of his own mind. He does not pretend to know exactly what reason is. But he does know that he is always able to conceive beyond what he refers to as mere instinct.[84] He contends that reason is present in all human action.[85] Humans act not simply with respect to external stimuli but through intellectual deliberation, through which judgments may be made.[86] Hence, human reason itself cannot be in time. It is rather, determining of states, as opposed to determinable by them.[87] Thus, he contends, humans, insofar as they are rational, enjoy a practical freedom, because reason itself must be understood to act freely.[88] Additionally, Kant holds to the assertion that no organ or faculty is to be present in a being unless it is best adapted for the end of that being.[89] He therefore submits that:

> Nature has willed that man should produce entirely by his own initiative everything which goes beyond the mechanical ordering of his animal existence, and that he should not partake of any other happiness or perfection than that which he has procured for himself without instinct and by his own creation.[90]

Moreover, Kant maintains that:

> It seems as if nature had intended that man, once he had finally worked his way up from the uttermost barbarism to the highest degree of skill, to inner perfection in his manner of thought and thence (as far as is possible on earth) to happiness, should be able to take for himself the entire credit for doing so and have only himself to thank for it.[91]

He surmises that given the fact that he, as a rational being, conceives his own purpose and takes steps toward that purpose on his own accord, it is important to make sense of himself as one who not only divines his own nature but also as one who himself brings about this essence to his being.[92]

Kant argues that the fact of freedom is demonstrated through experience.[93] Freedom is therefore an idea—in fact the only idea of speculative reason, in this regard—whose possibility is actually known a priori. Thus, freedom provides the actual keystone to the whole architectonic of reason.[94] As opposed to following natural law, which determines how things are, freedom places humans in the position in which they are to decide what *ought* to occur, giving rise to moral laws.[95] Kant may, then, feel validation in his assumption that there is indeed a natural primary cause and purpose in the world. This is because reason's role, in its practical application, is to determine a morality that is in concert with what this supreme and all-encompassing unconditioned condition must be. Furthermore, he determines the moral law to be "a law of causality through freedom and thus a law of the possibility of a supersensuous nature."[96] So that it may stay true to what Kant views as the necessarily systematic character of reason, human will must, thereby, command that such a law be fulfilled.

For Kant, then, the moral human being—a person who utilizes her or his practical reason in accordance with her or his deduced natural purpose—is one who is autonomous in her or his will. He writes: "The *autonomy* of the will is the sole principle of all moral laws and of the duties conforming to them."[97] It is so, because the moral law may be fulfilled by practical will only insofar as the will is determined with respect to the purpose from which history may be said to begin, the supreme being assumed by pure reason and ensured through the idea of freedom. Action willed with respect to material consequences (the pleasure and pain involved), as opposed to what is appropriately desired, pervert the freedom of the individual by linking that person's inclinations to mere natural law.[98] The supreme being must therefore be understood as also the highest good,[99] and all that distracts from a willing of the moral law must be known as evil. Moreover, the actualisation of this initial and unconditioned purpose, as the highest good, in the world is the necessary goal of a will directed by moral law. Thus, the history of humanity is to unfold.

Kant deduces four fundamental steps in the historical development of human beings that provide the grounds for such an evolution toward the highest good:

1. Dissatisfaction with the bounds of instinct
2. Mastery of instinctual drives (such as sexual appetite)
3. Anticipation of future events
4. Realization that humanity itself is the true end of nature[100]

As expressed in these progressive stages, Kant's history is the tale of beings who have fallen from the bliss of an all-caring and good prehistorical nature. It describes the struggles of people to construct the same natural comforts for themselves with the faculties with which nature has provided them. The development of reason is a struggle toward individual freedom, self-causation, with respect to moral law. Each individual has therefore only her- or himself to blame for the lack of goodness around her or him.[101]

Yet, Kant also claims that even if this freedom should lead to a regression away from goodness, even if this independence occasionally or often leads to hostile and impoverished circumstance, his prediction loses none of its force.[102] He hopes that what might appear as a confused and often erratic unfolding of events in human lives and the history of humanity may be considered, in a larger scheme, only as parts of the trials of reason attempting to reach autonomy with respect to morality.[103] In this analysis, the freedom that reason provides for persons disallows the deduction of any beginning to human history other than one that points to self-perception, in accordance with the highest good. With the realization that one can and does deduce one's own nature, linking concepts a priori to their possible objects, one already establishes both the essential rational character of one's being and inherently a progression in that being.[104] With such a rational achievement, it would actually be logically impossible to deduce an origin to human history that excludes that freedom.

The centrality of the independent self-possessed beings familiar to students of Kant's political theory therefore becomes quite manifest. Kant's world must be filled with people who desire and plan for themselves. Yet, as he notes, "Since the earth is a globe, they cannot disperse over an infinite area, but must necessarily tolerate one another's company."[105] The rational actors of Kant's world each necessarily project their own respective wills and grounds for acting according to such wills. And no individual possesses a final escape from the activities and intents of others. Hence, for Kant, conflict also necessarily arises in history. It becomes natural that politics must be engaged to avoid catastrophe altogether, to evade forces destructive to what each person may desire.

Kant insists that reflection on experience inevitably teaches one that all humans, once past the fourth step of reason, are indeed prone to violence and tend to fight among themselves.[106] Still he maintains that it is this "conflict of inclinations" that provides the foundation for good among humans as a whole.[107] The collision between persons in interest and deed show rational individuals that their respective ambitions to self-perfection cannot be sustained as a solitary affair. Kant observes:

> Thus the first decision the individual is obliged to make . . . will be to adopt the principle that one must abandon the state of nature in which everyone follows his own desires, and unite with everyone else (with whom he cannot avoid having intercourse) in order to submit to external, public and lawful coercion.[108]

Humans, by the imperative of refined reason, are compelled to seek concord with one another, while their very nature pushes them apart.[109] They must seek some form of convention that guarantees, to the greatest possible extent, the noninterference of one on the other, while promoting the freedom of each to fulfill her or his own nature.[110]

It is then here that one also sees the premises on which the analogies often drawn by international relations scholars between Hobbes' *Leviathan* and Kant's analysis arise.[111] Kant understands violence and war among humans to require no special motivation, by the fact that he sees these things to be thoroughly ingrained in the human nature he has deduced.[112] Further, Kant concludes that development in reason must finally lead to the practical maxim that "*There shall be no war*" between autonomous parties.[113] He believes that people are destined to finally commit themselves to forms of stable community, not unlike Hobbes' commonwealth, finding themselves to be able to achieve the fullness of their respective beings when in society more successfully than when alone.[114]

The humans of Kant's history do not seek out one another so much from fear, though, as do Hobbes' in the state of nature. Rather, the persons that Kant imagines strive to honor themselves as much as to protect what they honor.[115] Whereas the human beings in Hobbes' *Leviathan* only truly become persons once they have submitted to sovereignty, those that Kant describes already know themselves to possess the potential for human greatness and seek legislative society in order at least to express their respective perfection in the good of humanity as a whole. But this is also only a representation of what Kant ideally holds as the future of humanity. He also understands that the practical movements toward the arrival at such a state will likely demand a great deal more violence than is often admitted to in his writing.

In theorizing the practicality of the evolution of these freedom-motivated actors, Kant's emphasis strays far from any notion of persons joining toward the rationally necessary understanding and construction of a human order. He is not that naïve. On the contrary, Kant contemplates how particular orders of rules ought to be constructed and maintained to bring such forward-looking and honorable societies about, regardless of what manner of consensus may or may not exist among the populace. He writes:

> The difficulty . . . is this: if he lives among others of his own species, man is *an animal who needs a master*. For he certainly abuses his freedom in relation to others of his own kind. And even although, as a rational creature, he desires a law to impose limits on the freedom of all, he is still misled by his self-seeking animal inclinations into exempting himself from the law where he can. He thus requires a *master* to break his self-will and force him to obey a universally valid will under which everyone can be free.[116]

Kant considers how those few persons who have already developed sufficiently in their respective rational capacities to see the ethical necessity of human community, so outlined by him, may and ought to draw others into producing what a deduction of human history requires. His thoughts on the matter therefore not only allow for but insist on imposing certain orders of society on humanity.

It is thus in this way that Kant and Hobbes seem to reflect each other most. Certainly, as argued by Wolfgang Kersting, Kant does "denature" the social contract as construed in early modern political theory.[117] Kant develops a contract that *ought* to be and *can* be, in the face of Hobbes' contract that simply *is* or *will* be. But here Kant also only opens up the intellectual work that Hobbes suppresses in his emphasis on consistency and permanence in the definition of social political categories and functions.[118] Like Kant, Hobbes recognizes the danger present in the fact that each person is able to narrate the world and conceptualise the purposes therein. Hobbes therefore seeks to find a state in which only one narrative is possible, where concept and object may find final agreement in the proper use of names.[119] With both Kant and Hobbes, the sovereign makes history possible.

Yet there is a further important difference between the two. Kant does not agree that a concept may so easily be fixed to its practical object and certainly not in such a confined field of possible experience as the nation-state. Kant takes the productive power of reason in conjunction with experience far more seriously than does Hobbes. Keeping in mind the incommensurable division he identifies, in terms of the understanding, between imagination and things in themselves, Kant strives for conditions in which concept and object may at least come to *possible* agreement. In this fashion, while Hobbes seems satisfied—and necessarily so—with his focus inside the state, Kant is impelled to direct his attention both inside and outside at the same time.[120]

Conditions for the Possibility of Theorizing International Relations

The pacific world order of humans and sovereign states that Kant ultimately conceives in terms of an international federation is not, I contend, a theory of international relations as such. I argue, rather, that in tracing the reasoning that brings Kant to an analysis of states and inter-state politics, one can see that his now famed idea of a peaceful international federation is a 'solution' required by the problems of epistemology and morality that initially stir his thought. Each step in his political theory—each of which point toward an international politics—is part of an attempt to establish the conditions under which agreement between supposedly necessarily assumed ideas in reason and their possible objects may be achieved, given the field of possible experience offered through space and the capacity of men's minds to utilize a priori categories.

Among international relations theorists, the fundamental importance of the questions of reason and morality to Kant's work regarding international politics is articulated best by Gallie. As seen in the previous chapter, however, Gallie really only situates Kant's writings as "inspirational" to the spectrum of debate within the discipline.[121] He describes Kant's work as offering important challenges to the thinking that must go on, as more practical scholars grapple with the physical realities of international relations. With this sort of treatment, though, Gallie also triggers the most unfortunate of misreadings to which Kant is consistently subject. Despite his sensitivity to the function of epistemology and morality in the development of what are known as Kant's political writings, Gallie maintains that Kant's analysis is indeed only to be read as a theory *of* international relations. In this, Gallie also neglects the full challenge that Kant's works pose. For Kant's writings do not go along with the notion that "international relations" as a study is itself something that has an object to which it may be applied. I submit, rather, that his writings present the argument that *international relations is itself theory*.

Kant's texts disclose international politics as an idea that any human mind must finally form for itself in order to justify itself as the free entity it perceives itself to be. And the function of what one might call international relations theory is, therefore, through Kant's Copernican shift in reason, to establish a practical object for itself in the world with which international relations *as theory* may find agreement. Rather than being descriptive of a world that one may assume in developing one's theory of politics, international relations, in Kant's case, is a discourse through which one may struggle in the hope of someday being able to appropriately engage and fully understand the world one experiences and knows already in a local fashion. And it is this discourse that constitutes perpetual peace. For perpetual peace is not simply an international order. Rather, it is a practice whereby one may finally come to appreciate a world-wide community with others as practicable and morally necessary.

As established in the previous section, in order for Kant to secure the possibility of knowledge for the human being he experiences himself to be, it must be possible for one to realise one's own nature by way of guaranteeing the natural teleology that logically follows thereupon. As that which may make the accomplishment of such an end conceivable, human reason is able to produce a will that may drive humans to this final product, to accord with the highest good. Kant therefore asserts that the final purpose of the practical faculty of reason is to generate a will that does not simply provide a means to a point that is good in itself but is, rather, to stir a will that is itself good.[122] For humans truly to create the fulfillment of a telos that ought to be, the will that drives each of them must be itself the self-causing antecedent to the absolute good of nature.

Kant believes that in order for such an event to occur, however, people must be in some form of society with one another. He writes:

> The formal conditions under which nature can alone attain this, its final design, is the arrangement of men's relations to one another by which lawful authority in a whole, which

> we call a *civil community*, is opposed to the abuse of their conflicting freedoms; only in this can the greatest developments of natural capacities take place.[123]

More directly, Kant explains that, whether persons are disposed toward violence in the state of nature or not, pursuit of the good dictates the formation of lawful society:

> The *a priori* rational idea of a non-lawful state will still tell us that before a public and legal state is established, individual men, peoples and states can never be secure against acts of violence from one another, since each will have his own right to do *what seems right and good to him*, independently of the opinion of others.[124]

In this manner, Kant claims that the production of a civil constitution is the highest task set by nature for humanity.[125] Again, he sees that it is the inevitability of association, the eventual clash of desires and inclinations, that allows for reason to grow in the first place. Accordingly, the perfection of nature through humanity is also not something that can be single-handedly accomplished by a solitary individual or provisional grouping of them. Kant notes that it is hard to imagine how any single person or company of them might be able independently to produce a will good in itself without falling back on interests peculiar to that unit.[126] Acting in an insular fashion of that sort, such persons will ultimately deny the wills of others. The exchange supposedly required for the awakening and furthering of reason will be stunted. Moreover, this will, which is the only thing in humans that may itself be good, cannot be fragmented but must be held in common.[127] As the perfection of a singular nature through the potentially perfectible capacities of all respective rational beings, it must be a will with a general source.

It is on this basis that Kant therefore appeals to states as the sites of such a will. In fact, Kant claims that civil community, regulated through lawful authority, provides the formal conditions under which nature may attain its goal.[128] It is within the confines of a legislative union that the freedom of each human is supposedly protected from the caprice of others. He writes:

> A high degree of civil freedom seems advantageous to a people's *intellectual* freedom, yet it also sets up insuperable barriers to it. Conversely, a lesser degree of civil freedom

> gives intellectual freedom enough room to expand to its fullest extent. Thus once the germ on which nature has lavished most care—man's inclination and vocation to *think freely*—has developed within this hard shell, it gradually reacts upon the mentality of the people, who thus gradually become increasingly able to *act freely*.[129]

Kant presumes that it is within a constitutional state that conflict might be so regulated that each citizen may be free to reason independently and, at the same time and at least to some degree, may be free to act autonomously. For, inspired by Rousseau's vision, he believes that civil society may be founded through the union of individual wills into a general will, through an original social contract, wherein all gain sovereignty as One.[130] Thereby, Kant imagines, it is possible that that which is good in itself may eventually be produced across the species and thus realized without substantive opposition. In his estimation, all that is required is that social conditions are so legislated that the maximum freedom of each individual is guaranteed with the least amount of coercion.[131] Within such an order, a social rule may be developed with respect to how each person imagines and wills her or his welfare, as opposed to what suits the inclinations of one or a few.[132] Each citizen is to have mutual coercive rights over the others.[133] A general plan for what is to take shape in society thus becomes indispensable.

As discussed with regard to *Perpetual Peace* in the previous chapter, the rule that Kant conceives as eventually structuring human political community is that of *right*. In more precise terms, he defines this as "the restriction of each individual's freedom so that it harmonises with the freedom of everyone else (in so far as this is possible within the terms of a general law)."[134] Put another way, "Right is therefore the sum total of those conditions within which the will of one person can be reconciled with the will of another in accordance with a universal law of freedom."[135] It is a dictate founded in the notion that, while the desires of one person with respect to others may contradict one another greatly, their respective wills ought to coincide in form and find agreement in their external expression.[136] Consequently, he indicates that the type of government that ought to be formed to administer right rule—in fact, the only one, in his opinion, that can carry out a rule based on right—is a republic. Kant claims that republicanism guarantees the three principles required by right: freedom, mutual dependence on common legislation (coercion), and equality from the point of birth.[137] He trusts that, on the basis of these axioms, republicanism can secure political community as a shared enterprise.

In this regard, contrary to those, such as Doyle, Russett, and Sørensen, who think that Kant is somehow looking forward to the liberal Western-states of the twentieth century, Kant most vehemently rejects state sovereignty based on democracy. And he thus fully rejects the "peace-loving democracies" hypothesis of world order that is so often now attributed to him and which in fact serves as the most significant source for the recent revival of his works in international relations theory.[138] While an argument may be made that Kant establishes, here, a distinction between "direct" or "representative" democracies, denying the former while not necessarily excluding the latter,[139] it remains the case that Kant does not himself argue for the democratisation of states at all. In fact, Kant takes democracy to be the greatest instance of despotism, by the fact that the majority in such a rule may always impose legislation on an individual without that individual's consent.[140] But, most important, as John MacMillan outlines in some detail,[141] the heart of Kant's position here consists only in a call for the proliferation of sovereign states capable of instituting right rule, regardless of the specific electoral system under which such rule is implemented.

As Guyer argues, the force of governing politics alone is not enough to achieve the kind of community Kant has in mind here. Mere politics is only a violence. Rather, his vision requires political conditions of some sort in which social moral development may occur on the basis of individual self-discipline.[142] Kant therefore is not simply committed to the notion that each citizen within the state should have a vote but, rather, to the idea that the commonwealth, whether its government be autocratic, aristocratic, or democratic, truly represents the universal will of the people in the spirit of the social contract upon which civil society is rightly formed. Kant argues for the rule of universal law as the only ground on which a lasting constitution may be accomplished, regardless of individual desires.[143] And he believes that the republic is the best model for the propagation of right rule, while still not negating the idea that nonrepublican states may in part make up a global federation.[144]

This sense of the republican state as a mutually sanctioned project is important for Kant, first, because he therefore believes that the state practices most harmful to the rationally productive elements of human society will gradually cease. As noted previously, he observes that if public consent is required by the state for it to engage in the highly destabilizing efforts of war, as is ideally the case in a republic, the executive is less likely to have permission from the legislative body to proceed with such action.[145] In addition, this sense is significant because such a commonly engaged politics insists that legislation gain constant public hearing. The opening of law-making to public discourse ensures the possibility that laws conform to the ideal of a general will.

However, it is not the idea of a well-ordered populace itself that allows Kant to see good in a republic. It is, rather, the will that such a rule may provoke and ensure from a populace that has submitted to right rule. Thus, again, what is of initial value for Kant is the convention of governance and not necessarily the moral state of the community itself.[146] Aside from the moment of final perfection, he doubts that a fully moral society that has wholly agreed to right rule is even likely:

> But we need by no means assume that this contract (*contractus origniarius* or *pactum sociale*), based on a coalition of wills of all private individuals in a nation to form a common public will for the purposes of rightful legislation, actually exists as a *fact*, for it cannot possibly be so. Such an assumption would mean that we would first have to prove from history that some nation, whose rights and obligations have been passed down to us, did in fact perform such an act, and handed down some authentic record or legal instrument, orally or in writing, before we could regard ourselves as bound by a pre-existing civil constitution.[147]

Kant claims that such a public union is also best understood as a concept offered by reason, based on practical understanding.[148] It is an ideal that the sovereign, be it comprised of one, several, or many persons, must hold as a guide to forming a right rule.[149] The most urgent element is that the sovereign, informed by practical necessities revealed in reason, ensure a rule in which legislation (and thus the state) is constructed so that all members of the community *could* agree with the rationally determined balance of coercion and freedom.[150] The state must not only provide the grounds on which absolutely moral conduct is possible. It must also make the general will that is itself good unavoidable.

In view of this, it is Kant's position that the formation of a republican right rule wherein politics emerges as an applied arm of right, regardless of popular inclination, is a matter of moral *duty*.[151] Hence, conformity with moral law is insufficient for the expression of the good. To be truly moral and, thus, directed toward nature's end, activity must be performed *for the sake of* moral laws, as derived through reason.[152] The sovereign of Kant's republic therefore has the duty to structure the state and its rule in such a manner that it may come to determine (through public discourse) nature's end and, thus, the rational ground of one's duty. The sovereign must also structure the republic in such a way that the moral laws to which nature's end compels one themselves found the state.

Given this analysis, the difficulty in structuring the state is thus that the precise content of nature's end and perfection, as noumena, cannot be known in any manner whatsoever. There is no certain pattern to this teleology. Kant therefore announces that it is only duty grounded in a categorical imperative that could in fact dictate specifics in action.[153] The imperative that commands action toward absolute good must be without contingency. Thus, he comes to the conclusion that there can be only one imperative from which moral duty follows. It must allow for universality in the law.[154]

This categorical imperative on which the state must be ordered reads: "Act only according to the maxim whereby you can at the same time will that it should become a universal law."[155] From this follows the "universal imperative of duty": "Act as if the maxim of your action were to become through your will a universal law of nature."[156] This is exactly what the principle of right expresses directly in the political realm.[157] The categorical imperative thus entails a constant critical examination of one's will and the actions that follow that will with respect to the equally independent wills and actions of other rational beings. More precisely, the categorical imperative, from which the moral politician's duty flows, takes into regard what all citizens ought to will as the beings to which they ought to aspire. This is not, however, to suggest that all legislation in Kant's republic is directly based on the categorical imperative. But, the power from which legislation is enacted must be regarded as first grounded within the general will.

Accordingly, Kant's theory takes him to a stronger defense of the state itself than any one person in that state. He has no trust in the potential power of private means to condition citizens into well educated and morally upright individuals. Instead, Kant recommends that progress to perfection will be best served "from top to bottom."[158] The particular must be formed by what should be generally prescribed. He advises:

> Rather, the whole mechanism of this education has no coherence if it is not designed in agreement with a well-weighed plan of sovereign power, put into play according to the purpose of this plan, steadily maintained therein; to this end it might well behoove the state likewise to reform itself from time to time and, attempting evolution instead of revolution, progress perpetually toward the better.[159]

Kant finds that he must show interest in protecting the state from the fate of individual desire. Moreover, he must also guard against the dissatisfaction that may be engendered in rationally evolved members of the community who will the progress of the state to moral ends.

Further, Kant is directed by his logic here to reject all internal opposition to the law of a particular state. On his criteria, in view of nature's supposed end, such action is essentially and preeminently unlawful by the notion that resistance to the state is contrary to what men ought to will. Again in concert with Rousseau, Kant finds that the origin of a state's power structure is simply not available for citizens to view. It is always in the past. Yet, he reasons that to regard a state as present is to already assume that it was once rightfully established through the exercise of a universal will. There is thus no source of doubt in its foundation to deligitimize its current rule. Furthermore, there is no legitimate grounds from within the commonwealth to disobey the law. For to do so would be to put one's own desires against the will of all.[160]

In apparent contrast, it is the case that Kant certainly does express a strong enthusiasm for the French Revolution of his day.[161] But as Dieter Henrich argues, it may well be the case that, in Kant's eyes, the only revolution that occurred in France in 1789 was the abdication of Louis XVI without an heir, an abandonment of the state by the sovereign.[162] Although Kant is clearly against the execution of the aristocracy, as it is contrary to the categorical imperative,[163] he may in this case see the revolutionaries in terms of reformers of a state shifting albeit violently toward republicanism. He certainly sees the revolution itself as a striking moment in the development of the species.[164] And as Howard Williams suggests, Kant's comfort in doing so may be simply a result of viewing it retrospectively,[165] not having to endorse specific actions over others but, rather, being able to applaud eventual outcomes. In any event, Kant insists that resistance is truly acceptable only in a lawful manner within parliamentary channels.[166] Even if the sovereign emerges as a tyrant and contravenes the social contract that duty demands, Kant claims that no subject may justly revolt.[167] Revolution as such, he reminds his readers, "would be dictated by a maxim which, if it became general, would destroy the whole civil constitution and put an end to the only state in which men can possess rights."[168] Such a maxim could not be willed universally and, therefore, would work against the possibility of a shared idea of society.

In addition to the categorical imperative and his universal imperative of duty, Kant submits what he calls "the practical imperative." It reads: "Act in such a way that you treat humanity, whether in your own person or in the person of another, always at the same time as an end and never simply as a means."[169] This version of the categorical imperative underlines the consequences he places in willing that *all* rational beings be embraced in the construction of nature's end. Without action that assumes the perfectibility of each human being, there is no possibility that the deduced telos of humanity may be so constructed. Kant is committed to the idea that the development of natural capacities in humans can only practically, hence morally, be achieved on the level of the entire species.[170] The achievement of right rule within a republic, although admirable in Kant's account and in harmony with moral law, is therefore itself inadequate as a moral end.

As a unit with borders that face on and against the margins of other political communities, a state, on its own accord, is obscured to the larger history of humanity. Kant can therefore ill afford to leave his focus on the singular moral state for long. He asserts that the states do themselves exist in a state of nature, not dissimilar to that experienced by individuals before submitting to state rule.[171] As noted above, Kant concurs with traditional theories of international relations, defining the condition between states as anarchical.[172] Thus, he urges that, regardless of the diminishing of warring interests within a given state, any state must still face the hostile threats of others. This Kant identifies as the greatest oppression that states must confront.[173] He then recognises that the internal stability and, thus, moral future of any state is also dependent on the integrity of relations external to it.[174] While still championing the state, Kant is compelled to extend his understanding of right beyond national borders.[175]

Kant sees that it is in fact the same problems that drive people together to realise the idea of civil community that will propel state actors toward achieving what may be imagined as an international order. He is convinced that one may predict that the will to minimize violence in favor of general codes of conduct will also arise between states.[176] Kant beholds this as a rational necessity arising from each state's ultimate desire for internal security.[177] Moreover, he observes, through population growth, trade, and associations of all kinds, humans have created or are well on the way to creating an idea of "universal community," wherein "a violation of rights in *one* part of the world is felt *everywhere*."[178] With particular interest in the effects of the flow of capital, Kant remarks on how global forces knit states into inescapably interrelated political spheres wherein such notions are automatically fostered.[179] As a result, he charges that the conception of an international right *between* states is also morally required,[180] in order to avert the damage that the domineering interests of respective states may incur in one another.[181]

In this respect, Kant does indeed reject the notion that a single global state that might subsume all others could offer a suitable alternative to the state system. He criticizes such ideas on two basic premises. First, he claims that such a massive state would simply be too unwieldy to establish any hope of right rule, leading to war in any event.[182] Yet, second, and more significantly, Kant declares that a global state would be rationally contradictory to moral duty, by the fact that it would require a hierarchy of a worldwide ruler over those who obey. He admits that this division between superior and inferior is precisely analogous to the condition of affairs as it ought to occur within the nation of a state. However, Kant does not see how this is conceivable on an international scale, where no global national community naturally exists.[183]

One must understand here that his argument consists in the idea that human rational faculties have arisen in the conflict that has divided human beings and thereby has allowed nation-states to emerge. And Kant sees in nature the progressive diversification of persons and races, rather than the gradual assimilation of all into one family.[184] A global nation would therefore be possible only if no conflict were naturally present. And if there were no natural conflict between human beings, on this reasoning, there would not be any association of nation or state, regional or global, to begin with. Or, as Kant himself succinctly puts it:

> Yet while natural right allows us to say of men living in a lawless condition that they ought to abandon it, the right

> of nations does not allow us to say the same of states. For as states, they already have a lawful internal constitution, and have thus outgrown the coercive right of others to subject them to a wider legal constitution in accordance with their conception of right. On the other hand, reason as the highest legislative moral power, absolutely condemns war as a test of rights and sets up peace as an immediate duty.[185]

A global state does not fall within the realm of possible experience. Hence, Kant expects that states ought to develop, through the moral standpoints proper to each, an atmosphere among one another that could support an international federalism on the basis of state will. And this will is to be one founded in the general will to which each respective national group could agree, without appealing to any higher authority than the good that humanity ought to work out for itself.

This is precisely the ideal that Kant terms *perpetual peace*. And, as indicated in the previous chapter, by this he does not refer to an international peace treaty, which he rightly understands as a mere halting of fighting, but, rather, a complete elimination of the conditions required for warfare.[186] Kant denies that a peace can be said to exist truly when materials for the purpose of a future war are maintained.[187] In this sense, he quickly admits that qualifying "peace" with "perpetual" in fact produces a redundancy.[188] However, despite Kant's caveat, the word "perpetual" should by no means be trivialised here. It draws considerable weight with respect to how Kant expects this peace ought to function as a matter of duty. As a confederation that gains its 'sovereignty' only through a partnership of independent states and by the lawful rational consent of what the individuals therein ideally will, the rule of international right—that which aims toward the constitution of perpetual peace—ought to be one that can be dissolved at any point.[189] It must truly rest on the equal willing of each participant, as opposed to higher authority, so that it is continually endorsed. Without the persistent effort of each sovereign to will that peace exist between states, danger to the moral aims of right hangs on. Without action constantly directed from this will, threat to the contingency of generating the good will in general terms must survive. Thus, the possibility of ultimately constructing an end to human history that agrees with the deduced nature of human beings also vanishes.

It is also on this level of reasoning that Kant flatly rejects any faith in a balance of power between states.[190] For, contrary to George Modelski's claim that Kant theorizes an evolution of politics toward a peaceful *organization* of states[191] and conflicting with Negretto's representation of Kant's perpetual peace as a reformed manner of collective security,[192] Kant argues that support for a balance of power between states takes a dangerously static attitude toward the goal of peace. Its stability rests on the assumption of a particular set of conditions that are present in only one point of human history. Such a condition is therefore always vulnerable to collapse as conditions within and between states alter with the course of events. In the stead of such a stalemate, Kant puts his faith, rather, in what he sees as the *initial* positive force of war.[193] He remarks:

> War itself, if it is carried on with order and with a sacred respect for the rights of citizens, has something sublime in it, and makes the disposition of the people who carry it on thus only the more sublime, the more numerous are the dangers to which they are exposed and in respect of which they behave with courage. On the other hand, a long peace generally brings about a predominant commercial spirit and, along with it, low selfishness, cowardice, and effeminacy, and debases the disposition of the people.[194]

Kant believes that, as something sublime, war or at least its threat, faces people with something that is beyond everyday comprehension—something "absolutely great."[195] It motivates a feeling of respect for what the final destination of humanity might be.[196] Hence, whereas the stability of treaties or a cold war may allow individuals and states to lower their respective interests to simply matters of personal pleasure and pain, he is convinced that the experience of war or its possibility forces a thoughtful focus on matters of universal weight that course through the very freedom of each rational being.

One might then understand that, ideally, perpetual peace is the resolution of all possible human experience into a fully politicized world, a world that:

> must be represented as having originated from an idea if it is to be in harmony with that employment of reason without which we should indeed hold ourselves to be unworthy of reason, namely, with the moral employment—which is founded entirely on the idea of the supreme good.[197]

And, this is an idea that should itself be understood to rest necessarily on the concept of a *globe*. For it is a peace wherein the totality of possible human actors and their actions are effectively *contained*. From perpetual peace, one can imagine specific limits to the source of appearances made available to the mind through space. And, insofar as one wills toward the objective validity of the global context delivered by the idea of perpetual peace, one could conceive these limits as bounds to which all rational beings are subject. In this fashion, perpetual peace is a concept that provides those who will it with the practical grounds on which to insist on specific limits to the ideas one generates. Certain concepts, histories, properties, and events could be thought to occur and others could not. The possibility of what one ought to know and what one ought not to know are all the more closer to certitude.

The global conception that perpetual peace avails allows one finally to bring the idea of a singular supreme unconditioned condition closest into agreement with a singular and final realm of experience, infinite though it may be within itself. The conceptual confinement of what is practically possible narrows the arrangement of what one may imagine as true. It is therefore far easier for Kant to imagine human nature, in history, to be produced by humans themselves. At least, it is considerably more practical to find with surety that the rational determination of any sort is in the end possible.

Still, as I argue in some detail in the following chapter, it is not at all conclusive that Kant actually has a right to appeal to such a final globe and, hence, to this global will and thought. If a singular concept of a globe, as a field of possible experience, becomes widely accepted as rationally necessary, for whatever cause, it may be a much lighter task for the persons who populate this planet to begin to come to some sort of sense of what must follow politically from contemporary experience and from pondering these events. However, it is not incontestable that only one concept of what might be referred to as a global experience is possible in such conditions.

On Kant's own account, reason acts freely. And the judgments that form reason's objects arise from intuitions that, while a priori, are subjective in character. Thus, even if a person accepts that there are limits to what is objectively real, there is no globe that becomes necessary to that person's understanding. Despite Kant's final insistence that one must think in terms of one world, one space, and one time,[198] there is no one globe per se available. Rather, that states and a global arena for the actions of these states may be theorized and constructed by any individual who understands her- or himself as rational and free may be more easily read, in this regard, as yet another moment in the ability of humans to operate in both empirical and rational terms. It does not prove in any way that the determinations of theory and experience may be reconciled as such.

Enlightenment and the Impossibility of International Relations Theory

Kant's perpetual peace must finally be understood as itself part of what he refers to as the process of *enlightenment*.[199] In brief, enlightenment is the very progress he observes people to make toward transforming their respective innate capacities of moral discrimination into practical principles that can be universalized.[200] As such, it is concerned with the free and public discourse that Kant believes is possible within the apparatus of community impressed with the idea of republicanism. Enlightenment is the practice through which humans are supposed to come closest to a determination of the practical principles duty requires of them and, thus, knowledge of the reality humans experience, as something identified and sought through their own reason. Thus it is enlightenment that reveals the necessity of the "moral whole" that a global politics of states may allow.[201] And it is this ideal that perpetual peace is meant to serve.

Enlightenment, however, should not in this case be interpreted as a particular stage or description of what a fixed state of good politics may be. Kant emphatically notes that, in the condition of modern social and political affairs, one could not truly speak of an enlightened age. Rather, he affirms that human civilization has reached an age of enlightenment, wherein an enlightened age may be conceived.[202] It is characterized by a drive toward what reason shows is necessary. Enlightenment does not constitute a moral resting point in itself. It is actually doubtful that Kant could hold certain hope for an enlightened age of humans, as such, whatsoever. For, this process of public discourse, which Kant believes is to bring humans out of ethical immaturity,[203] is ideally a persistent critique of what human beings are and what they must do and will in the present in which they find themselves. It is most definitely a *process*,[204] a constant putting into question, by each generation,[205] of how persons are to understand themselves with respect to the particular history and nature that supposedly defines them.

Kant fears what he sees as the all too common and easy occurrence of thought which has become immobile and incapable of self-reflection. He complains against fixed ideas of the world which engage in debate only to win out over others and command rational thought:

> Thus it is difficult for each separate individual to work his way out of the immaturity which has become almost second nature to him. He has even grown fond of it and is really incapable for the time being of using his understanding, because he was never allowed to make the attempt. Dogmas and formulas, those mechanical instruments for rational use (or rather misuse) of his natural endowments, are the ball and chain of his permanent immaturity.[206]

Kant therefore hopes for an enlightenment in which individuals use their rational faculties to release themselves from the authority of what human history and nature is generally or particularly received to be, so that each person may constantly work to create these things independently as reason suggests. Above all, reason must prevail, not as autocrat but as inquisitor.[207] As perpetual peace must be persistently and generally renewed through will, Kant deduces that one can truly hope to enjoy the process of enlightenment only so long as one refuses to allow a set way of thought to emerge, privately and, most important, throughout the human community. This, he claims, is one of the "original rights of human reason."[208]

Onora O'Neill underlines this aspect well, arguing that Kant's notion of critique, which resides at the core of his focus on enlightenment, is not about reaching a "transcendent vantage point" from which reason may finally find knowledge unconditionally. It is rather an unending willingness to shift one's point of view, to take on other potential points of departure in thinking about the world and one's place in it—a willing commitment always to consider the otherwise.[209] Reason, in Kant's analysis, is incapable of actual finality, though systemic unity may be its necessary goal. Through experience and thought, he sees, humans develop knowledge through intuition and concepts. But humans do not in any way grasp the in-itself. That which defines humanity and the exercise in which humans establish the possibility of their inherent good as a species is always a *pursuit* of what is noumenal. However, it is always a pursuit through indirect and, thus, uncertain means.

Accordingly, the most fundamental obstacle that stands in the way of perpetual peace, and, hence, that which at the root of human life must be eradicated, is the reification in absolute terms of any definitive concept of what the world is or must be. No systemic or patterned view may be accepted in such a strong sense. Kant associates the dismissal of other ideas on the mere basis of dedication to one theoretical opinion with the clearest signs of insanity.[210] Thus "the globe" inherent to the idea of perpetual peace, as well as international relations theory in general, itself must be questioned as a true and real point of theoretical departure.

Even though the general idea of a contained world is what allows for progress in bringing persons' concepts into agreement with the objects they necessarily and inevitably deduce, Kant could never legitimately be satisfied in the progress toward peace with any particular vision of a globe and the politics that sustain it. A globe must be thought to free oneself and to provide oneself with the confidence in the advance of one's reason. The concept of a shared globe may allow one to think one's way toward the possibility of truth. However, it is also that progressively free thought, which the globe avails, that requires a further critique of the specific limits to thought that are provided for by a particular global organization of individuals and state structures. For enlightenment to proceed and, thus, for the object of perpetual peace to be realized, that same globe must be forever brought into question and undermined with refinement and further evidence. The possibility of the globe must be revealed in the subjective conditions in which it was surely produced. From that point, further possible human worlds and the ideas concerning the nature of the politics that there inhere may and must be entertained. In such a manner, all possible experience that could produce the multiplicity of worlds that may well be experienced by the multitude of rational beings could be further accounted. Collectively, rational beings could slowly come to an increasingly better understanding of what may hold universally, hence, what may stand in truth.

It follows that a particular manifestation of international relations, formed ideally and willed practically, is indeed crucial for what Kant sees as the development of humanity. Yet, in terms of developing both a peaceful and a good life on this planet, it is impossible for him ever to identify a schema of international relations that would suffice in this capacity. International relations in some form or another is ultimately required to begin to address unavoidable difficulties in the respective being of each human. However, the structures that are required to generate such an inter-state rule or domain also develop the conditions under which any and all rules and domains of international politics are to be morally challenged. Any determination of international relations is *impossible* by the fact that it is necessarily *always possible* to produce yet further such determinations. In this regard, international relations as an object and field of study is perhaps best replaced, for Kant, with an international relations as an ongoing practice.

With this general sense in mind, Kant admits that perpetual peace itself is an impossibility, that it is a concept "incapable of realisation." However, in the same breath, he claims that this does not mean that the *approach* to perpetual peace is impracticable.[211] On the contrary, Kant insists that the approach toward a peaceful international politics is demonstrative of the good in human beings and, thus, it has objective validity. While pronouncing such a cosmopolitan society an "unreachable idea," he sees it as at least a "regulative principle" that humans necessarily maintain if destiny is to be fulfilled.[212] Again, it concretely expresses the human ability always to make possible the confirmation of the rationally deduced nature of persons. The will toward an inter-state relations that may prepare for an absolute peace throughout the human community may always allow for that which is already good in itself.

This apparent impossibility of any particular understanding of international politics pervading Kant's thought does not, however, mean that Kant's analysis allows for a final stronger focus on the autonomy of states and individuals, from which a perpetual peace, it is hoped, will be formed. Despite his obvious and constant reference to staunch and independent individual and state units, Kant's analysis betrays a very different sense of what each actually is. As Kant represents the development of these things, it is the case that both individuals and states gain what come to be seen as their respective autonomy and freedom only through recognition of and action based on the radical interrelation of social and political units. Both individuals and states find freedom through the course of human history insofar as they each learn to negotiate with the inescapable conflicting inclinations of others. The progress of a rational individual depends on the extent to which she or he is able to will the progress of others. Once Kant faces the ultimate problem of international relations and the globe, it is the case that each individual must take into consideration even how she or he affects and is influenced by others who are thoroughly strange and unknown to her- or himself.[213] It is for this reason that the categorical imperative becomes necessary. This is the very doctrine of right.

Similarly, Kant's focus on republics requires an understanding of the inability of states ever to independently determine social and political life within their respective borders. Their strength, rather, lies in the extent to which they are able to interpret the necessity of moral law into inter-state and trans-state structures. The state's independence is contingent on its relative capacity to negotiate a role between what, hence, comes to be known as the internal and the external. Further, Kant's republic is free and autonomous insofar as it is able to perpetually contribute to the formation of a partnership of nations. As much as it requires the confidence of the national population within, Kant's republic has no stable existence outside of its relations with the external.

In the end, the source and foundation that Kant contributes to theories of international relations may be significantly complex, but he is also short-spoken in terms of providing positive solutions. That is, he offers little that is familiar or recognizable in traditional ways of engaging international relations as a discipline of social science. In Kant's study, the realm of international relations, as such, does not figure as the exigent point of politics in the world. On this account, then, it should really come as no great surprise that Kant's writings are so contested and seemingly problematic as points of reference for theories of international relations. What is surprising is that his writings are so consistently interpreted as somehow congruous with the traditions and conventions of international relations theory.

By Kant's reason, traditional theories of international relations must appear as hopelessly insufficient attempts to examine the political phenomena that may and do indeed occur within the world. As an aggregate of exercises that aims *first* to determine the units that constitute international politics, examines the relations between these units, and predicts the events that manifest within a particular object that contains these units, known as the world, a theory of international relations informed by realism/idealism, perpetually, necessarily, and systematically attempts to discount the possibility of the many alternative worlds that human beings will, experience, and on which they act. Contingency is displaced in favor of a presupposed or predetermined and whole reality. For Kant, this is just being immature.

His writings pose a different tack altogether. Kant implicitly requires that anyone concerned with international politics recognize the politics of her or his own theory. His work demands an always challenging political theory—one necessarily directed to a world—that prescribes a willingness to be claimed by the interest of an other. Kant offers little room for the calculation and estimation of what constitutes the world around one. There is only the possibility of responding to one's world on the level of a duty toward all that may possibly occur within it, whatever *it* may be. His theory legislates that one always be inclined to take on the concerns of others before one's own:

> It is our duty to regard them [the rights of others] as sacred and to respect and maintain them as such. There is nothing more sacred in the wide world than the rights of others. They are inviolable. Woe unto him who trespasses upon the right of another and tramples it underfoot! His right should be his security; it should be stronger than any shield or fortress.[214]

In this analysis, one's own interests in gaining knowledge and supporting action based on that knowledge are practicable only with the serving of foreign concerns. And, thus, one's politics must be first and always oriented toward forming the necessary structural conditions under which one may, first, best come to appreciate the claims that others could make on one and, second, best be in a position in which to act responsibly toward those claims.

The point that one may finally draw from Kant is that one can never know precisely what one's others are, nor what one's relation is to them. In larger terms, one can only imagine these things in terms of actual and possible experience. However, if one values the possibility of an identifiable meaning for one's own life, as a member of a human community—a desire that Kant sees as fully unavoidable—the same must be granted to all possible others. And this can only be a task without resolve. What exact form this politics must take is never to be certain, but it is always to be the crucial question.

3

Critique of World Politics

Bartelson provides what is certainly and by far the most helpful, insightful, and refreshing intervention into recent debates regarding the value of Kant's thought to the discipline of international relations.[1] He seeks to show that the various versions of modern internationalism,[2] most of which take up the peace-loving democracies hypothesis on one level or another, not only owe great debt to a Kantian root but also gain their troublesome shapes on the basis of unfortunately narrow misreadings of Kant's texts. Understanding all elements in the general spectrum of internationalism to rest on some systemic[3] and/or societal[4] interpretation of inter-state politics, Bartelson suggests an inevitable paradox within the theory. He contends that those taking up conventional liberal positions in contemporary international relations theory find themselves inescapably in the bind where they must both seek to overcome anarchical relations between states and exploit this perceived anarchy as the necessary condition under which it may be abolished.[5] And it is precisely this sort of paradox, I would argue, that so many recent proponents of an allegedly Kantian perspective, mindfully or not, seek to hide within some notion of the individual human being, as I indicate in chapter 1. In the hopes of offering some remedy, Bartelson goes on to recommend a return to and precise shift in the reading of Kant's texts. For while he finds current internationalisms (calling back to a Kantian impetus) to be fundamentally hopeless, he also discovers a richer and largely neglected ground within the breadth of Kant's texts for a fully renewed internationalist approach to state politics.

Specifically, Bartelson summons scholars of international relations to take serious note of Kant's theory of judgment, as it gains prominence in his *Critique of Judgment*. The Third Critique, being a text whose outward concerns are predominantly those of aesthetics and teleology, has not traditionally been included as a member of Kant's so-called political writings—far from it. However a recent revival of interest in the political implications of this philosophical work has been launched, most evidently in writings of Hannah Arendt and, to some extent, Jean-François Lyotard.[6] And Bartelson finds inspiration here with much justification. As I argue in this chapter, it is in judgment that Kant finds the grounds on which the trajectory of humankind is to be appropriately imagined.

For Kant, judgment offers the *critical* purchase from which his politics of right may deliver the possibility of perpetual peace, wherein peace is understood as a goal never guaranteed yet for which one must incessantly strive. Moreover, especially with respect to what he takes to be the beautiful, he understands judgment to offer humans the possibility of a species-wide community. In this regard, Bartelson takes the enlightenment politics of Kant very deeply and finds "reasonable hope" within his thought for a form of "internationalism [that] avoids the limitations of a political experience singularly circumscribed by present identities without succumbing to the temptations of an unrestricted utopian expectation."[7] Bartelson accepts the position that Kant's political theory is both skewed within the discipline of international relations and that it is likely quite critical of the precise ways in which Kantianisms have taken shape within it. Beyond this, however, he also tries to show that there is a true Kantian theory of international relations to be found across Kant's writings that provides a much more suitable and encouraging option to internationalists than those otherwise available, whether proposed under the appellation of "Kantian" or not.

Missing in Bartelson's very strong reading and analysis, however, is a sufficiently attentive perspective toward the grounds on which Kant's own theory of judgment, as it pertains to the political, rests. Enthused by the critical energy that informs Kant's political theory on the basis of judgment, one might say that Bartelson offers the best possible reading of the internationalist politics available in Kant's work. He provides a sketch of the Kantian approach to politics on an international scale of which Kant himself would most likely approve. My underlying argument in this chapter, though, is that this approach to politics, while potentially exciting, is defeated on its own principles. The activity of judgment that gives rise to what Bartelson correctly reads as the crux of Kant's political theory is based on a political position that is in itself neither acceptable nor tenable. Thus, the direction that Bartelson resuscitates from Kant's texts and recommends must also be thoroughly reexamined.

Accepting and reviewing the arguments presented respectively by Bartelson and myself so far, instead of offering a specific theory of international relations, Kant may be said to be ultimately *making an attempt at* an international approach to relations and theory. While certainly not appreciative of all cultural and national standpoints, he is trying to see how grounds for thinking the politics of humanity on a total scale may be established in a way sensitive to the standings of humans from all points on earth.[8] In the best light he can give it, this is a procedure that may permit one to adequately engage and negotiate the political circumstances that emerge around one's philosophical commitments and the practical claims made on one's activities. For it is an approach that, ideally, recognizes not only the impact that all human lives could have on one another but, more important, that things change (in time) and that there are limits with respect to what a person may know. Kant hopes that, with constant and, above all, critical attention toward these points, human beings and humanity itself may finally be able to avoid the enslavement of dogmatism and the fatalism or relativism potentially spawned by skepticism. He trusts that a rule instituted nationally and willed internationally, grounded in sustained attention to the manner in which the international is both inherently implicated within and brought to bear on one's theory and practice, may keep at bay those interests which seek to formalise human life as either fixed or purely a matter of contest between points of view.[9]

The advantage that Kant locates in this approach is enjoyment of the freedom he takes to be expressed in the reason of each human being. In this manner, he deduces, each human may finally come to command the benefits of truly creating one's own world as one knows it ought to be. But, he may do so with full respect for the rational determinations of others and, no less significantly, with regard to what is empirically possible.[10]

The form of this benefit is universal peace. However, as Kant describes it, this peace is by no means supposed to be an end point at which the conflict of particulars is finally mediated in a completely general form. He maintains that a global Leviathan is contrary to his view.[11] Rather, this peace is understood by him as a condition of process, in which the universal limits on experience and thus reason are elevated only as tools of social discipline.[12] Kant has faith that such discipline may then allow each individual to actively partake in the struggles, contests, and negotiations necessary to constantly build a human world in honor of the agonistic energy and dynamics promised already in nature.[13]

This enlightenment politics which, in the previous chapter, I suggest Kant proposes and which I believe Bartelson also outlines, however, is less free of the dogmatic than Kant apparently assumes. And it would be a mistake to think otherwise. I contend that, despite his exceptionally strong attention toward the necessity of persistent critique, Kant ultimately founds his politics on grounds which, after all, are not wholly contrary to those of Hobbes' commonwealth. Intended or not, Kant's approach leads him into a position where questions of difference and change in the circumstances of human lives do become fixed to a final realm of a sort. Just as the *Leviathan* seeks to establish what is inside and what is outside the domain of politics and society, Kant's theory betrays a description of the very shape in which enlightenment *must* manifest.

Kant does not preordain the rules under which the freedom of reason and activity may appropriately operate. But he does come to dictate the precise *kind* of conflict and contest that may be considered truly *of* the international presupposed and produced in human practice. Kant does not simply seek the disciplinary modes under which enlightenment may operate. He effectively confines enlightenment in such a manner that reason is not only brought into concert with possible experience but that it is also reigned into accord with a very specific and autarchic sense of human political territory. Hence, his undertaken approach to relations and theory is actually far from being one of international perspective. Rather, it is in constant risk of universalizing a narrow and singular position for all. He takes a specific point of human experience and reason as a model for the universe in which all human practices and ideas ought to be disciplined.

In substantiating my charges here, I will first and most comprehensively explore the precise grounds that underlie the presumed promise of Kant's analysis of politics as international phenomena. My aim here is to delve more deeply into the exact philosophical moves that support his efforts, as are identified and given rough sketch in the previous chapter. I wish to establish the extent to which the crux of Kant's theory regarding politics is situated within philosophical concerns. In particular, I argue that what I am reading as his attempt at an international approach to relations and theory must be understood, as Bartelson advises, most centrally in terms of the role that judgment plays in Kant's solutions to critical philosophy. Furthermore, I submit that, when read in terms of the attention Kant places in the concerns of geography and geometry, it is judgment that provides the specific contour to the politics he finds he must envision. And it is finally the geopolitical idea that Kant generates in these terms that betrays the acritical rigidity of his theory.

In these regards, I continue to admit that Kant certainly does go beyond Hobbes, in that Kant recognizes that there can be no discrete line drawn between domestic and foreign or between republican politics and anarchy. Kant shows politics to always invite the international and, hence, the unbounded contingent within human experience. However, on the bases of this reading and interpretation, I wish to also demonstrate here that Kant's perpetual peace enacts something at least akin to the sovereign of Hobbes' *Leviathan*. For Kant at length invites an international 'rule' based on what is inside and outside the international, as if the international is something that can in fact be determined, known, and measured as such in terms of what it is not. The conditions of Kant's perpetual peace first gain positive expression against the terms of what supposedly are *not* legitimate grounds for freedom. Thus a divide is already constructed between the human world and the nonhuman world, providing an inert yet not undeniably valid fullness to both terms.

In establishing the final Hobbesian character of Kant's peace, I will demonstrate how this peace is, thus, inconsistent with Kant's prior commitments to enlightenment critique, as deepened through attention to judgment. I recognize that a fundamental appreciation of the limits of human experience and reason are, of course, required by Kant for the possibility of the critique necessary for freedom and, thus, peace to emerge out of anarchy and despotism. However, I do not agree that this very human set of boundaries provides for the sort of sense of political possibility that Kant finally espouses. I charge that the grounds underlying Kant's supposed international approach to relations and theory suggests a forced universal structure that frustrates the full energy of his critical aims and, therefore, only reproduces the archetypal paradoxes that give the modern discipline of international relations apparent substance and standing.

It is therefore my position that what Kant posits as perpetual peace must itself submit to a far more radical level of critique. And I conclude that this critique may produce a yet more refined and far more successful understanding of world politics. However, such a deep critique also demands, for those interested in maintaining any semblance of the Kantian project, a fundamental reconsideration of the very function of political theory on any scale.

Attention to Kant's challenge shows in the end that his and any other view to the international is not soundly grounded from the start, that it is impossible to establish an empirically correct concept of international life, relations, and politics from which to build theories of the same. Rather, it shows that the world of politics from which international relations is invariably conceived may never be measured, analyzed, or presupposed in an adequate manner. Through his own failure, Kant only betrays the fact that politics may be known in the world without the comforts of such limits. The final challenge is thus to produce an approach to international politics without a final territorial sense.

Judgment and the World

As I note at the beginning of this chapter, Arendt is responsible for much of the current excitement regarding the impact of Kant's theory of judgment within his political philosophy. But she takes the position that Kant actually does not offer an overt political philosophy. Arendt claims that he simply never wrote one.[14] She argues, rather, that it may only be detected as something hidden within the *Critique of Judgment* and, presumably, read back into his so-called political writings. In this regard Arendt opens important debate. However, a significant part of this debate is a stark refusal of her suggestion that there is indeed anything hidden about Kant's political philosophy in the first place. For example, Riley takes great exception to Arendt's analysis.[15] He accepts the thesis that it is within *Critique of Judgment* that the most sophisticated spin of Kant's theory of politics emerges. But, taking the basis of Kant's position on politics to revolve around the promotion of "eternal peace and universal republicanism as a legal approximation to the 'kingdom of ends,' "[16] Riley insists that Kant's thought on the matter is already publicly broadcast in his writings on history, ethics, and the state. As he writes elsewhere, Riley suggests that *Critique of Judgment* is extremely helpful in establishing what he sees to be the pivotal role of public justice in Kant's political philosophy.[17] But, for good reason, as the work of Allen Rosen alone will attest,[18] Riley remains convinced that the importance of this legal aspect of a culture fueled by critique is already announced in a variety of ways in Kant's various other works.

Public justice along with other related components such as autonomy are undeniably foundational to what emerges as Kant's theory of politics. The experience of autonomy must be respected, protected, and promoted as the political condition that humans ought to enjoy. And the practice of public justice is necessary in the first place for the enjoyment of such autonomy through the institution of right rule. However, as Arendt attempts most strongly to illustrate, it is really only in *Critique of Judgment* that Kant finally begins to theorize fully *how* it is that the distance between the rationally determined theories of justice and autonomy and the political practice of right and critique may be bridged. And it is in this regard that her potential response to Riley's sentiments gains most inertia. For without any grasp on *how* Kant believes theory and practice may be joined, without a sense of the very politics of this central point, it remains both possible and likely to read his otherwise articulated political theory in the unresolved manners reviewed in chapter 1. And the paradoxes that irritate Bartelson may, thus, continue to stagger along unchallenged.

Arendt finds described in Kant's Third Critique a process in which, via judgment, the free thinking of humans is finally and appropriately tempered in a balance between an idea of the world and the full empirical requirements of the objects to which this idea seeks correspondence. At root, this would be the resolution that he requires between understanding and reason introduced in chapter 2. And it is therefore the point from which perpetual peace may be anticipated. But, as also indicated in the previous chapter, it is in addition a process that cannot be accomplished by any one person. Rather, it must remain open to the great multitude of potential and actual experiences of humans and the array of purposes to which individuals and groups attribute them. The political promise of judgment, for Kant, lies in interaction between or, at least, sensitivity toward the multiplicity of perspectives that people may have of their world and the diversity of worlds that they may in turn describe as an account of such impressions that lies at the root of perpetual peace. While keeping the requirements of universal unity in mind, it is the perceived need to constantly work through the reality of differences and change that makes international politics both imperative and truly possible.

Open as Kant's requirements may be in developing this accord and unity, though, it is possible to identify an uncomfortably harnessed mode remaining in his work. And it is the resulting stasis that gives the first signal of an unfortunate rigidity in his general project of enlightenment. There is evidence to suggest that the very context in which Kant seeks resolution is strictly presupposed within the functions most central to his critical work. At base, Kant neglects to fully consider and acknowledge the rudimentary ways in which his approach may seal-off particular possibilities and levels of difference across the lives of human beings. Thus, Kant's ostensibly unflagging approach to a resolution of the political in judgment may not necessarily proffer the radically persistent energy that it understands enlightenment to avail.

At the most elementary level of analysis, it is indeed through the faculty of judgment that Kant sees the possibility of unity being struck between understanding and reason. In short, Kant identifies judgment, first, as "nothing but the manner in which given modes of knowledge are brought to the objective unity of apperception."[19] What this means is that judgment functions as a faculty by which one is able to appropriately subsume many appearances under specific concepts and distinguish them accordingly in one's mind. This is the very act of understanding, wherein immediate representations are portrayed together under a "higher representation" for the sake of knowledge.[20] Judgments thus provide unifying forms for knowledge in which the categories provide unifying content. And, in its practical mode, it is judgment that evaluates whether or not maxims may be universalized and thus gain moral worth under the categorical imperative. However, as Kant explains somewhat differently in *Critique of Judgment,* judgment may also, in general, be understood as "the faculty of thinking the particular as contained under the universal."[21] It is the way in which one is able to think the specific instances and moments of sense, as offered through the understanding, within a supersensible framework which is to hold for all representations. Judgment is thus the faculty through which it is finally resolved how the freedom of reason ought to conceive its appropriate function in the practical world.

Holding to the notion that there is a fundamental and immeasurable gap between sensible phenomena collected under the concept of nature and the supersensible realm of the concept of freedom, Kant admits that there could be no transition from the sensible to the supersensible.[22] But he does not claim the same for the reverse. On the contrary, he writes:

> The concept of freedom is meant to actualize in the world of sense the purpose proposed by its laws, and consequently nature must be so thought that the conformity to law of its form at least harmonizes with the possibility of the purposes to be effected in it according to the laws of freedom.[23]

One must remember that, for Kant, the realization of freedom is embedded within the notion of spontaneity in causation.[24] To repeat, reason, from which the idea of freedom arises, is itself not within time. It does not appear as an object for sense but, rather, is simply already present in all human action.[25] Reason, Kant claims, is not subject to natural causation but creates for itself an idea of autonomy.[26] Hence, there is within the concept of freedom an inherent disposition toward thinking what *ought* to be in the world of sense.[27] To think freely is to constantly think how things should be and to, therefore, legislate appropriate actions toward the fulfillment of such ideas. The world, as understanding renders it, is automatically an issue for reason. With the understanding as its object, reason functions to marshal concepts with respect to the objects that understanding has ordered within them. Reason provides a unity amongst the concepts, so as to provide a total picture for the heterogeneous objects of understanding made available through sense.[28] Through judgment, then, reason gives itself an arrangement to the world so that it may not only conceive how the appearances categorized in understanding make sense to one another in space and time but also so that it may conceive how its own spontaneity may be conceived as a part of that pattern.

As Bartelson reminds his readers, judgment, in this role, provides a "middle term" between understanding and reason, wherein the antagonism between the two may be finally brought to some fruition.[29] And this functions without question, where the appropriate universal is already provided a priori. For example, in the fundamental concepts of the understanding Kant outlines in *Critique of Pure Reason* judgment simply determines the appropriate order under these given laws.[30] This *determinant* judgment therefore is not autonomous and risks no contradiction with itself.[31] But, the work of judgment cannot proceed automatically where there is no given principle for the occurrence of the given particulars. Thus, the ultimate task of judgment is not served until the thinking person becomes open to the political risks of her or his own thought.

In order to act productively on the aspects of knowledge provided through respective determinant judgments, Kant explains, the mind must be able to also understand them with respect to one another. An overall principle for knowledge of the world must be gained. But, the principle that could underlie all matters possible in the realm of sense would itself be beyond what is legitimate for reason to know. This could only be wrapped up in the in-itself unconditioned condition. In this case, then, reason has no recourse to a given determination of how it is to conceive of itself within this world. Rather, Kant claims, that the mind must resort to *reflective* judgment, wherein it creates for itself a law.[32] It must make a political judgment regarding the limits to this universe, based on rational deliberation:

> As universal laws of nature have their ground in our understanding, which prescribes them to nature (although only according to the universal concept of it as nature), so particular empirical laws, in respect of what is in them left undetermined by these universal laws, must be considered in accordance with such a unity as they would have if an understanding (although not our understanding) had furnished them to our cognitive faculties, so as to make possible a system of experience according to particular laws of nature.[33]

Thus it is in reflective judgment that the very idea of the international and the moral value of world-wide peace must begin. And, Bartelson is absolutely correct to locate the crux of Kant's political concerns at this very point.[34] For it is in such ideas that the particular events of nature and human society that one may come to understand are possibly brought into line with the Copernican view of the world that, as Kant explains, reason requires for itself. Moreover, it is only with such a cosmopolitan perspective that this exceptionally broad self-founding judgment could hope to succeed. And it is then through this specific sense of judgment which the international arises for Kant as a necessary object for thought and how it is that he finds himself compelled to approach this object with a politics of enlightenment.

To briefly recount and emphasize in a different way some steps introduced in chapter 2, what is at issue here is the question of natural ends. Kant explains:

> Now the concept of an object, so far as it contains the ground of the actuality of this object, is the *purpose*; and the agreement of a thing with that constitution of things which is only possible according to purposes is called the *purposiveness* of its form. Thus the principle of judgment, in respect of the form of things of nature under empirical laws generally, is the *purposiveness of nature* in its variety. That is, nature is represented by means of this concept as if an understanding contained the ground of the unity of the variety of its empirical laws.[35]

When taking into consideration natural phenomena represented through understanding, the concept of freedom leads one to posit a more general idea of the finality of nature as a whole. For Kant, nature may be defined most generally as "the existence of things under laws."[36] And the laws regarding the natural relations of cause and effect between particulars may be evident and manifest to sense. Kant admits that even an ultimate purpose may be determined for the movement of these natural things.[37] He shows that it is possible to link such an end to the existence of human beings, as rightfully partaking in the very top of a chain of natural being. He also shows, conversely, that one could take the view that it is the welfare of the more base and inanimate levels of life that pose the true ends within nature, with humans and other higher forms of life serving as the natural grooms and caretakers of the whole.[38] However, Kant argues that the central debate over whether nature serves humanity or whether nature has its own mechanical dynamics which have only incidentally served humans in certain ways cannot be concluded decisively and, thereby, really only goes to show that human beings cannot conceive the movement of nature without view to final causes.[39] And this substrate to nature, since it cannot be found within nature but only underlying it, must itself be supersensible. Hence, reason needs to create for itself an idea of such a principle of purposiveness. Reason must furnish an idea of the substrate underlying the dynamics that may be sensed.

Accepting the fact that humanity cannot be situated within the aims of nature by means of determinant judgment, Kant seeks a rule for judgment on this point from the inescapability of reflective judgment itself. And he sees in this fact justification for viewing humanity as not only a natural purpose among others but as the ultimate purpose of nature overall:[40]

> If now things of the world, as beings dependent in their existence, need a supreme cause acting according to purposes, man is the final purpose of creation, since without him the chain of mutually subordinated purposes would not be complete as regards its ground. Only in man, and only in him as subject of morality, do we meet with unconditioned legislation in respect of purposes, which therefore alone renders him capable of being a final purpose, to which the whole of nature is teleologically subordinated.[41]

What Kant understands to be the necessity of reflective judgment proves to him that the very freedom of human beings in their thinking must at length provide the basis from which purposiveness in nature could be judged in the first place. Hence, all phenomena of nature will always be thought in reference to thinking humans themselves. And, thus, judgment will always posit a system of purposes in nature with respect to the freedom of rational beings.

Kant therefore indicates that it is the happiness of humans that is the first purpose of nature.[42] For, according to him, happiness should be understood as a concept signifying the state that one will be able to enjoy once the greatest possible freedom is achieved.[43] It is the one single end in which all of one's desires are united. And, as such, happiness is the concern of the whole enterprise of reason with respect to questions of practicality.[44] Happiness is the idea of a state in which the freedom of an individual has come into adequate relation to the empirical conditions in which that person must live.[45] But, as Kant indicates further, such an idea is not so easily achieved when it serves as its own foundation. If happiness be the ultimate interest of the practical concerns of reason, it must lead to that which is good in itself. Not just any desires must be satisfied. Rather, Kant explains that reason may only approve of an idea of happiness once it is brought into accord with a worthiness to be happy. And such worthiness is possible only once happiness constitutes a concept of the satisfaction of desires which are themselves established with respect to one's moral duty.[46]

There must then be a larger context than the egoism and dogmatism of a single person's mind by which the appropriate satisfaction of desires may be realised. Kant claims that this context is culture and, thus, labels culture as the second purpose of nature.[47] He reasons that culture provides for each human the atmosphere in which that person may indeed set out to judge the final purpose of nature with regard to a general condition for all such rational and free beings.[48] And Kant trusts that the social inequities established in the formation and development of any and all human cultures will in the end bring about violence and dissatisfaction from both within and without. This collision of wills and desires will then bring about sufficient misery through which the lawful authority of civil community will be required. And, thereby, Kant imagines that the formal conditions under which nature is capable of achieving its final design—whatever that might be—will be accomplished.[49] For it is from this point that he sees that the rule of right may emerge nationally and thus the need for right rule to arise in the international sphere.

Kant argues that once the conditions necessary for a cosmopolis of humanity has been established, it then becomes possible that all humans may gain access to the discipline sufficient for truly being worthy of happiness. They may also then procure a sense of what specific collection of desires will provide for happiness. And, in this manner, humanity may finally be able to understand its whole series of movements as a gradual process toward the perfection of nature. For, in choosing practice in accordance with ideas created with respect to the final requirements of sense, Kant imagines that humanity may be able to establish for itself what the beginning of history must have been for current social reality to emerge and for human freedom to develop as it ought to.

Kimberly Hutchings suggests that this judgment has an inevitably arbitrary quality, that one judgment with respect to the purposiveness of nature is as groundless as another. She thus concludes that theorists of international relations who seek foundation in a Kantian resolution must still risk a great deal of failure insofar as a distance between morality and politics is left unbridged.[50] However, as Bartelson also notes on this very point,[51] arbitrariness in judgment is precisely that against which Kant wishes to guard.

The reflective judgment that Kant imagines can establish the final purposiveness of nature and, thus, the proper activities and thoughts of human beings is not founded in mere strong opinion. Rather, he describes a process by which such judgment is founded and gains validation through immensely rigorous comparison and debate. Kant argues that both cognitions and judgments, as well as the tenets which follow from these things, must be available for universal communicability amongst rational beings. He thus admits that the idea of common sense is legitimate.[52] This is precisely one of the central points emphasized by Arendt. She notes that for Kant to commit to the notion of public criticism he must also make contract with the notion that the ideas of each human may be transmitted between and possibly held by any other.[53] Hence, Kant believes that it is possible for a person to weigh his judgments against all possible others—not only the actual judgments made by others around one—by taking the various positions that other rational beings could assume and by abstracting from the limits inherent to one's judgment.[54] Supposedly, he may do so via imagination.[55] In this manner, although the judgment that one might make with respect to the finality of nature lacks absolute grounding, one may be able to make this judgment with sufficient discipline to adequately challenge the alternatives.

Difficulty persists, however, given the fact that the reflection that underlies this sort of judgment cannot provide for the objective reality of nature.[56] The final end established in the process of reflective judgment can never be more than a regulative principle through which the teleology of nature and human history are subjectively constructed in retrospection. This judgment, therefore, offers no more than what Kant refers to as a "guiding thread" toward how the future of nature and humanity ought to be understood with respect to the beginning of history.[57] The precise form and appropriate movement of the progress towards natural perfection is not made absolutely clear in judgment. For, as the objects of sense and, hence, understanding are subject to the movement of time, further possibilities in nature and human history come to bear on the discipline that Kant hopes will buttress the validity of reflective judgment. Thus it is that judging the purposiveness of nature with reference to humanity, through culture, within civil community, and open to a world-wide society of rational beings does more than necessitate a context of international politics; it also requires that international politics always be a perpetual project of enlightenment, in which rational beings seek to appropriately write a global reality for themselves in consideration of one another. Hence, in this manner, what Kant describes is without doubt an essentially ethically oriented politics in the constant pursuit, thereby, of discovering its own foundation.

Despite the very deep commitment to critique prominently exhibited in his idea of the necessary role of reflective judgment, though, a surprising level of implied constancy remains through Kant's position here. He calls for a sustained interest toward how different forms of the international and world activities are legitimately thought within different perspectives. He further admits that received notions of what it is that constitutes human happiness cannot possibly have legitimacy without full exposure to the court of a global enlightenment. Still, within Kant's position, a greater defining identity is allowed to stand in an unchallenged manner. The notion that there is *a world* out there in which and in reference to which such a radical practice of judgment is to occur is left as a strict and unquestioned reality by him. And, in this way, the foundation of his ethically oriented politics is already prescribed. He allows and, in fact, requires a particular ethic to prevail prior to the social ethos of critical discourse from which such a universal ethic is supposed to finally emerge.

Kant does indeed hold that human political life and experiences proliferate the earth. Moreover, he presupposes that this activity is, thus, contained within and saturates the surface of a globe.[58] Therefore, Kant does not simply anticipate unavoidable contact and conflict between human desires, movements, and ideas; he also casts a kind of shape to the possibility of this conflict as an extended dynamic. As a result, one may be tempted to conclude that Kant further provides for a universal space *in which* the specific challenges of human life are to take place. Hence, it is possible that he takes up a vision of human reality that already rests on boundaries that are not themselves necessarily subject to reflection at all.

In Kant's writings, the world in which humans live does not appear only as a mere principle or idea in the formation of his "guiding thread." Rather, there is a fashion in which he also upholds it as a very real general condition for all human life, already described by Kant himself, which has a specific role in propelling human reason toward a deduction of the purposiveness of nature. The risk of an arbitrary quality in Kant's vision of judgment that Hutchings raises is thus not so quickly dismissed after all. Perhaps it merely needs redirection.

The idea that there is *a world* prior to reflection in reference to which reflective judgment is made may not seem so nonsensical. It is likely even an automatic and unthought commitment in most ways of thinking. But, there is a central danger for such a project as Kant's in allowing an idea of that kind to remain unexamined or fixed, intentionally or unintentionally. To allow for and require perpetual debate over views to the purposiveness of nature produced through activities of judgment in the context of a world suggests that there exists a containing realm *in which* such activity takes place but which is not itself subject to the same elements of reflection.

A world itself, as the object of and the arena *within which* judgments are supposedly made, remains a neutral and potentially definitional ground upon which or in spite of which debate about purpose and finality may continue. This world is the idea of not simply what the world ought to be with respect to reasoned principles but, rather, what it is in an effectively determinant manner. Hence, inherent to this idea is that there is an objective world that is available for mapping as such, if the appropriate form of mapping could only be developed. It is a universal category in which the particulars of human life, whatever they might be, may all be finally organized. Thus, the need for persistent critique is placed into question. And interest in projects of explanation, reminiscent of realism/idealism, is again provoked.

Kant literally refers to the world as "the sum-total of all appearances."[59] He thus does not intend to posit the world as something existing in an independent fashion. Rather, Kant insists:

> If, therefore, I represent to myself all existing objects of the senses in all times and in all places, I do not set them in space and time [as being there] prior to experience. This representation is nothing but the thought of a possible experience in its absolute completeness. Since the objects are nothing but mere representations, only in such a possible experience are they given. To say that they exist prior to all my experience is only to assert that they are to be met with if, starting with perception, I advance to that part of experience to which they belong.[60]

In this sense, the world is most definitely not "a whole existing in itself."[61] It is very much an idea in service of the unity required by reason for Kant. He thus denies and denounces efforts by those he understands to be "cosmologists" to determine the magnitude or exact physical dimensions of the world.[62] Still, within this idea of all existing sensual objects in all times and places, Kant posits a *planet-world* which describes very specific limits to what he believes humans can experience. He explains:

> Through the spherical shape of the planet [people] inhabit (*globus terraqueus*), nature has confined them all within an area of definite limits. Accordingly, the only conceivable way in which anyone can possess habitable land on earth is by possessing a part within a determinate whole in which everyone has an original right to share.[63]

It is this set of limits he grants to the world of humans that make politics possible and politics in the form of perpetual peace necessary in what he judges to be the dynamism of nature.[64] And it is from this premise that a level of constancy emerges in his own understanding of what the world in fact is for humans.

In addition, Kant habitually offers evidence to suggest an absolute sense of the condition of human life, which is not simply a principle open to debate but, rather, one that must necessarily inhere. And this tendency arises at no better point than when he discusses the question of differences between nations in the world. In describing how it is that peoples ought to treat one another in the settling of nation-states along side one another or in the sharing of lands, Kant comes to delineate the possibility of human experience within a place that can be represented in little more than total terms. It appears that Kant can tolerate heterogeneity in perspectives and communal outlooks only insofar as such peculiarities may all ultimately fit within one universal outlook.

At first Kant suggests that differing perceptions, desires, and structures of community ought to gain the respect and toleration of each other. He claims that new nation-states may quite legitimately establish themselves and their independent cultures on previously unsettled lands neighboring older territorial communities. Kant also states that if a specific nation wishes to colonize the land traditionally utilised by nomadic and hunter/gatherer communities, such settlement should proceed only on the basis of a treaty negotiated between the groups. He is adamant that what he takes to be the "ignorance"[65] of the aboriginal persons of Africa and the Americas not be exploited for the gain of colonial Europeans.[66] Presumably, Kant is of the mind that the different ways in which these "natives" view their relationship to the land and world ought not to be abused for the sake of imposing Euro-centric notions of property and tenure. He denies that the violent seizures of land can be justified by allegedly 'benevolent' gestures to spread European civilization or the government of Western laws. Kant refuses to accept violence against the wills and perspectives of others for the sake of "the best interests of the world."[67] However, this issue remains a simple matter of tactics and conduct for him.

Kant certainly does not rule out the idea that such civilization and laws *should* ultimately embrace the globe and all people. He does in fact understand the excuse of benevolence in colonization and the work of cultural missionaries to be theoretically "plausible."[68] It is just that he is unable to justify such direct imperialism in light of the categorical imperative. Kant believes that such a process should only advance gradually, without overt violence. Just as he argues against the validity of violent revolution as a means to reform states to right-rule in favor of gradual reform, Kant looks forward to how "the best interests of the world" may be established within each human community across the planet through the growth of cosmopolitan spirit.[69]

Thus, there is finally a very deep level of tension in Kant's position. It is unclear whether or not the reader ought to understand Kant's vision of the dynamism of nature and its purposiveness as a matter for reflection only. For the judgments to which Kant believes humans must eventually come, in the service of perpetual peace, seem to still also finally rest on precise limits that exist empirically through time. The central issue at the heart of Kant's politics then appears to be the extent to which his idea of the world, as a guiding principle for knowledge and reason, comes to be confused, conflated, and/or reduced to what he attributes as necessary and final limits to the very shape of human existence.

Kant's Geopolitics

The guide needed to discover the relationship between what Kant takes to be the world, insofar as he posits it simply as the sum total of all appearances, and the strict and determinate planetary limits that he also places on human conduct lies in a consideration of the relationship between history and geography in his thinking. For the movement of the world that becomes an issue for reason in the form of nature and which is subject to judgment in reference to a history requires an extended realm in which to occur. The character of that space is thus crucial to understanding how Kant's image of the world actually does function in his theory and what this image, therefore, provokes and/or allows in terms of critique and enlightenment. As it turns out, despite Kant's warnings that the world ought not to be subject to measurement as such, his own theory betrays a highly specific notion of what the geographical limits to practical human experience are and how these determined dimensions must produce political life for all persons. As a result the enlightenment practices which fuel Kant's vision of perpetual peace are confined from the very start. A geopolitical ethic prefigures what is possible in terms of conducting a practical ethos, as opposed to the other way around.

It remains quite clearly the case that "the world" is for Kant just an idea and, therefore, has no true determinant reality. It cannot be an object of legitimate knowledge for him simply because of the fact that the sum total of all appearances could never be an object of possible experience. No such whole could ever be perceived without condition[70] and, thus, without a conceptual regress toward the inconceivable unconditioned condition.[71] However, it is not so clear that the bases from which the world, in this sense, is judged to exist is as equally stuck beyond the grasp of reason. For, as signaled in the previous section, there remains a very definite realm for Kant in which reflective judgment must function.

In judging the purposiveness of nature, the mind must not stray from the limits of human experience. And, although he can accept human experience to be possible beyond the confines of the surface of this earth, Kant cannot accept any suggested appearance from such potential experience to be more than merely a problematic conviction. For example, he states:

> To assume [the existence of] rational inhabitants of other planets is a thing of opinion, for if we could come closer to them, which is in itself possible, we should decide by experience whether they did or did not exist; but as we shall never come so near, it remains in the region of opinion.[72]

As a matter of opinion, although opinions for him do consist in a very rudimentary type of judgment, the potential appearances of other beings and things beyond the confines of earthly existence are simply insufficient as evidence for the serious work of judgment Kant describes leading to political theory:

> Opinions and probable judgments as to what belongs to things can be propounded only in explanation of what is

> actually given or as consequences that follow in accordance with empirical laws from what underlies the actually given. They are therefore concerned only with the series of the objects of experience. Outside this field, to form *opinions* is merely to play with thoughts.[73]

It thus follows that judgment is prescribed as a solely *earthly* practice. The focus from which the larger principles are to be derived is necessarily inscribed within terrestrial borders.

These limits are not simply conceptual themselves, however. On the contrary, Kant establishes the bounds in which human thinking may and ought to occur with very unequivocal and mathematically determined boundaries and, thus, space. He acknowledges that the earth itself can never appear as a whole either.[74] However, Kant does believe that, unlike the more general category of "the world," the sensual realm in which human life is limited may be charted, measured, and described with great detail by purely intuitive and, therefore, prediscursive means.[75] He explains:

> If I represent the earth as it appears to my senses, as a flat surface, with a circular horizon, I cannot know how far it extends. But experience teaches me that wherever I may go, I always see a space around me in which I could proceed further; and thus I know the limits of my actual knowledge of the earth at any given time, but not the limits of all possible geography. But if I have got so far as to know that the earth is a sphere and that its surface is spherical, I am able even from a small part of it, for instance, from the magnitude of a degree, to know determinately, in accordance with principles *a priori*, the diameter, and through it the total superficial area of the earth; and although I am ignorant of the objects which this surface may contain, I yet have knowledge in respect of its circuit, magnitude, and limits.[76]

Kant understands the propositions of Euclidean geometry to already hold purely a priori. He takes this to be demonstrated by the fact that, according to Kant, all mathematical judgments "carry with them necessity, which cannot be derived from experience."[77] In addition, he takes geometry to be "a science which determines the properties of space synthetically, and yet *a priori*."[78] And, since, for Kant, all objects given to the senses via intuition are characterised with the property of spatiotemporality, it naturally follows that he anticipates the world in geometric form.[79] He claims that "the objects [of the outer sensible world], so far as their form is concerned, are given, through the very knowledge of them, *a priori* in intuition."[80] And it is geometry, "the mathematics of space," that provides the rules under which magnitudes represented and apprehended in an extensive manner will be constructed for the mind.[81]

One then ought to take seriously Béatrice Longuenesse's point that, for Kant, the objects for understanding and the objects for the mathematical sciences arise from the very same mental capacities.[82] Or, as Rudolf A. Makkreel suggests, a view to the beautiful inherently draws out an "affinity" between mathematical and aesthetic forms for him.[83] From principles of Euclidean geometry Kant believes that he may, with certainty, develop an idea of the bounds of experience to which each human must ultimately admit.[84] As Guyer points out, Kant cannot allow himself to think extended reality outside of this particular spatial form.[85] Thus, the possible realm and order of particulars from which reflective judgment must be produced are therefore sketched and allegedly guaranteed from the start.

Kant's notion here is that one not only may encounter one's experience and consider possible experience within prescribed dimensions but that one also ought to buttress one's understanding with the discipline of such an a priori rule to begin with. In the introduction to his *Physische Geographie*,[86] Kant underlines this all the more. He writes:

> We say of the person who has travelled much that he has seen the world. But more is needed for knowledge of the world than just seeing it. He who wants to profit from his journey must have a plan beforehand, and must not merely regard the world as an object of outer senses.[87]

In this respect, Kant is aiming his comments directly against Hume, "one of those geographers of human reason,"[88] whom Kant views as having illegitimately quit any attempt to understand what the horizon of human perception may represent and imply. In this instance, Kant insists that "consciousness of my ignorance . . . , instead of ending my enquiries, ought rather to be itself the reason for entering upon them."[89] And the profit that he anticipates in this instance is nothing less than an actual intellectual map to guide one's judgment and the judgment of all like rational creatures terrestrially confined.

As J. A. May draws to his readers' attention in his study of Kant's theory of geography,[90] Kant goes so far as to suggest that the minds of children are best disciplined with suitable maps of the world.[91] Kant explains that a young mind can only hope to actively conjure for itself a sense of the relation between its practice and duty if that mind is first impressed with maxims. And he further identifies geography as the discipline which can appropriately provide the most fundamental of these maxims, suggesting that playing with maps is the best manner through which to curb the child's imagination.[92] More to the point, however, what Kant is at base claiming here is that actual experience of the empirically available world through travel is of little use unless one is first in possession of an instructive scheme for knowledge on this planet that can teach one how to actually know the human species.[93] In this respect, his point is that "universal knowledge will always precede local knowledge."[94]

Kant argues that a man may "know the world" through his travels. But the content of this knowledge may only be trivially understood unless he first "knows his way about the world." And such a prior plan is best arrived at via rational discourse prior to one's journey.[95] Reflected similarly in his theory of mathematics, Kant explains that without admitting to a synthetic a priori geometric guide to one's study of such a thing as a triangle, one would be forced to accept the triangle as something in itself—that it is *not* an appearance—and, thus, completely beyond one's knowledge.[96] In this regard, he again insists on the primacy of the subjective conditions under which one encounters the world.

As always, Kant appeals to the necessity of respect for an architectonic sense to the function of reason and the building of knowledge. He likens this geographical sense to the plans drawn in preparation for building a house.[97] But the idea proposed here is less in need of critical examination than are the future conditions and requirements of a house or the trajectory of nature and, thus, humanity which Kant imagines is to be "staged"[98] on this planet. It provides stable and timeless limits that merely need to be colored-in with specific items and situations that the traveler and his fellows may come across in space and time. Geography is the substratum and foundation of history,[99] wherein particular physical accidents within may alter. But the geometrical design of the totality remains constant.

It seems to be the case that, for Kant, knowledge of the precise character and integrity of the global world is ensured by the constitution he attributes to reason. For Kant, reason is also limited within a very specific geometrical reality. He chides Hume for treating human reason as if its limits, because unobservable in total themselves, are similar to a receding ungraspable horizon surrounding one's field of sensation.[100] Kant claims that such a notion rests only on an examination of what reason may show to be the case in any one circumstance. It is expressive of how reason can be used in its sceptical form to prove and disprove claims in daily affairs, wherein the total condition of reality is itself not available as an object. Hence it is an investigation of the facts of reason but not of reason itself.

In contrast, Kant contends, in a tone identical to that used in his analysis of geography, that:

> Our reason is not like a plane indefinitely far extended, the limits of which we know in a general way only; but must rather be compared to a sphere, the radius of which can be determined from the curvature of the arc of its surface—that is to say, from the nature of synthetic *a priori* propositions—and whereby we can likewise specify with certainty its volume and its limits.[101]

His point here is that from the 'experience' of the manner in which human reason functions, it is possible to delimit its potential extension in the service of creating knowledge also. For, presumably, just as Kant understands that no edge to the earth's surface may be found, he discovers that he never confronts a final obstacle in reasoning either. Yet, since he knows that he may not experience all that he can think, he concludes that reason must most definitely have an end of a sort as well. It thus occurs to Kant that reason too must be a working whole (a sphere) which simply does not contain all that possibly exists. Therefore it must be possible to determine the limits of reason in terms of what is within and what lies without. Hence, he urges:

> Outside this sphere (the field of experience) there is nothing that can be an object for reason; nay, the very questions in regard to such supposed objects relate only to subjective principles of a complete determination of those relations which can come under the concepts of the understanding and which can be found within the empirical sphere.[102]

Thus, it appears that for Kant both reason and the geographical unity of the earth must be understood to describe the same political realities and necessities. For, calculated correctly, they necessarily extend to the same dimensions. And the history that takes place within that which geography describes will necessarily amount to the total movement available for reason's view.

The point for Kant then is to devise a method by which one may indeed determine these mutual boundaries and limits between the globe and reason accurately. And this method is, as should be familiar by this point, critique. In this regard, he generously refers to Hume's skepticism as a "resting place" at which reason "can reflect upon its dogmatic wanderings and make survey of the region in which it finds itself, so that for the future it may be able to choose its path with more certainty."[103] But, this stay does not provide the potential certainty Kant requires for the hope of a permanent repose. The point remains for him to seek, simultaneously, a way of thinking that may stay within the lines of the earth and a geographical knowledge that is complete. As Arendt suggests, what Kant's critique then requires of one is the training of one's imagination to "go visiting" through this world,[104] as if all the points at which Hume and others might find rest could somehow be scheduled for stopovers in advance.

Beauty and the Beast: Extending Leviathan to the World

The conditions under which critique may truly furnish such an alignment between the earthly sphere and the sphere of reason must include not only a unity within each but, furthermore, integral unity that is universalizable for each human being. For if Kant's critique is to come of any practical fruition, it must be possible and practicable for each person to not only think the globe within a reason limited to possible global experience. It must also be feasible for each human being to do so in the same way. Perpetual peace requires the fact that all could genuinely will to live under the same principles and natural order.

Kant does offer grounds upon which such universality may be expected. This is found in his attention to aesthetics. He appeals to questions of taste and beauty that he supposes guarantee a universal communication between rational beings and a universal language for the highest good. However, as hesitantly anticipated in chapter 2, the legitimacy of these grounds is not evident. Examining further the geometrical foundation on which Kant's geopolitics rests, it becomes quite clear that there is no global human realm to which his theory may validly appeal. Rather, it is in this case that the acritical character of Kant's theory begins to shine through most impressively. For the universal unity he requires within and across the practical and rational spheres rests eventually on a dictatorial view. Kant finally does contract with a Leviathan. And, it is on this basis that the spirit of enlightenment, fundamental and necessary for perpetual peace, must be dashed.

The key to Kant's belief that there can be a common total view of the limits of human experience as well as a conjoint frame through which to judge it ought to be understood to rest in his theory surrounding pleasure with respect to taste.[105] It is exceptionally difficult to provide a strong and exact understanding of what he takes pleasure to be in this case. But, in general, Kant comes to suggest that it is a "feeling of life,"[106] offering mediation between the theoretical and practical faculties.[107] To be somewhat more precise, he takes pleasure to result from the ordering of the heterogeneity of nature in terms of principles discovered through judgment with a view to purposiveness. Kant takes the feat of understanding to attain such design to be thoroughly "bound up" with pleasure.[108] It is a feeling generated when one comes to witness how it is that particulars may be collected under broader and ultimately the broadest sense of the purpose of nature. He explains that pleasure is the result of something within human judgments regarding nature that draws attention to a successful picturing of nature's harmony. In contrast, Kant continues, judgments in which representations of the laws of nature are irreconcilable under universal empirical laws must give rise to displeasure.[109] Pleasure is, thus, an initial mark indicating progress toward correct reflective judgment, that is, judgment in which the principles and movement of nature are understood with respect to what it is actually possible for a human to sense.

Kant admits that this feeling of pleasure is not simply ever-present within the comprehension of unity. It is not a governing state of being. Still, he contends that pleasure is always enjoyed at each moment in which elements of such unity are themselves recognized. Kant states that one cannot possibly undergo the process of any level of experience without some form of pleasure/displeasure arising around it.[110] For, at root, experience for him is knowledge derived from the connection of particular perceptions.[111] There is always a process of ordering, even at this basic event.

Kant clarifies that pleasure may occur in at least three forms. There is an interested pleasure, wherein personal gratification is found within an object,[112] which is otherwise known as something pleasant.[113] Where there is pleasure through concept alone, where something is to be esteemed, the object of this pleasure is known as the good. And like the pleasant, the good is caught up with the faculty of desire.[114] However, Kant explains, where there is a feeling of *mere* pleasure with respect to judgment, wherein both interest and concept are of no concern, this is a judgment not bearing the same sort of situated character of the previous two. From the feeling of mere pleasure, he tells his readers, one has view to the beautiful. And, in this respect, Kant is quick to note that this object ought not to be confused with that which may simply reside within the eye of the beholder.[115] The beautiful is that which must please outside of all concern.[116] It is thus through the example of this feeling that he identifies the possibility of a universal approach to a singular and unified world.

Kant recognizes the fact that the beautiful, as derived through a judgment of taste, may after the fact be combined with either empirical or intellectual interest. He thus notes that, on the one hand, the inherent inclination toward society that he perceives within human beings may render a sense of beauty into that which is only valued within communal discourse, providing a vague passage from the pleasant to the good.[117] And Kant suggests, on the other hand, that the feeling for the beautiful may be unjustly conflated with moral feeling.[118] With respect to the latter case, he does agree that an "*immediate interest* in the beauty of nature (not merely to have a taste in judging it) is always a mark of a good soul,"[119] that "if . . . the beauty of nature interest a man immediately, we have reason for attributing to him at least the basis of a good moral disposition."[120] However, Kant is concerned that regarding the beauty of nature with a prior sense to the moral good is mostly just an expression of pleasure in the *presence* of the natural objects one beholds.[121] His complaint is that the concern in intellectual judgment for natural form gives way ultimately to producing an interest in the laws that ought to objectively hold for all human beings. As such, Kant argues that this feeling must in reality be something available to only the very few persons whose minds have had the fortune of already having been cultivated toward the good.[122]

Prior to these possible combinations, though, Kant takes it that there is a feeling for the beautiful which demonstrates necessary universal assent for rational beings, regardless of theoretical object or practical satisfaction. And the type of necessity he has in mind here has to do with a feeling of a universal rule prior to any concept of the content or the direction of that rule.[123] In this manner, Kant associates taste with what he refers to as *sensus communis*.[124] And, by the use of this term, he is careful to indicate that what he means is more aptly referred to as a sense common to all, rather than the more "vulgar" notion of common sense. Kant's point is that within the judgment of taste, wherein only the form of the given representation and the representative state are taken into consideration, there is a feeling for the beautiful that asserts the necessary communicability of the pleasure.[125] He states, "We could even define taste as the faculty of judging of that which makes *universally communicable*, without the mediation of a concept, our feeling in a given representation."[126] Mere pleasure is thus a feeling toward the unity of natural order and the unity to which all rational beings must admit.[127] Furthermore, the beautiful is an example of this dynamic whole.

In this regard, Kant defines beauty as "the form of the *purposiveness* of an object, so far as this is perceived in it *without any representation of a purpose*."[128] What he means by this is that beauty is that which produces a feeling toward the fact of purposiveness itself, that there is purposiveness in nature to begin with. He argues that, for example, "a flower, e.g., a tulip, is regarded as beautiful, because in perceiving it we find a certain purposiveness which, in our judgment, is referred to no purpose at all."[129] And to feel purposiveness in one object is to bring further attention to the necessity of such pleasure in the similar judgment of others for all persons. For, by definition, natural purposiveness must be for one and all.

Kant actually goes so far as to claim that "the beautiful is the symbol of the morally good."[130] Different from how beauty may be combined with intellectual interest in the service of moral instruction, he takes the object of mere pleasure to give rise to a higher mental sense of the necessity of agreement between rational beings. In this way, the judgment of taste bound in mere pleasure inspires its own law, as opposed to submitting to simply empirical laws, with a mind toward satisfaction in the purest sense.[131] And, it is thus with regard to the beautiful that Kant believes the fundamental accord between the freedom of reason and the requirements of sense are shown to be bridgeable for each rational agent. He concludes:

> Hence, both on account of this inner possibility in the subject and of the external possibility of a nature that agrees with it, it finds itself to be referred to something within the subject as well as without him, something which is neither nature nor freedom, but which yet is connected with the supersensible ground of the latter. In this supersensible ground, therefore, the theoretical faculty is bound together in unity with the practical in a way which, though common, is yet unknown.[132]

It is thus through beauty and the pleasure received in its view that Kant's hope for a universal unity in human judgment is given ground. Moreover, it is within this question of beauty that the alleged practicability of perpetual peace is given purchase.

This fundamental unity, expressed and indicated in a feeling which is supposed to be universally communicable, however, rests on assumptions which do not necessarily hold. To start, Kant must assume that the pleasure he associates with beauty is a feeling that not only can be but is enjoyed by all humans in the same way. And, since this feeling is specifically prior to interest and concept, he remains on relatively stable ground in that regard. Such a feeling does not require a definite disposition or perspective. It merely requires the simple active perception of a rational creature. But it is here that the difficulty begins. For underlying this set of precepts is the notion that all rational creatures must, at least, naturally perceive in the same way regardless of conditions. As Makkreel argues, the common sense that Kant requires here does not mean that each subject be able simply to appreciate the standpoints of others. Rather it means that all members of the community be able to take up an intermediary position that could be common to all.[133] Kant's theory requires a fundamental equality among rational beings insofar as they may all come to reason in the course of the exact same mental exercises and at all points and times. His analysis does not offer sufficient support for that idea, though. Nor is it apparent how it could.

As Bernard Yack argues, the attribution of common identity to all humans is problematic for Kant's interests from the start. For, the claim to identity between rational actors begins to erode the idea that humans present to one another a vast array of difference from which morality is to be worked out through political society.[134] Guyer bolsters this point considerably further from another angle, showing that Kant cannot hold onto the universality he attributes to mere pleasure in a particular object and, at the same time, the contingent quality of the experience in which beauty may be recognized.[135] Placing this complex of issues to the side for the moment, though, one can see that the mutual equality Kant attributes to each rational human is based on the idea of spontaneous freedom he believes to automatically emerge in rational thought.[136] As a being who may a priori conceive of her- or himself as free,[137] each human, for Kant, possesses equality with all possible rational beings, "because he could claim *to be an end in himself*, to be accepted as such by all others, and not be used by anyone else simply as a means to others ends."[138] But, even if one grants to Kant the idea that there is a thing one may call human reason that inheres in each sound example of a human being, it is not clear that this reason does lend itself naturally to the same structure of thought in all cases.

Kant himself implicitly offers stark evidence to the contrary. While he identifies women as rational beings,[139] Kant argues consistently that they are incapable of the same quality of rational functions as enjoyed by men. He believes that men are vastly superior to women on this accord, just because of the fact that they are male.[140] Thus, just as Kant presupposes a particular vision of the world, he also assumes a sex-specific perspective behind the view. Women are thus to be ruled by a masculinist discipline in a way similar to how Kant believes European civilization must naturally come to dominate the world over. And global peace between the sexes is, thus, eliminated as a possibility.

Even, if one accepts his insistence that reason be understood as analogous to a sphere, it is still not necessary that the thinking of each and every rational individual can lead one to the same radius, circumference, and volume in each case. The arc that Kant believes can lead one to describe the limits and shape of reason must constitute a particularly unified segment of what understanding may avail. Functioning to represent the necessary complete determination of things[141] and, through unifying the manifold of concepts by means of ideas, to posit a certain collective unity as the goal of the activities of the understanding,[142] reason, in this view, strives always to completion and final unity. Hence, it seeks a whole that may support the objects of understanding. Yet the whole that one may mathematically extend from one such arc need not match that which is extended from another. Any one segment of reason may lead one to the positing of a spherelike order. In this way, all reason may undeniably admit to a total and containing singularity. But the curvature of one arc may not match that of all others. Each description of what appears as the bounded horizon of reason may offer an enclosure that, while not totally exclusive to others, is unique with respect to the alternatives.

As is evident from his observation of the possibility for differing judgments across humanity, Kant must acknowledge that the contour of one's ordering in reason from any one position is susceptible to the information available at that site. Although he comprehends reason to be something that searches for unity of knowledge in accordance with ideas that extend far beyond possible experience, such as when determining astronomical movements,[143] the specific objects reason finds in understanding remain fundamentally informative of the ideas reason employs. Reason seeks a position from which to make sense of that which is ordered by understanding of appearances.

One may develop a critical method wherein all arcs and the spheres they describe are compared to one another as a manner by which to generate a finally corrected sphere to which all instances of reason ought to be understood to realistically conform. Or one could through this comparison describe a larger sphere that could contain all the overlapping and intersecting ideas of the totality of reason that rational individuals may generate. But one then runs into the difficult question of determining how many arcs one needs to take into consideration in such an enterprise. Furthermore, one needs to evaluate the length of arc that is suitable for comparison. Need all possible horizons be taken into account? How could one measure them all? Perhaps these troublesome questions fit within the scope of the incessancy of the resolution Kant ultimately frames with perpetual peace, that the search for final unity is likely to be an inevitably persistent exercise undertaken, ideally, by all rational creatures. However, the worthiness of coming to conceive the final dimensions of reason as a sphere is still dubious.

To be fair, Kant would not advocate that the sphere determined through the arc of local experience ought to be used as the solid definition from which reason constructs the delineation of its own limitations and the definite aspects of its spheroid structure. For Kant, this would consist in the development of knowledge directly from concepts, which would amount to the dogmatism he deems as despotic and seeks to eliminate from thinking at the start of his critical project.[144] On this basis, Kant would resist Longuenesse's point that his mathematical cognition is illegitimately extended to precise quantitative determination of what the world really is.[145] In this regard, he takes mathematics to really offer only a guide for philosophy with which the work of critical inquiry might finally be able to establish definitions for itself as its final function, if that function could ever be completely served.[146] However, adherence to such a guide as this in one's philosophical efforts to determine the political conditions and necessities of humanity gives geometry and the concepts it avails far more assured life within philosophical inquiry than critique itself can bear. And Longuenesse's challenge in the end is not so easily put off.

As Howard Caygill reminds one, "The prime motivation of the critical philosophy, what makes it 'critical' is the recognition that we cannot simply deploy our existing categories globally—we cannot extend them without a careful examination of the limits within which they may be used."[147] And, as he further points out, Kant seeks rudimentary limits to categorical judgments through what he calls the Concepts of Reflection. In short, the Concepts of Reflection offer the matrix through which "we first set ourselves to discover the subjective conditions under which [alone] we are able to arrive at concepts."[148] Moreover, it is through these Concepts that one may begin to correctly determine the respective relations of the sources of knowledge to one another.[149] They achieve this by directing judgments through four oppositions: identity/difference, agreement/opposition, inner/outer, and form/matter.[150] However, as Caygill continues, these oppositions make sense only in terms of the three-dimensional space described within the principles of Euclid. Once, time is admitted as a fourth dimension, as Kant has already done via intuition, the matrix provided by the Concepts of Reflection must also allow for a great deal of flux and change.[151] The structure of consciousness that Kant suggests must inhere through reflection must submit to movement, as all appearances for him are conditioned by time. But to admit to such flux, change, and movement would be to push beyond the Euclidean description of possible experience. And, for Kant, do to so would, thus, be to push judgment beyond what he understands to truly limit reason to possible experience. Still, the priority of Euclidean three-dimensional space is not demonstrated. The tension generated between time and this description of space is unavoidable for Kant. And, as already argued above, the principles of Euclidean geometry need not securely develop a unifiable projection of human experience in any event.

If it is the case that innumerable arcs of reason may in fact generate similarly innumerable spherical descriptions of the actual limits of reason, it is not obvious why a final sphere should be the goal from the start. It may well be the case that there is this pleasure of the beautiful, as Kant describes it. And such pleasure may certainly inspire a simple sense of purposiveness and unity, without a directive content in any case. It may further hold that this feeling could lead human beings each to will singular concord with one another and with respect to the purposiveness of nature. And, on that basis, morality may be appropriately founded within a categorical imperative, as Kant provides it. Yet, it is still not necessarily shown that such ultimate concord or universality is possible. For, that one could judge the limits of reason to either trace the nexi of all possible arcs or outline the furthest limits of all spheres that may be possibly generated from such arcs, does not mean that those limits do relate to the actual limits within which any given rational being may act. The idea of such a generalized sphere would be abstract to the various instances in which humans do think. This principle may not provide an adequate guide for any one rational thinker, let alone all.

In the very same manner, as is more loosely anticipated in chapter 2, one may conclude that Kant is not really entitled to rely on such a universal idea and, hence, guiding principle, of the globe either. It is all the more evident in this case that the arc one may describe from one spot on the earth cannot generate the same sphere as may be calculated from any other. The topography of each point on earth and the horizon that extends around it do not necessarily follow the same quality of curve as all others. The only manner in which one can truly come to the same measurements of diameter, circumference, and volume from any point of the planetary geography is if one already supplies the principles of a sphere to one's calculations and accommodates the mathematical requirements through an exclusion of rises and dips that skew the geometrical purity. Thus, the idea of a globe on which Kant's theory gains such solid support could not truly be an appropriate principle for the learning of each and every traveler. It is not an idea that can offer objective validity. For it does not rise from or shows itself adequate to the possible subjective experiences of the members of the species at all. It is simply a principle along which all may order their perceptions in a similar fashion and not a guide to experience, as such, that could offer objective validity for any one point.

This is not to suggest that one cannot make proper measurements of the earth based on the principles of geometry to which Kant is faithful. With the building of non-Euclidean alternatives to the science of geometry in the work of, for example, Riemann,

Hilbert, and Einstein, Kant has been greatly criticized for the command he allows Euclidean geometry to take in his view on mathematics.[152] Along with Newtonian physics, Kant's mathematical convictions now appear antiquated.[153] However, like Newtonian physics, Euclidean geometry, while limited, does of course have widespread practical application. The physical properties of this planet may be calculated and described in such a way as to accurately anticipate the fact that one will not fall off an edge in one's travels. And one may calculate the approximate distances that must be traveled in the circumnavigation of its oceans precisely on the bases of such principles. But, antecedent to the introduction of extraterrestrial travel, the geometric equations can only explain the fact that human life is bound to a specific and closed physical existence. That the processes of one's thought impress one with the notion that life may be contained within a sphere does not in itself identify what are the precise limits to experience. The *actual* shape or shapes of possible experience across the species is not articulated by this figure. Similarly, the recognition of a unity in reason does not show what must be the full extension of that whole.

Caygill draws attention to the fact that Kant, of course, realizes that the demarcation of space in one's activity consists in a limit whose final shape is introduced subjectively. Emphasizing the idea that the geometrical limits in such a construction are to be merely treated as if they were objective, Caygill suggests that Kant expects potential excess to the subjectively inscribed boundaries and that such excess may be "felt."[154] Still, there are no grounds here to show that each and every human can and must ultimately feel the same practical deviations from the pure geometric form. And, even if this point could be supported, it is not clear that each person could feel these points of excess in precisely the same way.

Pursuing the question further yet, it is not even clear that Kant's rational subject is necessarily capable of gaining the unified recognition of what ought to hold universally within her or his own experience let alone the experience of all possible rational beings. Gilles Deleuze provides a provocative analysis in this regard, indicating that the common sense generated through judgments of taste is not the singular ground through which a person may enjoy the mere pleasure associated with purposiveness as such. He argues, rather, that "Kant's enterprise multiplies common senses, making as many of them as there are natural interests of rational thought."[155] His point is that, while common sense must always be understood as a general form of recognition in which the various faculties collaborate, any one of imagination, reason, or the understanding may respectively provide that form. It all depends on the nature of that which is to be recognized, be it an object of knowledge, moral value, or aesthetic effect.[156] As a result, Deleuze suggests that there is no one *generality* to the general form of common sense that may be presupposed.

Whether or not Deleuze's cautions hold firmly,[157] reason to doubt the necessary unity and, hence, universality of recognition is demonstrated more directly with a return to the concerns of morality. The universal recognition of common sense that Kant believes is made available through the aesthetic is tenable only insofar as he is able to maintain the initial separation between the posited sensible and supersensible realms. There must be a unity that exists outside of particular sensual interests, for which all humans may practicably strive. It is the aesthetic judgment of beauty that secures Kant's commitment to a moral law to which all rational beings ought to submit. For beauty expresses the fact of ends that hold beyond the apparent physics of nature and which must do so for all humans. But as William E. Connolly argues, the initial separation between the sensible and the supersensible, which is to be mediated only through rational autonomy, is not guaranteed in Kant's theory.[158]

Connolly's central inspiration here is Gordon Michalson's analysis of radical evil in Kant's moral theory.[159] What Michalson attempts to show is that the propensity toward evil that Kant attributes to humans at each moment of judgment, as described in chapter 2, endangers the possibility of approximating or realizing the moral universe more fully than Kant admits.[160] Remember, this propensity to evil is radical, because "it corrupts the grounds of all maxims."[161] For Kant, humans are in a position wherein each maxim is always susceptible to the pollution of inclinations grounded in sense as opposed to law. There is, as Connolly notes, an inescapable "wildness" at the heart of this will.[162] But, Kant insists, one may still enjoy a hope for grace from God, as a deliverance from this crookedness.[163] One demonstrates one's worthiness of grace (one's "holiness") in adopting a purity to one's maxims, in attempting to do one's duty for the sake of duty alone.[164] However, Michalson draws attention to the fact that Kant is then caught within a paradox of his own making. Kant wants and needs to maintain the autonomy of the rational being, positing the struggle between a fall to radical evil and the freedom of self-legislation under moral laws as a matter internal to that being. Yet, he must also condition the relative success of one's struggle for autonomy within the guarantee that there is a God who could externally offer the grace needed.[165] As Michalson summarizes, "[Kant] goes 'outside' this world in order finally to underscore an obligation that can only be met *in* the world."[166] Hence, again one witnesses the troubled assumption of a universal and unified supersensible prior to and as a poorly substantiated guide toward its recognition. Thus, Connolly justifiably asks: "What makes Kant so certain that morality must assume the form of a *law* we are obligated to obey? Why not pursue a practice of ethical life in which the equation between morality and law is relieved?"[167]

Morality, as law, is necessary for Kant, as it allows him the certain point from which to legitimately theorize the supersensible and autonomy in the ways he does. Yet, as Deleuze anticipates elsewhere,[168] Kant's rational subject, given that this subject's will is the site of its own morality, remains in a poor position from which to ever know or appreciate grace as a true possibility. The subject's hope for grace can only be grounded on the belief that there is a universe that makes sense.[169] But such sense, even if it were actual, could not be easily or even likely recognized without the act of grace from God first.

It is thus worth entertaining Connolly's notion that:

> Kant can now be interpreted first to project persisting elements of a Christian culture into a 'common sense' projected as constitutive and then to invoke this projected accord of the faculties to justify a Christian-inspired rendering of the moral life.[170]

In conjunction, returning to my prior comments on geometry in Kant's thinking, one can see all the more that the Euclidean principles that Kant wishes to establish as girding both reason and geography are then imposed as boundaries on these things rather than simply recognized within each. The general plan and structure of the universe is not found within the limits of experience or feelings of beauty but, rather, in the prejudice of Kant's own project. Or, as Guyer notes, Kant can anticipate that judgments of taste will provide a universally valid pleasure only on the basis of an aesthetic judgment he has already and independently made about the experience of pleasure itself.[171]

As summarized by Philip Kitcher, Kant puts himself in a position where he must suppose that the series of spatial representations that one does in practice receive from one's own standpoint could be extended in such a way that the fundamental properties of the space that one may possibly experience would be revealed. But, this is as circular as Kant's resolution of morality and freedom with respect to the subject's struggle between radical evil and grace. For, in extending these representations so, he already informs such an extension with the properties he seeks to discover in the process.[172]

Another form of this circularity is evident in Kant's commitment to the essential identity of each (rational) human being. He trusts that each human must ultimately be able to admit to the same sphere, given the a priori validity of Euclidean propositions to what Kant takes as the human mind. Yet, what this discussion also brings to light is the fact that at least part of Kant's reason for assuming the identity between human minds is the presupposition that humans all must admit to the same planetary limits.[173] The sphere that is suppose to limit and guide human reason is also taken universally and is presupposed as the grounds from which one can speak of a human universe to begin with.

While working from a perspective more deeply motivated by questions of cognition, Deleuze traces this circularity yet once more. Broadly put, Deleuze's point here is that Kant approaches the problems inherent to reflective judgment and the recognition of natural purposiveness and unity as already *solvable*. He already presupposes the solvability of judgment with respect to taste without considering the ways in which his own critical theory disallows such a position.[174] Deleuze correctly argues that Kant's Copernican shift demands that problems in judgment be understood as themselves sites of potential solution.[175] Taken as only possibly true, only optionally asserted within the unity of understanding,[176] problematic judgments must be tested on their own 'grounds'. Whether or not such judgments may be admitted to the understanding then must not rest on a prior general assumption about truth as a unity that may be found through critique but, rather, on the success of asserting such a proposition with respect to other local propositions availed through possible experience. Otherwise, the Copernican Revolution is indeed without force,[177] and a 'geo-centric' position remains asserted in veiled form.

Kant's principles for understanding the necessary unity between reason and sense are thus inspired by an effectively despotical root, benevolent though it may be. Therefore, the possibility that Bartelson sees in Kant's thought for a new internationalism, wherein a "commensuration between value systems rather than a source of universal values in itself"[178] may be achieved, is simply not available. The unresolved tension between universalism and pluralism that Bartelson views in Kant's writing does in fact have a prior resolution of a very strong sort toward the universal and a priori. For, instead of developing the grounds of his critique with respect to the multiplicity of limits to experience that humans verily live, Kant seeks an investigation of what sort of a universe it is that may be implied by the consideration of all potential experience taken together. He looks toward the description of a literal sphere of human life in which all activity and perception may be expressed in singular terms. But Kant does not persist in his efforts to confront how it is that rational humans possibly differ in the very grounds of their respective perception, thought, and actions, regardless of content or interest. Rather, the boundaries of earth, geometrically conceived, remain the limits in which Kant understands the communal discourse of reflective judgment ought to proceed. It is only within this sphere that difference will be recognized. And all points of difference will be mediated within this universe via a series of republican states, which, as Makkreel points out, represent application of the overall aesthetic ideal Kant has in mind.[179]

In a spirit consistent with the line of criticisms taken up above, Richard K. Ashley identifies Kant's philosophy with a universalizing turn of modern thought that supports one of the most acritical moments in international relations theory.[180] Ashley submits that the reception of state sovereignty as the axiom of modern international politics is not the inevitable fact of some natural forces of conflict. Rather, he states that its condition lies within a particular Kantian understanding of reason, extended to all human beings:

> In all its varieties, modern discourse holds that the sovereignty of the state, including the citizen's duty to obey the law, does not derive from any source external to man. Instead, the state's claim to sovereignty obtains in its establishing as the principles of its law and its violence those historical limitations that reasoning man knows to be the necessary conditions of his free use of reason. It consists, put differently, in subordinating *raison d'état* to the reason of man, making the former the guarantee of the possibility conditions of the latter *in history*.[181]

Ashley's point is that there is a fundamental "compact" between "reasoning man" and the state, wherein each rational person comes ultimately to support a set of territorial and juridical limits as those necessary for the function of reason and wherein the singular state structure will itself act coercively only to ensure that activity and thought contrary to the critical vigors of reason do not gain sway.[182] And he notes that this compact may be made in various guises, be they, for example, Marxist, Christian humanist, radical communitarian, or ecological.[183] For it is simply a matter of *a* singular voice being accepted as the expression of the needs and direction of the species within *a* particular space.

In response, Ashley complains that there remain many "transversal struggles" which do not agree with and are inconsistent with the singular view of man that is spoken in any one place. He draws attention to the idea that there persist elements in any territorially unified and single-state society that are not and cannot be fully embraced by its limits. These are, as a result, pushed outside the political and deemed as essentially apolitical, for they compete with the historical judgments that direct the particular sovereign power.[184] Ashley, thus, challenges others to take up what he receives to be the audacious call to admit that no one really knows who "we" are.[185] For, as long as a "we" remains an assumption, violence toward the actual spatial experience and legitimate understandings of human life is sustained as a politically sanctioned reality. There are many of the "we" that then become "them." And this opposition between us and them is what comes to fuel modern discourses of international relations.

In this mode, however, Ashley's attention can be seen to not take into account the broader planetary territory from which the sovereignty of Kant's rational human speaks the story of Man in nature. Ashley's comments are perhaps better understood as directed toward Hobbes' interests in resolving difference and anarchic motion within his vision of a commonwealth. Hobbes claims that the natural conditions of motion that exist within each person require that each submit his or her individual authority along with others to a singular sovereign. In this manner, Hobbes maintains that a group of persons is able to construct a unified and monolithic Person in the state, that may speak for all as All.[186] And, in doing so, he suggests that the constant clash and stirring of bodies in time, which Hobbes likens to the unpredictability of weather, may be subdued into a universal progression of a whole body of Man accountable in the form of History, a state of Peace.[187] Still, in this manner, one can see how it is that Ashley's comments against Kant are perhaps quite relevant after all. For, in this light, Kant's theory may at base be understood as a broader and certainly more perfect form of the sovereign Hobbes limits to the state.

Kant does indeed locate the authority for signifying a description of the necessary direction of the species within the thinking rational man. As noted in the above discussion of judgment, rational man contains the appropriate end of nature for Kant, because it is only with rational man that the purposiveness of nature can even be judged. It is essentially this point that encourages Arendt to view at the centre of Kant's philosophy *the* individual, who is a world citizen on the basis of being the spectator for whom the whole historical world is his object.[188] And as Kant recognizes true state sovereignty to legitimately consist in the union of all wills within that territory,[189] the sovereignty of the species is made practicable with the union of all national wills toward the requirements and duties of the species, as articulated through the authorship of rational man. In other words, Susan Shell's observation that the appropriate function of Kant's republic requires the existence of a "shared reality" embraced by all,[190] may be extended equally, if not moreso, to his cosmopolis. His primary interest in providing this alleged international approach to theory is to bring about the conditions under which state sovereigns, while thoroughly avoiding any sort of universal government as such, will give themselves over to the authority of rational man. In such a circumstance each nation would then supposedly find union with one another with respect to the territorial limits of possible experience on a practical level: the globe.

If this arrangement of sovereignty can be achieved within the perpetual form in which Kant envisions it, the commonwealth of humanity that would result would indeed be far superior to Hobbes' Leviathan. For the practical danger of the outside would have been removed. Hobbes' resolution may be seen as akin to what Kant describes as Hume's resting place for reason. *Leviathan* is concerned with a pragmatic solution of motion and conflict within a particular horizon of thought and activity. It remains constantly vulnerable to further experience and movement beyond its borders and beyond the moment in which the covenant is formed. On the one hand, Hobbes' commonwealth is susceptible to war and questions of difference posed from without. Kant, on the other hand, theorizes a domain for human beings in which neither regional identity nor humanity are themselves threatened. The political form of planetary community is founded only on the fulfillment of right rule within each and every state. And humanity as a universal political bond gains and maintains stable definition by the fact that it may be conceived only in terms of the containment of the globe. Humanity does not offer universality in itself. Rather, there remains an entire world beyond planetary existence that is possible for humans but of which they have no part. Insofar as humans are understood as rational beings, there are no human *others* outside of the sovereignty of man that may be able to bring its authority into question. It is also the case that there persists an entire world full of *potential* rational others, beyond earth, *against which* the species may understand itself as a unit.[191]

Employing the geometrical set of axioms that he believes are available a priori to one's mind as a guiding principle for philosophical efforts, Kant hopes that it may be possible to ultimately establish final definitions regarding the human species and the political conditions surrounding it. In this "sisterly union"[192] between mathematics and philosophy, he appears confident that the grounds may be established upon which humans may legitimately come to form a singular and unceasing motion toward peace and, thus, the perfection of nature. But this motion would not amount to the simple linear and eternal progression of the unchanging and unchangeable commonwealth as imagined by Hobbes. Rather, the motion of perpetual peace, as authorized in rational man, would consist in the cultivation of the very ground on which human history, as a concept adequate to the species, may finally take hold.

However, cultivation of this ground requires the rational identity between each person that has already been shown to be impossible in numerable ways throughout the discussion immediately above. And, just as Hobbes' Leviathan rests fundamentally on the assumed equality among human beings, without the assurance of equality and without the guarantee of sameness in rationality, there is no complete and final globe for Kant. Furthermore, without this globe there is no true basis for the unity and order that his universal federation of nations requires. Hence, there is no ground from which to actually expect perpetual peace, as Kant has conceived it. The lawful procedure obliged by the advance of critique remains unsettled. Thus Kant's enlightenment traveler must still contend with his own skepticism in a far more central manner than might be hoped. This traveler may merely be stuck in a perpetual denial of possible worlds without ever being able to find repose and without gaining the comforting evidence to suggest hope in an eventual rendezvous with the human community he presupposes.

Beginnings of a Critical Approach Toward World Politics

One may be able to undermine the legitimacy traditionally granted the sovereignty of rational man within world politics and, therefore, disturb the promise of Kant's project as he envisions it. However, in doing so one does not also take away the force and grounds that propel his work. The freedom experienced and conceived by each human being does not inevitably lead to the foundation on which a categorical imperative may successfully be justified. But such freedom may still very well confront each human with the inescapable problems that fuel both Kant's philosophical interests and his political resolutions. The notion and sensation of experience still bring up choice of action and the question of the results of one's actions as issues to which one must respond. Relations of cause and effect are prominent in any reflection on activities within life. In addition, in coming to make sense of oneself with respect to one's idea of what one experiences in and as "the world," either one denies the possibility of knowing the world in any way but how one cares to, or one must consider what the world must be in order to support the freedom one thinks one enjoys. In the former case, one leaves oneself open to constant war and conflict with others, as in the battle between skepticism and dogmatism. Hence, it is only in the latter instance that one may find some hope for a manner of being that allows one's freedom to truly flower. Thus, a very serious set of political questions arise regarding the possibility of lawful and disciplined thought and action in the face of a lack of center to either reason or practical life.

To begin with, one really must consider whether or not a Hobbesian construction and defense of order against disorder is the final practical reality to which one must admit. Given that Kant cannot ultimately offer a justifiably centered view that may rationally speak what all ought to will, regardless of inclination, it is quite easy to slip into the pessimism that sees authority ultimately falling heavily into the hands of those who gain the advantage of rule over others. Struggles between ruler and ruled for authority may arise. Competition between assertions of sovereignty are inevitable. Still, it is not clear that uncentered freedom must imply simple chaos either. That struggle and conflict occur certainly means that lawful life and thought is most difficult to achieve. But, this does not mean that discipline in these realms is not possible or that it has no practical ends.

At heart, what is at issue here is whether or not thought can maintain the freedom from traditionally understood power politics that Kant argues for in his *The Conflict of the Faculties*. There, he contends that, unlike the "higher" faculties of theology, law, and medicine—faculties that he claims are of primary interest to government—the "lower" faculty of philosophy must not submit to the censorship of the state. Rather, Kant insists that philosophy maintain the right to critically evaluate what is done in the higher faculties as well as government and how these institutions are structured. His point is that, while philosophy itself should gain no executive political power, it is only in critical work that the governing laws may be appropriately described. In the same manner, one must then investigate whether or not it is possible to derive a rule for reason and conduct from freedom other than that offered by categorical imperative. It is important to examine the extent to which critique can indeed survive, in the face of no legitimate universal idea, as a procedure that does not simply defer to a hopeless skepticism.

In precise terms, what is at stake is the possibility of developing an ethos that does not rely on the ethic of personal autonomy at its base. For it is the autonomy of the individual that, despite Kant's hopes, places philosophy in a position where it must in the end tip its hat to Hobbes. Necessitating respect for the alleged equal personal freedom of each rational being, this notion of autonomy is the idea that leads to the unjustifiable universality required in the categorical imperative. Hence, critique must not start its project from the limits to rational thought in general, as if these boundaries are proper simply to the thinker her- or himself. These limits are never generalizable, as each rational being has a view to differing horizons. It is also the case that these limits cannot be extended to a singular position of rationality, as such absolute concord is an impossible achievement. Rather, critique needs to examine how reason is limited by the motion of possible experience and the constant rational activity of others.

The judgments and points of view that may be and are generated by one person cannot be exclusive to that person. Drawing once again on Kant's attention to geometry, one may see that no singular sphere may be inscribed as an adequate guide for all persons, if any at all. Still, on the basis of this position, it must be the case that the sorts of worldviews and guiding principles that each person may and is likely to describe from local experience and specific thoughts are inescapably in contact with one another. The very laws of geometry, insofar as Euclid's propositions remain valid on a practical day-to-day level, show that each must intersect, as each projection is traced from an arc of the same mass, so to speak. There is a standpoint from which each rational person could consider her or his respectively perceived condition of freedom. Through the experience of asserting one's own worldview and, thereby, showing problems in the assertions of others, it is evident that one is in constant touch with all possible descriptions of the world and ideas of the world. Furthermore, one is invariably entangled with the imperatives that are shown to be required from such judgments. Therefore one may take it as a rule that one's freedom is in continual relation to the freedom of all possible rational others.

On the basis of this information, one may respond in the Hobbesian fashion and defensively locate all others 'outside' one's standpoint, as if they are natural threats to one and can only be understood as either friend or foe. But to do so, in this analysis, would run contrary to what experience tells one. For, if one finds that it is universally true that one's own judgments and determination of guiding principles are in constant potential conflict with those of any and all others, that only goes to demonstrate that these others can never be on the outside of one's perspective but, rather, are always possibly coursing through it.

The implication is that, as a rule, one might consider how one's freedom is always constrained through conflict with others and through the alternative information that others may bring to bear on one's experience and thought. Without recourse to the possibility of a final globe/mind, instead of finding a position from which one may think in a critical fashion, one might situate one's critical project within the exchanges that give rise to the perception of conflict and struggle to begin with. For it is at the points in which one discovers the limits of dogma and the skepticism that possible experience is realized. Through conflict with the motion of others and the intersection of ideas one necessarily discovers collision, contention, and struggle as the foundation of possible experience. For the sake of politics, critique must then come to consider more seriously the radical role that such anarchy can have in the theorizing of ethics in the beginning as well as the ends.

4

From World Politics to Politics (in 'the World')[1]

If one must ultimately deny the viability and legitimacy of rational autonomy as the universalizable ground for Kant's understanding of international politics, one presents an equally halting challenge to the mainstream bedrock of international relations theory overall. For, both realist and idealist traditions themselves pivot on what is assumed to be an inherent rationality in human beings. Rational man remains the foundation on which some predict a constant anarchy of self-interest and from which others anticipate a universal progression toward peace.[2] The critique of Kant's work that I produce here, then, demands something far more complex than a dismissal of his ultimate position as a guide for international relations theory. Neither removal of Kant from the discipline's den of "founding fathers" nor the outright rejection of all things deemed "Kantian" sufficiently meets the task. It also demands a reformulation of the basis from which theories of international relations are to be built.

Presumably, it is in this light that such writers as Linklater, as discussed in the Introduction, seek a theoretical base on which a global set of differences in outlooks may be entertained and appreciated. As is evidenced in the growing literatures focused on culture, ethnicity, globalism, gender, or social movements in international relations, the inability of "rational man" to explain all politics in the world is provoking a swell of new analysis dedicated to the multitude of accounts human beings across the globe have told, are telling, and will tell about political life. However, whether one is committed to rebuilding a tradition of rational autonomy minus Kant's foibles or whether one seeks an alternative to the theoretical ground inherent to him and the traditions of international relations, the importance of his critical approach remains inescapable. While his answers may be unacceptable, Kant's questions remain unavoidable.

As shown in the conclusion to the previous chapter, a dogmatic approach to international relations is not only illegitimate but impractical. Likewise, a disciplinary metaphysics, wherein scholars submit political phenomena to a map of the international world drawn prior to a complete investigation of it, is unacceptable. Rather, an adequate approach to international politics can be derived only from the experiences and consequences of human freedom that give rise to the concern of politics in the world to begin with. And the challenge in this regard is to discover some manner of understanding this freedom within its own empirical yet changing and indeterminant reality.

The geographical limits, extended through geometry, that form the disciplinary ground for Kant's critical project falter, because, at the very least, they cannot adequately account for movement and change in the lives of human beings. They cannot satisfactorily describe the dynamism and inconstancy that first gives rise to the experience and appearances to which, Kant hopes, human minds may ultimately provide an order and purpose. The social and personal conflict that Kant wishes to resolve through the persistent work of judgment may not be overcome by way of establishing a universalizable standpoint.

Scholars of international relations may seek such a viewpoint. But the effort is surely without point, in reference to the ever-potential mobility of human perspectives and reflections. To start work on establishing such a discipline in one's critical efforts would not result in simply bringing to fruition the perfection which all humans might and ought to achieve for themselves. It would amount, ironically, to searching for singular command over the species from private reason and not the public discourse that Kant so values and that international relations theory is obliged to cultivate. It would require a repetition of the problematic universal/particular matrixes underlying any conventional theory of international relations.

This is not to suggest, however, that a critical approach to world politics is altogether out of reach. By no means do I want to suggest that attempts to address politics in the world is a hopeless venture. On the contrary, as I indicate in the previous chapter, the point merely shows that critique must finally find its discipline in a much less stable and inert vein. The Kantian and international relations projects simply face very difficult challenges. And, for the sake of developing a strong understanding of politics on this level, it is important to recognize and take up these responsibilities. As Kant takes Hume's empiricist limits as the point at which to consider the problem of knowledge anew, it is important that theorists of international relations learn from the failures of Kant and consider the conditions under which a politics of critique with respect to international politics may be successfully remade.

In both cases, one must accept as one's rule that the limits to possible experience are always made in the constant confrontation of human wills with one another and with apparent horizons. The guide to critique must be formed in full appreciation of the mutability and even irrationality of the limits that are daily established in human living. To accept such a guide in one's critique of world politics, however, is also to embrace a most radical turn of perspective. For, absurd or contrary as this may sound, a discipline of this sort commits one to push critique away from any focus on the world and back toward *politics* minus the global qualifier.

This is not now to say that, while one may conceivably recreate a critical approach to international politics, one must for this purpose ultimately deny the existence of the international. Clearly problems of international politics cannot be denied and are the objects of concern here. But, it is important to finally understand that it is impossible to approach the international from an international perspective *first*. As Kant would note, such a point of view is unavailable without a process of reflection. And critical reflection can begin only on the basis of local sense and an as-yet unlimited imagination.

As I argue in chapter 2, international politics is not something to which Kant applies his ideas. It is not a subject as such that he presupposes worthy of consideration. International politics is a moral problem that he finds inevitable in the taking up of fundamental questions of epistemology and in the derivation of meaning for oneself as a rational being. The politics of living as a human inescapably escalate to world-wide ethical issues. For Kant, the source of international politics is always to be found both in the domestic and the personal. Hence, strict distinctions between the international and the national is unacceptable for him. However, if one is to take seriously the critical work he advocates and obliges, it is manifestly imperative that one never accept the international or world dimension of politics as simply interrelated with the domestic or personal, regardless of how radically the interdependence is posited. For, on this account, the world is never anything experienced but only ever a judgment made in the contest of human discourse.

The world of world politics is a description of limits always contingent on the politics of personal and cultural debate, never available for possible universal assent. The world, hence the limits of the international, is always only a contingent image generated in the movement of politics. It is an image offered as a means to establishing the ends of politics. But these ends are of course themselves always already subject to the throws of practical political life. Thus, to engage in a critical study of world politics, in these terms, is to approach the political struggle of all persons to provide meaningful contexts to their lives and interests. And it is to do so in a manner that is perpetually aware that the 'domain' of "all persons" can never possibly be described in universal form. It is certainly required that the attention to world politics be shifted to studies of politics in the world. But on the basis of that directive, no world may itself be posited in which politics, the struggles of all persons, may be provisionally or finally contained.

Accepting the idea that Hobbes' attempted divisions between inside and outside and between friend and foe, let alone rational and absurd, are unacceptable orders to the politics experienced in human life and refusing the geopolitical limits of Kant's ethical position, I then seek in this chapter to outline and contemplate the possibility of maintaining a critical approach to world politics as indicated immediately above. I wish to give some shape to the meaning of engaging *world politics* as primarily a function of *politics*. And, in so doing, I aim to assess the likelihood of being able to finally establish an engagement with politics in 'the world' that avoids *both* the self-righteous violence of dogma and the nihilism of mere skepticism. Thus, my project in this chapter is to attempt to learn whether or not Kant's hope for a truly mature approach to thinking the meaning of one's own identity, one's relations to others, and the direction of human society is in the end a worthwhile pursuit.

Of course, such a project presents a magnificently huge task. And I do not pretend to offer a fully accomplished effort in this short deliberation. Rather, my intent is to merely establish a substantial opening for such work in reference to studies currently occurring under the perhaps troublesome rubrics of "international relations" or "world politics." I essay only to provide some completion to my own examination of the relations and potential relations to Kant's thinking and the discipline. And it is my hope that this modest exercise may then provoke further productive contemplation and debate on the implications of this position in wider fields and activities of greater depth.

Initially, I set out what I find to be the theoretical ground necessary for taking up the requirements of Kantian critique successfully in this context. Here, in contrast to the alternatives offered by Arendt and Jürgen Habermas, I offer the enlightenment politics of Michel Foucault as both provocative and appropriate. Subsequently, I read two sets of literature in international relations theory that, taking seriously Foucault's reading of Kant, offer the substantial potential for an examination of the dual move I set out in the previous chapter: to, first, reject what I view to be the unfortunately static discipline of Kant's critique and, second, to call for a critical guide accepting of the movement and change of human life.

Primarily, I look at the theoretical engagements with international relations of Ashley and Walker. Together, I argue, they herald the call to critique offered by Kant but simultaneously remain highly suspicious of the sort of universality that he requires of an international/world perspective. And, in doing so, I suggest that Ashley and Walker provide examples of the least problematic aspect of Kant's critical project, to always maintain a rigorous public examination of the limits under which the human species is said to be appropriately organized and administered. Second, I turn to a consideration of the work of David Campbell who aims, along with others, such as Michael Dillon, Jim George, Patricia Molloy, and Daniel Warner, to retheorize international ethics. It is in their efforts, I submit, that one may witness highly vigorous attempts to provide the very mobile guide to a critique of world politics—which finds world politics always first within politics—that I contend is necessary. Through an account and evaluation of the work of these writers, I aim to offer initial conclusions with respect to the actual viability and practicability of the critical approach I argue are exhibited in Ashley and Walker's writings and which Kant's failures require.

On the bases of my studies of the works of Ashley, Walker, and Campbell, I then seek to think through the implications of these conclusions for the study of politics in 'the world'. The final movement of this chapter focuses on analyses of the positive and helpful points that may be drawn out of a review of the above mentioned authors' analyses. Here I further contemplate the political conditions of critique itself, as it may not only both provide and discredit views of the limits of human life but, more important, how it also establishes a way of living. I am interested here in what critique may itself offer as a politics. And, in this manner, more than I am interested in considering the potential 'worlds' that critique may provide for the imagination on the basis of practical experience, I am concerned to investigate the 'worlds' that critique allows one to live as a politic.

In the end, my point is to show that, from the perspective of examining politics in 'the world', Kant perhaps gives up on the role of skepticism in critique too early.[3] I suggest that the maturity in reason that he seeks is not to be found in something beyond radical doubt. Rather, it may be found in taking on doubt as a rigorous and perpetual project itself. I do not claim that skepticism will provide the more proper path to perpetual peace or its possibility. But I do wish to indicate that it is, perhaps, only with a conviction to the skeptical aspect of Kant's critique that politics in 'the world' may be engaged well. In this way, I am by no means suggesting that we can only ever respond to questions of international politics with doubt and, hence, pessimism. To the contrary, I claim that it is only by embracing the skeptical force of critique that international relations theory may be advanced in a truly productive and empirically relevant manner. And in this regard, I recommend continued pursuit of Ashley and Walker's investigations as sources for the strongest critical work and less so the guide offered by Campbell, compelling and attractive as his example may be.

Enlightenment as a Limit Attitude

There are recent responses to Kant in political philosophy that attempt to address and correct the acritical foundations of his enlightenment project. Perhaps the most important and certainly the most influential of contemporary neo-Kantians in this regard is Habermas. Uncomfortable with the notion that there could ever be any knowledge or rational position that is not subject to interest, he seeks a critical guide that may employ the true interests of all humans in the determination of knowledge, truth, and meaning for all.[4] Habermas provides an engaging return to the political potential Kant perceives in public discourse. However, the sort of position Habermas offers does not lend a sufficient address to the requirements of the project taken up in this chapter.

He insists that there is indeed much promise where social-political structures are such that they allow for and encourage incessant debate and consultation on a community and, ultimately, world-community level. Habermas' point, crudely put, is that, outside of deceit and humor, within acts of communication humans necessarily presuppose that their statements contain truth and that, under the appropriate conditions, this truth could be conveyed successfully to others. On this basis, he suggests that, with persistent effort, an intersubjective discourse may evolve across human community in which truths and agreements might be generated that could hold for all persons.[5]

Habermas sees that human language manifestly demonstrates the possibility and practicability of an ideal speech-situation, in which all humans together could, through ongoing critical discourse, contribute to the formation of social-political agreements appropriate to both the differences between them and the linguistic reason they all allegedly share. He writes:

> My reflections point toward the thesis that the unity of reason only remains perceptible in the plurality of voices—as the possibility in principle of passing from one language into another—a passage that, no matter how occasional, is still comprehensible. This possibility of mutual understanding, which is now guaranteed only procedurally and is realized only transitorily, forms the background for the existing diversity of those who encounter one another—even when they fail to understand each other.[6]

Despite his interest in a human knowledge that is founded through intersubjective discourse, though, Habermas retains the prefigured limits of the universal and particular. He presupposes a specific type of rational-communicative human being and generalizes that subject-position to all possible humans. Furthermore, Habermas prefigures the possibility of a human linguistic-universe, in which all human perspectives and experiences could supposedly be contained. Hence, in essence, the Habermasian position reproduces difficulties central to the critique of Kant offered here.

Arendt offers an alternative to Habermas on this point. Wary of the totalizing authority potential within the rationality adhered to by Kant and promoted through notions of linguistic community by Habermas, she seeks a guide for what she sees as Kant's critical political philosophy within reflective judgment itself. As a principled activity that submits to no determinant view from above, Arendt expects that reflective judgment may permit individual freedom to flourish in a politically responsible manner while coerced by neither reason nor nature. Appreciating the political quality that Kant locates within thought and theorizing, she is inspired by how reflective judgment immediately impels one towards an expectant concern for an entire species of possible others within a community of human beings. She writes:

> One can never compel anyone to agree with one's judgments . . . ; one can only 'woo' or 'court' the agreement of everyone else. And in this persuasive activity one actually appeals to the 'community sense.' In other words, when one judges, one judges as a member of a community.[7]

As a result, Arendt believes that taking judgment seriously may lead to a rigorous communal-political life in which all members of the species live the cosmopolis on equally willed terms. But, as with the case of Bartelson, this interest in judgment still neglects to take into account the deeply complex *terrain* of Kant's thinking in which judgment is understood as community-oriented in the first place.[8] Arendt would like to see the idea of "mankind" provide the very guide for critical political activity as humans seek to engage one another at all levels, whether within the confines of the state or not.[9] She trusts that it provides a general idea for all that is inherently willed freely by each. But it is not at all clear that the idea of "mankind," taken here to also mean humanity as a global community or species, is universalizable as such a cosmopolitan medium without presupposing this "original compact" of humanity determinately.[10]

To push toward a critique of world politics of the sort I suggest here, one that is without a static framework and one that pursues its guide with respect to the mutability of possible experience rather than an allegedly universalizable and atemporal ethic, places one's interests, instead, squarely within the purview of Foucault's response to Kant. Foucault, typically viewed in stark contrast to Habermas, finds much value in Kant's emphasis on the enlightenment aspect of critique. He too favors the constant public discourse on the limits of knowledge, emphasizing the notion that a final view to limits can never find legitimate standing. However, Foucault, unlike Habermas and more radically than Arendt, poses a serious challenge to any notion of a true human subject position or final limits to human community.[11] And in so doing, Foucault shows that a move beyond the theoretical anchors availed between universality and particularity pushes the whole project of enlightenment critique far more forcefully toward a politics of freedom than any resolution of meaning, knowledge, or certainty.

The aspect of Foucault's thinking in his response to Kant that suggests its relevance to the general aims of this chapter most impressively is found in his treatment of Kant's call to enlightenment as an *attitude*. In concert with and appreciating the importance of Kant's preference to speak of the modern age as one of enlightenment, rather than one that is indeed already enlightened, Foucault refuses to characterize it as a stage in the development of modernity. Rather, Foucault insists, it is better understood as the spirit or *ethos* that pushes the modern search for postcatholic truths and knowledge in all its actual and possible developments.[12] In this manner, he takes up Kant's call to enlightenment as a remembrance of the attitude that wrested European humanity from the dogma of medieval religion and the fear of the loss of the eschatological order that accompanies it. Foucault argues that all modern European knowledge of humanity, social order, nature, law, and so on has been established on the venture to question and to know differently, to not accept any particular domain of ideas until it has been established by humans for themselves for their own reasons grounded in the divers experiences they live. On this basis, Foucault, like Kant, finds it unacceptable that any truth be left unquestioned. For to do so would be to ignore the fact that all truths are first founded on questions and not true in themselves. In other words, to take seriously the motto of the Enlightenment, *Sapere Aude* (dare to know!), is to always and first honor the right to question the limits on which knowledge is founded.

It is here where Foucault and Kant also part ways most significantly. For, along with his unwavering commitment to the spirit of *Sapere Aude*, Kant is also wedded to the commands of obedience. While the critical activity of enlightenment must be publicly free, Kant is equally unforgiving in his insistence that in the use of private reason, consisting in the carrying-out and ordering of one's (even a public official's) occupation and social conduct, individuals must also obey the discipline he decides is necessary for the freedom of critique. And this is the discipline that finally finds its political form in the quite possibly heavy-handed right rule of the state and the potential right rule gingerly willed amongst states. In contrast, Foucault forces the full implication of Kant's critical stand and denies the surety that Kant finds in the limits of right rule. Thus, for example, Foucault also denies the sorts of principles which Kant lists as unquestionable in his three Definitive Articles of *Perpetual Peace.*[13]

Foucault's reasoning here is that enlightenment as Kant presents it is not only a political activity that need be protected at great risk but is also a political activity that is very sensitive to precisely how it is protected. In this regard, he is compelled to view enlightenment not only as taking up the exigent issues of knowing and ethics but, precisely on those bases, to also inescapably take on very practical issues of power.[14] Kant may understand the republican rule made visible through an Eighteenth-century European imagination to provide the only opportunity to protect public debate. However, for Foucault, such a republican commitment as Kant's is one that is merely historically contingent, as one may understand Doyle's trust in the liberal democratic state imaginable and/or desirable from the vantage of the United States of the 1980s. He would refuse the political limits judged desirable by Kant, or for that matter Doyle, as by any means necessary to the freedom of thought. To the contrary, Foucault would understand the order of each, while perhaps fostering vigorous debate and critique in certain manners, to disallow particular other inquiries, not the least interesting of which would be a consideration of the political form under which enlightenment should be permitted to flower.

Foucault's general interest is to point out that unquestioningly obeying any specific political structure as the condition under which the daring of an inquiring knowledge is to bloom assumes at least a bedrock of an already enlightened society. This is a stand not unlike that which I take against Kant in a more complex manner with respect to his assumptions regarding geography. And, similar to my argument there, Foucault suggests that this position is precisely against the drive of the enlightenment for which Kant so vehemently argues. Embracing Kant's persistence on this point all the more fastly, Foucault takes the primary function of critique to consist in the search for constant freedom from ideas and social constructs that would serve to prefigure one's ability to always question and know:

> I will say that critique is the movement through which the subject gives itself the right to question truth concerning its power effects and to question power about its discourses of truth. Critique will be the art of voluntary inservitude, of reflective indocility. The essential function of critique would be that of desubjectification in the game of what one could call, in a word, the politics of truth.[15]

His point is also that the conditions of human experience do not only vary in space but also in time. Thus it is that the very constitution of each human, as she or he views her- or himself, as a social-political subject is also prone to change. In order to truly provide oneself with the assurance that one may give one's own mind the opportunity to know for itself and not appeal to dogma, one must then ensure that one's imagination is never limited by the confines of any one historical example of human culture. Hence, Foucault knowingly seeks to push the commitment to autonomy in ways that are dangerously radical—almost adolescent—for Kant:

> If, properly speaking, Kant calls critique the critical movement that preceded Aufklärung [the Enlightenment], how is he going to situate what he himself means by critique? I would say, and it sounds completely puerile, that in relation to Aufklärung, critique for Kant will be that which says to knowledge: Do you really know how far you can know? Reason as much as you like, but do you really know how far you can reason without danger? Critique will say, in sum, that our freedom rides less on what we undertake with more or less courage than in the idea we ourselves have of our knowledge and its limits and that, consequently, instead of allowing another to say "obey," it is at this moment, when one will have made for oneself a sound idea of one's own knowledge, that one will be able to discover the principle of autonomy, and one will no longer hear the "obey"; or rather the "obey" will be founded on autonomy itself.[16]

On the very grounds of Kant's enlightenment ethics, Foucault refuses any final deduction of human subjectivity, perceived individually or collectively, and the imperatives that are therein implied. He takes the position of a thinking human to always be a question for that person. And, in this sense of the Kantian spirit, solution to that question should not be left to the authority of a subject constituted without regard to the specificity of the lived movement and historical conditions which underlie it. The duty of critique must first always be that of resistance. And it is through resistance that the critic may hope to realize her or his freedom.

In the context of Kant's aims, then, perhaps the most important or essential point of critical resistance for Foucault takes the shape of what he calls refusing the "blackmail" of the Enlightenment.[17] Understanding the Enlightenment to consist in "a set of political, economic, social, institutional, and cultural events on which we still depend in large part" as well as "a certain manner of philosophizing," of which Kant's critical project is a supreme example, Foucault refuses to accept the position that places one in simple opposition to this very important modern tradition if one is not wholly for it.[18] His argument, in essence, is that to posit the aggregate of traditions and institutions that come to form the Enlightenment as something open only to either support or rejection, is to accept the Enlightenment as something that does indeed exist as such. It is, so to speak, to view the Enlightenment as something in-itself. And Foucault denies such a view on the grounds that the set of political, economic, social, institutional, cultural, and philosophical activities that come to be gathered under the rubric of the "Enlightenment" does not and cannot exist independently of the historical character of these activities. Foucault can again be seen to employ Kant's warning that modern Europeans ought not to understand their societies and themselves to be enlightened but that they should understand themselves to be caught up within processes of enlightenment that may give rise to customs and views that, in contrast to the past, may appear enlightened, constituting the idea of an Enlightenment.

For Foucault, heeding this warning, however, implies a necessary reversal of Kant's queries regarding the limits of knowledge. And it is in this instance where the alignment between Foucault's inquiries and the requirements of critique that I finally lay out in the previous chapter is most strongly expressed. For, whereas Kant sets out to discover the boundaries which human reason must respect, Foucault calls for a no less persistent effort to trace the outline of sociohistorically constructed ideas and institutions which corral a person's ability to imagine the limits of reason to begin with. Instead of presupposing that there is a definite ground upon which the transgressions of reason may be established with certitude, Foucault stresses the importance of always identifying the limits described within a supposed enlightened context which must in turn be transgressed in the cause of enlightenment as a critical attitude.[19] This is the limit attitude he professes and claims to draw from Kant. And the crucial element of this limit attitude is its historicocritical aspect.

Understanding the Enlightenment to be conditioned by ongoing social practices that have neither singular origin nor unified telos that may be determined in advance, the point for Foucault is not to decide whether the Enlightenment is good or bad, to decide whether the Enlightenment should be maintained or replaced with a preferred ideal. He does not see such questions to be of much sense. For Foucault's analysis offers the Enlightenment as a set of sociohistorically produced limits to thought, imagination, behavior, and practice in which one's critical capacities are themselves embedded. Thus, it is of little use for those persons born of Enlightenment culture to judge it first on simple moral or positive grounds. The grounds of morals and positive reason are already limited by those enlightenment practices structured in a particular way under the heading of the Enlightenment. To judge the Enlightenment as an enlightened person is therefore to simply enforce the limits prescribed in the same.

In contrast to such judgment, Foucault therefore asks that critique take on the form of the question "how?" Finding the Enlightenment to necessarily describe and enforce specific spheres of intellectual and experiential possibility, he calls for diverse inquiries into *how* it is that such limits come to be taken as given or real to begin with.[20] It is Foucault's primary position that only when the limits to thought, behavior, and one's view of the world are shown to be formed in various practices and events that have no final or necessary ground that the possibility of one enjoying the freedom of reason may be truly delivered.

Providing a particularly interesting intervention on these very points of concern, Andrew Cutrofello argues that Foucault pushes the critical element of enlightenment so far that his radical questioning ultimately leaves one without a site from which to resist the domination of lawful discipline.[21] He contends that Foucault's enlightenment position finally leaves critique without a productive guide at all. Furthermore, Cutrofello suggests that Foucault's particular interests in enlightenment may be folded much more gently into Kant's own position in any case.

While accepting that Kant's adherence to a freedom sustained only in autonomous obedience of laws undercuts his primary interest toward a critical ethos, Cutrofello also submits that Foucault's unyielding efforts to trace and resist the confines of authority ignore how a disciplinary practice need not be also domineering.[22] Hence, he suggests that there is room for mutual supplementation between Kant and Foucault, wherein Kant's categorical imperative is recast as the basis for Foucauldian-style Kantian critique. Taking the maxims that Kant imagines fall from the categorical imperative to be unnecessarily narrow in scope,[23] Cutrofello suggests that the purity of the categorical imperative may be left behind and that it may then be used as a strategic tool for simply testing contingent maxims subjectively generated.[24] Foucault's rejection of rational authority and the determinant principles which confine Kant's thought remains appealing to Cutrofello. And Cutrofello's point is that this ethic may be served through an imperative that simply seeks always to gauge the acceptability of one's reflective judgments to all others.[25] In this way, experience would not be so limited by reason. And the categorical imperative could be interpreted as a mutually willed disciplinary safeguard against the domination of any one discipline, reading: "Always act in accordance with a strategy of resisting disciplinary domination that could be willed to become a general strategy for everyone to adopt."[26]

Put differently, Cutrofello's hope is that all might adopt a general strategy to "resist techniques of mutual betrayal."[27] And, in this light, one may see that his attempt to show a Foucauldian approach within Kant's fails to pay sufficient attention to the final implications of Kant's own theoretical difficulties. For, to reconstruct the Kantian imperative by way of bringing an enlightenment ethos into submission before Kant's ethics is still to presuppose that there is a We to whom a general strategy could hold. It is to suggest that, even if the practical institution of a universal ethics is not likely, such universality is a mutual interest before such universality or the commonalty across individual interests could ever be established through critique.

While Cutrofello presents a 'common-sense' manner in which to render the purity of Kant's ethics apparently more practical through the 'purified' enlightenment of Foucault, he still does not show a way in which the radical character of Foucault's critique may be in this context justifiably subdued. The importance of shifting one's view of limits from the global to those of anarchy and change is not successfully challenged. Still, as Cutrofello warns to begin with, it remains to be seen whether or not the radicalized critical position that I find necessary in overcoming Kant's contradictions and that Foucault enthusiastically supports may be, in the end, at all productive.

A Limit Attitude for the Study of World Politics

Despite the great difficulty that Foucault's approach inherently poses to the study of international relations, his position enjoys a marginal 'following' of a sort among scholars in the discipline. The writings of Ashley and Walker are revolutionary in this regard. Foucauldian readings of Kant's thinking within the studies of international relations, however, do not afford a new and improved Kantian point of analysis that may compete with those troubled forms engaged in chapter 1. They do not produce a Kantian perspective that may finally be applied as an appropriate framing for world-wide political activity. Rather, just as Kant's enlightenment position implies the impossibility of traditional international relations studies, as the study of inter-state politics, the Kantian enlightenment rendered by Foucault suggests even the impossibility of the more loosely conceived study of "world politics," wherein international politics is posited neither as activities exclusive to states nor primarily organized through states. As a result, while it may be said that Ashley and Walker provide exciting promise for the pursuit of a critical approach to international relations that both takes Kant's project seriously and largely avoids the confines of his own work, there is little evidence to show that their efforts provide an obvious alternative *rule* as such for a critique of world politics. Rather, they demonstrate the need for a very different kind of disciplinary undertaking wherein critique is itself a rule of a sort.

Ashley and Walker understand both the study and practice of international relations to be intricate aspects if not foundations to what Foucault, and to some extent Kant, refer to as *the* Enlightenment. Accepting sovereignty as the fundamental ordering concept for the discipline, they see in international order false pretense toward a ground from which truth, order, and knowledge may allegedly be pronounced by a universalized subject.[28] In these terms,

Ashley and Walker inevitably come to reject any notion that there is a set of practices and events named "international relations" that may, as a result, be followed and employed in a positive manner or rejected in the favour of a different world order.[29] They each work consistently to demonstrate that, traditionally, whatever is taken as a subject of study within the discipline of international relations is always embedded within and is a function of specifically modern exercises to establish what one may imagine as the political conditions of human life.[30]

In this way, it is precisely at the shift in inquiry from a question of "*Why* should the Enlightenment be accepted or rejected?" to an investigation of "*How* is it that the Enlightenment limits possibility in the way that it does?" that both Ashley and Walker may be seen to take up the Kantian critique as rendered by Foucault.[31] For Walker:

> Theories of international relations . . . are interesting less for the substantive explanations they offer about political conditions in the modern world than as expressions of the limits of the contemporary political imagination when confronted with persistent claims about the evidence of fundamental historical and structural transformation. They can be read . . . as expressions of an historically specific understanding of the character and location of political life in general. They can also be read . . . as a crucial site in which attempts to think otherwise about political possibilities are constrained by categories and assumptions that contemporary political analysis is encouraged to take for granted.[32]

And, for Ashley, truly critical analysis within studies of international politics will not be founded through an inquiry into what may be the most appropriate divisions between human communities on a global scale but, rather, will ask how it is that, in the context of European-Enlightenment thought, it is a natural-seeming convention to view humanity as a domain to be divided in a geopolitical manner. He writes:

> The questions to be asked are not: Where is the boundary? What marks the boundary? Or, why should this boundary (and not that one) be the line by which we mark off the "international dangers" that we should know to fear? Implicitly, all of these queries presuppose a boundary—and,

> with it, a state—because they presuppose the presence of a domesticated "we" who could definitely answer them, a "we" already constituted in opposition to some set of total dangers. Instead, the sort of question to be asked is, again, a *how* question. How, by way of what practices, by appeal to what cultural resources, and in the face of what resistances is this boundary imposed and ritualized?[33]

From these positions, Ashley and Walker embrace the Foucauldian-Kantian enlightenment attitude, seeking to produce the possibility of political freedom through the simultaneous transgression of intellectual and spatial borders. And in their respective efforts they indeed deftly show how it is that such transgression may be conducted. They describe paths of doubt that demand further debate on the primary questions that Kant himself seeks to engage.[34] Still, what Ashley and Walker also demonstrate in this work is that the freedom to be associated with the limit attitude is not one that engenders peace but, rather, one that calls forth exceptional danger.

In this respect, the intellectual and political association between Ashley and Walker and Kant should not be understood as something only mediated through Foucault. For example, Walker too goes to great efforts to demonstrate that components and conditions of human life typically understood in the discipline as inevitable on a global scale are the results of exceptionally rigorous efforts to maintain a particular kind of judgment about humans in the world, where no final ground for such judgment is actually available to human beings.[35] He writes:

> Concurring with the judgment that it is indeed necessary to take [the principle of state sovereignty] as the key feature of modern political life, I seek to show how this judgment tells us more about the constitutive imagination of *modern* political life than about the determinations and possibilities of the political worlds in which we now live.[36]

In this manner, Walker identifies a discourse of reflective judgment across international relations theory whose commanding principle ought to be open to further critique. Furthermore, he acknowledges the Kantian sentiment suggesting that the world and the political conditions of human life are things contingent on the manners in which human beings write them.[37]

Walker along with Ashley reflect Kant's critical pursuits in broader and ultimately deeper manners as well, though. Just as Kant shows the most fundamental debates regarding the limits of human reality to be fully irresolvable, what he calls the antinomies of pure reason,[38] Ashley and Walker begin their respective analyses of international relations in recognition that the discipline is plagued by a series of conventional antinomies, disallowing final agreement on any central point of international politics and fueling only constant and fruitless debate. Kant's point, on this register, is that questions pertaining to the full dimensions and structure of the human world refer to objects outside of human perception and are thus wrongly posed from the start and rest on groundless presuppositions themselves.[39] Likewise the antinomies identified by Ashley and Walker in international relations theory are not simply professional disagreements that could be sorted out with the appropriate evidence. Rather, as they described it, the foundations of the discipline rest on assumptions no less metaphysical or ungroundable in character than those addressed by Kant. Consequently, as in the case of Kant, Ashley and Walker then seek to engage the questions of limits from a recognition of how one's inquiry into limits of worldly life is itself confined.

In examining the potential for a critical social theory of international politics,[40] Ashley argues that the discipline draws one into viewing the world as truthfully both anarchical and communal at the same time.[41] His point is that in order to explore the relations of supposedly autonomous communities one thinks and treats these exclusive components as if social and political practices, ideas, and skills are common across them.[42] Otherwise, the critical inquiry could offer no judgments about international politics per se.[43]

In a more direct vein, Walker indicates this same antinomy between the theoretical poles of the discipline itself. His idea is that realism and idealism are not only two main competing theoretical engines, which just happen to contradict one another, for the study of international politics. Rather, Walker tries to show that realism and idealism arise as a necessary or, at least, unavoidable set of contradictory claims that together provide a pseudoground for the discipline in their historical and theoretical dialectic.[44] The community of the globe and the particularity of the state provide frames for one another. He writes:

> Like many prevailing attempts to make sense of 'the global,' this appeal [to global civil society] comes largely from

> a projection of a familiar form of 'inner' life onto an 'external' realm. Bounded only by the world itself, global civil society is envisaged partly as a check on the state and partly as an alternative to it. But of course, the appeal of this way of framing the concept depends on the assumption that the world itself can be constituted as a bounded political community modeled on the state writ large.[45]

The framing is highly problematic. However, as long as the debate between globalist and statist theses remains on the go—and, on this line of analysis, there is no reason to believe that the contest could ever truly be resolved within the discipline—the relationship may function well enough and feed its own tenability. The interminable antagonism between views to the particular (realism) and views to the universal (idealism) create conditions in which *the international* may gain a type of imaginable determinant semblance. Just as *Perpetual Peace* is given life as an apparent ground to modern theories of international relations through two-sided debates over its alleged statism versus globalism, conflict between realism and idealism more broadly provides international relations with a central content otherwise beyond sense and reason.

Not surprisingly, the content that Walker finds in the either-for-or-against pull of international relations theory are a series of oppositions that mirror the self-defining antinomies of anarchy/community and realism/idealism. He repeatedly claims that the best way to understand the constitution of the discipline is through the "Manichean" binaries[46] that he finds pervasive through constitutive theories of international relations.[47] And, on this basis of analysis, Walker's larger point is that theories of international relations and, thus, the practices of inter-state politics can be boiled down to inside/outside oppositions of one sort or another.[48]

Along with representing the general demarcation between the political society supposedly found within states and the anarchy between states, this dichotomy calls up the antinomy (or blackmail) between a position for the state and a position for the world. On the one hand, those for the state (realists) denounce the globalists for foolishly attempting to find politics in the realm outside. On the other hand, those for the globe attempt to show that the stasis associated with the politics inside the state may be extended to the world. Hence, there really are no contests between the inside and the outside but, rather, a series of oppositional discourses that amount to a contestation over where the demarcation between inside and outside is to be drawn. Even where globalists (idealists) successfully argue for a political community that embraces the planet, there remains an outside: that which is not stable, that which is not for the (global) state, that which is not with us.

As Walker describes it, the inside/outside dichotomy that results from and, in turn, substantiates the anarchy/community antinomy is irresolvable, because it presupposes that one can make an exclusive distinction between the inside and outside as well as the various opposed terms identified above. And, according to Ashley and Walker, what avails students of international relations such a lens for judgment is the presupposition of sovereignty.[49] As discussed in the previous chapter, in this way of thinking, sovereignty is a claim to literal authority, where the sovereign is in a position or *non*position from which to define the limits of all things within political community, including its order and, not least of all, the limits of political community itself. It is a final and, ideally, unquestionable authority whose naming of social and political phenomena provides a final stability and through a reduction of ambiguity between terms such as inside/outside, us/them, here/there, peace/war, ought/is, etc.

On the basis of its necessary pretense to autonomy, Ashley refers to this sovereign authority as a "heroic practice," which solicits its own form of blackmail.[50] For, to adopt sovereign authority as a legitimate point from which to critically examine international relations is to already and without question admit to the alleged objectivity of this subjective position. And to reject this intellectual harness is to, in the face of the dominant discourse of international politics as framed within this paradox, place oneself not only outside of but also against order, stability, peace, and, ultimately, politics, supposedly in favor of anarchy, war, and confusion.[51] In agreement, Walker notes that to even establish one's inquiry into international politics through the terms of state sovereignty is to already deny the possibility of any other resolutions to the conflict between universality and particularity.[52]

In the same manners that Kant refuses the legitimacy of taking the cosmos as an object of experience available to the understanding and that Foucault refuses engaging the Enlightenment as a concrete cultural phenomenon, then, Ashley and Walker also refuse the principle of state sovereignty and the world of exclusions on which it rests as a set of objects simply available for the critical theorist of international relations. Initially, as discussed in chapter 3, Ashley, also along with Kant, rejects the idea that a sovereign subject position is possible prior to critical investigation. But, going beyond Kant on this point in the Foucauldian-Kantian vein, he is committed to *always* question an authority who asserts the objective universal view claimed in sovereignty.[53] For, at base, such a sovereign voice gains its "heroism" from the very fact that it may stand against history, outside of the change which experience tells one is constant.[54] But as a voice that stands against change, Walker contends, the principle of state sovereignty must always be viewed as merely a historically specific definition of the tension and attempted resolution between universality and particularity.[55] It must always lag behind its own efforts to delineate the incessant information given through spatial and temporal experience.[56]

Ashley and Walker, in appreciation of Foucault's critique of subjectivity, must refuse the grounds of debate that form the antinomy between universalist and particularist views in the discipline of international relations, for the reason that the principle of state sovereignty claims to represent that to which no one or collection of humans could ever have a view. As they jointly write, in reference to the various sites different persons around this world live and the incongruities that any one person may live through the span of her or his individual being:

> One cannot speak as an economist might of rational individuals whose identities are given and who, in order to find their way and give meaning to their lives, need only deploy their available means to serve their self-generated interests under external constraints. One cannot speak as a moral philosopher might of the responsible human being who has a duty to ground his conduct in the transcendent principles of an ethical community. And one cannot speak as a sociologist might of social actors who habitually replicate an eternal yesterday, measure their practices by reference to a recognized norm, or project social values already inscribed in a coherent order.[57]

Accepting that their own rendition of the fundamental crisis of the discipline does not and cannot adequately represent all that the discipline is, on the same coin Ashley and Walker insist that no scholar or practitioner of international relations can possibly ever represent the reality of international politics in a final and sufficiently total manner that could avail credence to the claim of sovereignty.[58] It could only be a representation of representations, a judgment based on reflection. Hence, the necessity of critical inquiry is once again called on, and thus persists the crisis facing any hope for a certain ground for such critique.

Consequently, Ashley and Walker each seek to open up for debate, in the spirit of enlightenment, international politics through the very antinomies and contradictions that provide the appearance of its ground.[59] Walker aims most directly to show that the terms that come to form the more general opposition of inside/outside may be shown to always face one another with far greater ambiguity than a sovereign voice could ever afford.[60] In this regard, he remains particularly attentive to how very difficult if not impossible it is to discover the boundaries of identities, cultures, nations, territories, and institutions without possessing some sort of organizing metric—be it Euclidean, Newtonian, or Cartesian—already in one's mind. Ashley works most effectively on tracing the conditions under which the perennial "anarchy problematique" functions.[61] His point is that, while the contest between theories of community against anarchy come to prop up a general vision of international politics and sovereignty, the initial dispute over the anarchy problematique rests on the fact that there is no first principle that organizes human life and society, that human life is truly *an-archic*. In this way, Ashley seeks to draw the students of international politics into finally taking the significance of anarchy more fully.[62]

For Walker, the opening of debate with a Foucauldian enlightenment ethos inevitably leads one away from strict discourses of inter-state relations, governed as they are by the principle of state sovereignty, to imagining international politics as "world politics."[63] He claims that it is something like "world politics" that far better represents the inescapable questions and experiences of world-wide interdependence than "international relations" ever could.[64] However, in this respect, it is incumbent on the critical theorist of international politics to also question the potential determinative function that an intellectual guide such as "world politics" itself may have.[65] Although it is certainly a less rigorous idea than that which Kant relies on in his geopolitical vision, Walker's idea of "world politics" also provides a limit to thought and presupposes an identifiable domain of human experience. Hence, while he asks that students of international politics begin to make vulnerable their theories to the "transformations, dangers, and opportunities" that pervade the possibility of political community and concentrate less on the coordinates that discipline recommends for the categorization of such phenomena,[66] Walker also reaches out for a container in which such changes may be examined and understood. Still, he remains acutely aware of this problem, noting that:

> both the presence and the possibility of something that might usefully be called world politics or human identity flatly contradict the understanding of political identity affirmed by claims to state sovereignty. Yet, paradoxically, it is precisely the possibility, and in some respects the presence of some kind of world politics and common human identity that has continued to produce an account of the world as a spatially demarcated array of political identities fated to clash in perpetual contingency or to converge somewhere over the distant horizon at a time that is always deferred. This paradox continues to be the primary condition governing our ability, or inability, to think about struggles for political identity in a world in which it has become exceptionally unclear who this 'we' is.[67]

Walker writes further that "a politics that encompasses 'the world' cannot be envisaged on the assumption that that world already exists along with the categories through which it must be known."[68] He fears that "world politics" may just as easily allow for a translation of inside/outside into an 'inclusive' politics of 'high' and 'low' activities *within* the world, divided between sovereigns and nonsovereigns.[69] In this regard, Walker appears to simply offer the notion of world politics as an interruptive force in the midst of conventional disciplinary views. And, in turn, he seeks to invite similar interruption on his own closures.

Walker can do little else.[70] As Ashley notes, exploring the anarchy problematique critically provides questions that "do not invite certain answers."[71] Hence, together, Ashley and Walker, maintaining the rigor of Foucault's stand, refuse to provide an alternative paradigm, citing the practical difficulties of global representation, the theoretical problem of putting forth a paradigmatic view, and the ethical quagmire of asserting "alternative" limits within a politics that must refuse limits.[72] The best that both can do is to constantly open possibilities of thinking politics in this world otherwise that must themselves in time falter.

Walker finds some solace in this, suggesting that:

> There is certainly no possibility of becoming otherwise if that account is assumed to provide an accurate portrayal of

> where we are now. As the discursive strategies through which we have come to believe in the natural necessity of that historical claim become more and more transparent, however, at least we may be spared the interminable self-righteousness of those who know what we cannot be because they are so sure of where we are.[73]

It is the activity of questioning that shows promise to Ashley and Walker, at the cost of secured home, name, and direction.[74] What begins as critical departure through a consideration of "how?" ends still with the question "how?" In this regard, such an inquiry as this has no true beginning nor possible end.

It should, then, come as no surprise that Walker, for one, finds so much interest in how the writings of Machiavelli may be read against the grain of international relations, traditionally understood. While Machiavelli is so often treated as a realist, pure and simple, Walker reads him as someone who could never give in to such a positive idea of what is objectively real in politics.[75] He appreciates the only maxim that holds clearly in Machiavelli's writing, that things change. And, accepting the benefits Machiavelli identifies in cunning, ability, and virtú over the play of power, Walker concludes that:

> The future of world order discourse lies with its capacity for judgment, with its discriminations, its sense of the intolerable and the possible, its sense of timing in an era of profound spatiotemporal transformation.[76]

Walker, along with Ashley, must finally resist politics as a function of sovereignty in any form, particularly that offered in the form of rational man. But as in the case of Machiavelli's writings, this does not leave one with any definitive vision of politics between states or how to understand them. Rather, the Foucauldian-Kantian approach of Walker and Ashley offers at most wariness of any rule to politics in the world. They insist, and necessarily so, on the need to always watch for difference and that for which one could not expect.

Imperatives of Responsibility[77]

Central to the critical inquiry of international politics offered by Ashley and Walker, excited by a Foucauldian stressed Kant, is also the problem of autonomy. Certainly, the alleged autonomy of state sovereignty is strongly placed into question, as the legitimacy of any claim to autonomously view, understand, or determine human social and political life on either a micro- or macroscale is found totally suspect within this line of analysis. At a more mundane, yet no less important, level, though, the critique taken up by Ashley and Walker necessarily also asks for the displacement of autonomy as a subject position.[78] They must not accept human actors as discretely separate entities. It is also the case, that they cannot accept humans as self-limiting subjects, who are capable of engaging experiences and other humans beings on the bases of universalizable laws.

Fundamental to the Kantian-critical activity Ashley and Walker endorse and pursue in their writings is the notion that humans within the asocial-sociable strife of political life are always already embedded within cultural contexts that inform rational limits and guide judgments on reflection—a point already recognized by Kant himself. Thus, for a limit-attitude toward international politics, it cannot make sense to find its guide within principles that focus on the human subject as its center. Not only is the universal given up as a possible point of reference, there can be no autonomous or even potentially autonomous human subject around whom a critical project could gain its bearings. There is no fixed particular point from which an ethical drive for critique may gain direction and scope. Rather, a limit-attitude for international politics requires that the only driving principle for critique could come from attention toward the multiple areas of human intercourse that both build and also finally place into crisis the cultural contexts in and through which humans may variously live.

This call for a fully reoriented 'stand' with respect to international politics, one in which the guide for one's judgment and sense of what ought to be done is unhitched from an autonomous figure made possible within and acting as guardian of the presumed antinomy of international relations, is given a very strong answer in specific aspects of contemporary international relations theory concerned with ethics. In this regard, while the writings of Dillon, George, Molloy, Warner, and others are definitely of interest, the writings of Campbell prove most effective and compelling. Taking up precisely the same Kantian enlightenment ethos roused by Foucault and embraced by Ashley and Walker,[79] Campbell searches for alternative philosophical leverage that may allow for an international ethos which affirms change, incessant difficulties in judgment, and mutability of subjectivity with respect to identity and culture. In this regard, he finds further resources in the phenomenological strivings of Martin Buber, Emmanuel Levinas, and Jacques Derrida. And it is through this network of thought that he begins to effectively trace a more radically critical rule for the critique of world politics called for by Ashley and Walker.

The results of Campbell's efforts are without doubt refreshing and inspiring for those already compelled by Foucault's intervention into Kant's thought. He does an exceptional job at showing how international politics may finally be understood and imagined anew, dismissing autonomy as a central issue and embracing the interweaving of human experiences and views as the lifeblood of politics in general. And, in this regard, Campbell offers as strong an ethical rule for a critique of world politics that may be possible, as such. However, to be true to the Foucauldian-Kantian enlightenment practice, one must also admit that Campbell's efforts ultimately reintroduce the antinomy between universal and particular. And it is difficult to see how his theoretical invention could avoid this peril. Furthermore, one must conclude that it would be impossible for any such reorientation of ethics to finally meet the requirements of critique, so understood. And it is, thus, important to rethink the ground on which a principle of critique in this regard is even possible.

Campbell too may be seen to accept the general Kantian point that what anyone conceives as the international, including its limits and components, is subject to and grounded within reflective judgments. This idea is crucial to Campbell's point, as he pursues the critique of sovereignty offered by Ashley and Walker, pondering the alleged given identity and reality of sovereign states in the modern world. He writes:

> States are never finished entities; the tension between the demands of identity and the practices that constitute it can never be resolved, because the performative nature of identity can never be fully revealed. This paradox inherent to their being renders states in permanent need of reproduction: with no ontological status apart from the many and varied practices that constitute their reality, states are (and have to be) always in a process of becoming. For a state to end its practices of representation would be to expose its lack of prediscursive foundations; stasis would be death.[80]

Campbell argues that it is not the natural character of states and the requirements of sovereignty that provide, for example, the form for United States foreign policy. Rather, the foreign policy of the United States is validated through a constant repetition and representation of a specific narrative of "danger outside of the sovereign limits," as was articulated during the build up toward and the execution of the Persian Gulf War of 1991.[81] His larger underlying point here, as spelled out more fully in later writings, is simply that thinking and responding to affairs in one's world always includes "rendering the unfamiliar in terms of the familiar," "adopting one mode of representation over another," and employing a historically specific perspective through representation.[82] Campbell agrees that social/political phenomena, whether understood as truly real and objective or matters for debate, are always already embedded in the public discourse that Kant would have politically liberated.

A significant Kantian corollary of this point, which is already indicated by Walker but drawn out more pointedly by Campbell and offered support by Dillon and Warner as well,[83] is that social/political phenomena are also always embedded within ethics. Along this line of thinking, one must accept that, however the conditions and limits of human society are understood in discourses of international politics, the judgments on which such understanding is based emerges from a specific sense of how such conditions and limits *ought* to be understood or determined. In this manner, international politics may be viewed as a site or sites of ethical contestation, discourses through which hegemony for moral grounding is sought and lost. Yet, with its traditional focus on autonomy, Campbell and Dillon jointly argue that the discipline of international relations is theoretically impoverished in its ability to affirm and appropriately examine the ethical dilemmas called up within its core. Again echoing Walker, their initial point is that, insofar as conventional theories of international relations rest on autonomy as a rule, ethics is already divided from the discipline as a central issue for study.[84] By locating questions of judgment within individual persons and agents, the discipline systematically denies how social/political issues are themselves constituted in interpersonal struggles without a contained or ordered context, reducing the very agonized aspect of ethics to questions of reason proper to the supposedly independent, hence sovereign, mind.

For Campbell and Dillon, though, the problem here is not simply that a focus on autonomy allows, ultimately through the principle of state sovereignty, a theoretical neglect of the ethical they find already within assumptions regarding autonomy. Rather, they also are acutely aware of the practical implications of such assumptions with respect to the ethical issues from which they attempt such distance.[85] Foremost in their minds is the notion that a separation of the ethical from the political in the commitment to autonomy allows for and requires the reduction of all political thinking to the same logic or, at least, intellectual confines.[86] Put briefly, to understand judgments regarding the political to rest properly within the rational employment of independent minds is to suggest that there is a world which may be and, thus, ought to be viewed in the same way or in similar terms by all who make claims to the same rights of autonomy. Hence, within a privileging of autonomy is entrenched the political necessity for all agents to share judgments, whether that necessity is borne out in experience or not. And, therefore, legitimacy is granted to political action that seeks to quash and/or marginalize difference from the sphere of politics, as if such a boundary could be struck. Thus, as with Kant's attachment to the globe, the public discourse from which enlightenment and critical inquiry is supposed to flourish is soundly shackled.

This critique of autonomy, emanating from critical inquiry into perceived antinomies founding international politics and the discipline of international relations, leads Campbell to propose a new principle for study altogether. Understanding the identities of political subjects, agents, locations, and institutions to be the result of reflective judgments made through social conversance, he finds identity itself to be grounded within differences.[87] This is a central portion of the critique of autonomy. For to question autonomy is to question the existence of social/political entities who gain meaning independently of others and whose location is simply self-interpreted. The principle (discipline) that Campbell then offers as an alternative to autonomy and in the service of critical inquiry is constant encouragement in the recognition of *radical interdependence* between agents.[88] He is interested to see that all subject positions, understood autonomously or not and framed in terms of race, state, community, or individual, arise meaningfully in the crossing of inter-human experiences, that they arise through the limits both emergent and collapsing within the movement of human interaction.

Integral to this principle is a refiguring of the concept of responsibility, both as an ethical and political problem. For insofar as Campbell accepts the notion that identity and moral disposition is established through intersubjective activity, he must also see that each subject emergent within the course of human living is able to claim its identity only through interrelated encounters with others.

Similarly, he must accept the idea that the meaning, limits, and identity of others are made possible at least in part through the informative activity of oneself. As recognized also by Warner,[89] there is thus, a deep commitment within this principle to viewing any self as first and foremost a position of responsibility toward other identities, as such. Furthermore, the politics in which variously identified subjects find themselves situated must in turn be understood as grounded in the ways in which humans allow the process of identity formation to take place.

Although Buber proves of some initial interest in these respects, Campbell primarily looks toward Levinas for a way in which this *deterritorialization* of theory may be accomplished.[90] Campbell finds Levinas' account of human identity appealing, because, in his view, Levinas offers a de-centering of autonomous subjectivity in favor of attention to a heteronomy of responsibility.[91] Quoting him at length, Campbell recounts how for Levinas being, taken here as a radically interdependent condition, is made possible only because of responsibility to *the other*. In this way, Levinas' point is that one cannot escape responding to the other in being, because it is only with respect to the other, who is already there, that one may make a claim to being.[92] Campbell explains:

> Responsibility understood in this way refigures subjectivity: the very origin of the subject is to be found in its subjection to the 'other,' a subjection that precedes consciousness, identity, and freedom, and as such does not originate in a vow or decision. Ergo, it cannot be made possible by a command or imperative. In other words, subjects are constituted by their relationship with the 'other.' Their being is called into question by the prior existence of the 'other,' which has an unremitting and even accusative hold on the subject. Moreover, and this is what rearticulates ethics, this relationship with the 'other' means that one's being has to be affirmed in terms of *a right to be* in relation to the 'other.'[93]

Identity is itself then always ethically situated and actively and incessantly responsible for, in conjunction with the other, how the relation has and is to unfold.

Campbell remains hesitant in following Levinas too far, noting that Levinas finally allows societal borders to direct attention to intersubjectivity in some instances over others.[94] In this way,

Campbell finds Levinas to leave the prefigured communal identity of the nation-state untroubled and seeks to find a manner in which to make Levinas' position more fully "Levinasian."

On this accord, Campbell supplements the commitment to radical intersubjectivity he initially finds and celebrates in Levinas with the deconstruction of Derrida.[95] Acknowledging the affinity between Derridian deconstruction with Levinas' ethics in their mutual affirmations of alterity, Campbell believes that the fuller critique of identity as a present and locatable thing presented by Derrida may draw Levinas' commitment to responsibility to the radical point Campbell's project requires.[96] As Campbell recounts, Derrida, who also takes up the project of the politics of enlightenment critique while remaining wary of the limits an Enlightenment may itself impose, must refuse any self-identifying function to the state as much as Levinas denies it to each human subject.[97] And, in this manner, Campbell concludes, Derridian deconstruction may maintain responsibility as a question. The proximity of the various potential others called up in face-to-face encounters are not provided with convenient divisions between neighbor and foreigner. Rather, the identity of citizenship, kinship, and border are retained as dilemmas.

On this basis, deploying an ethics in the context of international politics may seem impossible. Yet, on the contrary, Campbell makes a very strong case, showing that a Derridean-fortified-Levinas may keep issues of ethics alive in the heart of a discipline and set of practices that typically exclude ethics as nonpolitical.[98] Campbell recognizes, however, that employing the Levinasian-Derridean perspective he develops here will not and cannot then offer a more certain approach to international politics. He readily admits that it makes such an engagement all the more difficult.[99] His position is not even safe among his sympathizers. Warner, while sharing many of his sentiments, criticizes Campbell for favouring Levinas' understanding of inter-human encounters over what Warner sees as a richer account offered by Buber[100] and for searching too quickly for supplementation in the form of Derrida to cover the difficulties in Levinas.[101] Campbell, in defense, offers counterevidence on these very points.[102] Regardless of how this particular dispute may be successfully concluded, though, one must recognize that a quarrel of this sort draws debate away from the issues of critical inquiry that is the occasion for such a contest of views. Entertaining this level of conflict brings far too much focus on the correct reading of principles that should be retained first as questions.

In this regard, I am more interested in a less conspicuous claim made by Warner: "Yet, [Buber and Levinas] are attractive alternatives mainly because the basic foundations of the alternative position are so unacceptable."[103] Although it is from this statement that Warner then goes on to place himself in opposition to Campbell and argue for a "developed ethic of responsibility," I see a way in which this observation moves to undercut them both. Indeed, the move toward a Levinasian reading of inter-human relations, whether it be invigorated with deconstruction, drawn back toward Buber, or anything in between, is primarily compelling in this context because it does *seem* to offer the sort of complex view that one would hope to entertain after recognizing the violence inherent to theories of international relations explained through autonomy and resting on the antinomies of international relations theory. And this is precisely the spirit in which Levinas, Derrida, and Buber are employed across this literature.

In each of these cases, including the writings of Campbell, Dillon, George, Molloy, and Warner, the perspective or radical intersubjectivity offered in Buber and/or Levinas is taken up for being compelling most substantially on the grounds that it both speaks against autonomy and articulates an image apparently helpful in redefining ethics in the context of international politics especially.[104] But, nowhere in these discussions is there actually an argument to demonstrate that a Levinasian description, or any other phenomenological description of human relations, is appropriate or legitimate. Hence, while the writings of Levinas may 'make possible' the sort of perspective called for in Campbell's principle of inquiry, there is no case here to suggest that this possibility is desirable in the least. There is no argument to show why this particular shift in perspective ought to be embraced aside from an indication of its "attractive" character.

The precise danger that I wish to indicate here is that Levinas, treated in whatever manner, is used ultimately as a guide for critical inquiry into the limits of conventional international relations theory in a most uncritical manner. Hence, the principle of always recognizing radical intersubjectivity sought by Campbell may unfortunately be confined within one specific view of human interrelation for which there is no justification. Molloy, for instance, does a remarkable job of showing how the ethics of Levinas forces a return of attention to the inescapable relational politics one has with others in the world, making such situations as the Balkans crises always a matter of concern for all.[105] But the question remains, why such an ethics should be given priority. It remains unclear why, for example, Levinas' description of human interrelations should be taken up as the heart of this exercise and not those proposed by others, such as Luce Irigaray or Maurice Merleau-Ponty. There are many possible phenomenological descriptions of intersubjectivity, each of which have very different political implications.

To be fair, one ought to recognise that Campbell does not wed his project so completely to the Levinas he augments with Derrida. He quite clearly notes that his turn to this complex of thinkers is meant simply as a "starting point."[106] Warner echoes this caution, admitting that, aside from what one might think of the final political implications of positions taken by Buber and Levinas, together "they are helpful basic tools for understanding different perceptions of international relations."[107] In this regard, Campbell appears to hope for further possible perspectives beyond the ones he champions. He does not argue for a new theory to replace old ones in the application of ethics to international relations. Rather, he strives for an *approach* that may conjure awareness of what he views as the inescapability of international ethics. And, Campbell remains open to the fact that his own ventures via this approach are more likely to perpetrate complicity with the concepts he opposes than to fully transcend the problem of autonomy and, thus, the antinomies of international relations.[108] He embraces the lack of completeness and finality to his own use of Levinas as expressive of the continual struggle that politics is and how political life cannot be divorced from theory either.[109] But regardless of their openness and nondogmatic attitude, the points of departure that Campbell and Warner offer do fix the type of debate and endless theoretical interruption that might follow this approach in support of a specific and unquestioned human model. Not only do they each recommend a specific phenomenological description for the rethinking of an ethics of responsibility, the general approaches that each respectively generates relies on a very specific sense of subjectivity overall.

At root, Campbell and others argue that the meaning, identity, and divisions between human subjects, societies, and communities are never certain and always in the process of emergence, through processes which can never be divorced from ethics and politics—that these processes of emergence are themselves ethical and political. However, the existence of subjects, societies, and communities is presupposed. Campbell would insist that such agents themselves emerge in social intercourse. But fundamental to his position is that he may assume social intercourse between such agents. For it is this idea of intersubjective relations that he uses Levinas to describe. It is a world of conflicting individuals and groups, in such places as Rwanda, the Balkans, and Kuwait, that motivate his call to a principle regarding responsibility. Hence, as laid out so far, Campbell's analysis allows him only to suggest how the significance of such agents is achieved in relations. That there are relations between human agents that offer such productive power must be accepted in a prior manner. Moreover, it must be universalized to all. In this way, he does indeed invite complicity with the very concepts he hopes to undermine.

Furthermore, it is also the case that Campbell remains apparently caught up within at least one of the Concepts of Reflection that illustrate the acritical nature of Kant's commitment to Euclidean geometry, namely identity/difference. Here, Caygill's analysis is once again helpful, noting how even the radical theories of global society have a tendency to reproduce this trap.[110] Campbell strives to perceive identity, hence ethics and politics, generated within relations themselves. Yet, his analysis is fundamentally limited and ordered through attention to the relations possible between agents who are already understood to differ as such. More significantly, these are agents who gain prior identity through the presumed fact that they may enjoy community of some sort (a community of responsibility?) with one another.

There may well be further insightful augmentations possible to the Levinasian position that propel the critical work inaugurated by Campbell and debated by Dillon, George, Molloy, and Warner. But, regardless of the intellectual inspiration employed, as long as this critique is guided simply by a principle to constantly reveal how inter-human relations are radically intersubjective, globalising dogma must germinate nonetheless. The central problem here is that the foci of any such work remain disciplined by the 'selves' and 'others' produced within the relations and identified with human beings in various manners. Efforts to examine and recognize how subject positions are conditioned by the nonpositions of relations and processes of differentiation may go to show that autonomy and the identities that may adhere to such an idea are less than stable ideas. And this may also show how human agents are inescapably embedded within one another's lives and judgments. However, there persists in such efforts the idea of all humans experiencing the movement of one another—while clearly having very different experiences and coming to differing judgments on that account—in the same manners. The problem of change and interrelation is universalized between subjects. Thus, a total image of human movement becomes the disciplining guide for critique, while the myriad and shifting experiences of the same are entertained in a secondary manner.

This being said, one can see the sort of critical discipline promoted by Campbell to be necessarily mired in the same difficulties that embraces Kant's international ethics as expressed in his third Definitive Article of *Perpetual Peace*.[111] Remember, here Kant states that an inherent principle to perpetual peace is that the citizen of each state has the right to claim hospitality, or resort, in other lands.[112] He reasons that, simply on the basis of being a rational human being, one's right to at least travel through and reside within foreign political domains must be respected. For, all persons have a right to "communal possession of the earth's surface."[113] Understanding that all humans are naturally equal and autonomous and that they each reside on this singular sphere, Kant sees that a right to hospitality follows naturally. And, thus, the cosmopolitan ethics and politics follow necessarily. However, as argued in the previous chapter, the equality and autonomy of humans and the commonalty of a human world are by no means made certainly manifest in his work. Rather, they ultimately remain only presupposed. Therefore, the cosmopolitan ethic of hospitality Kant supports is more akin to the political moralism he rejects in favor of truly moral politics. For, hospitality is an ethic that is offered here only in retrospect to having presupposed a particular nature to human agents and their environment. Likewise, the Levinasian ethic supported by Campbell, as well as any ethic which serves a radical interdependence of agents as its guiding principle, may be upheld only in retrospect to unquestioned assumptions regarding the existence of particular kinds of subjects existing in a particular kind of intersubjective world. The principle of responsibility underlying Campbell's political analysis gains its right not in the character of human life but, rather, in prior private judgments regarding how to view humans and their social/political locations with respect to one another. And like Kant's notion of hospitality, adherence to the notion of a responsible politics rests on the prior assumption that each human agent may stand face to face with one another in the same (intersubjective) way, that there is an essential equality among all members in individual being and in the limits of social life.

In essence, Campbell and his colleagues search for starting-positions from which a critical inquiry into international politics may begin. The starting-positions that they provide as points of departure in a general approach, however, are ways of seeing. These perspectives are, surely, left vulnerable and, through their own appeal, attract interruption. Campbell does not, for example, require the same kind of human subject as envisioned in Linklater's citizen. However, as the origins of a new approach, the descriptions of subjectivity promoted by Campbell are still means by which the possibilities of human experience are limited prior to a critical exploration of such limits. Hence, they have the same function as Linklater's citizen. As ways of viewing human life, these various glimpses at a radical intersubjectivity confine one's imagination to entertaining an intersubjective human world, which, while surely far more appealing in many ways to the competitive images provided via notions of autonomy, itself offers a sphere of closure.

Here the traveler introduced by Kant may not be able to simply paint within the circles, triangles, and squares she or he has charted on her or his map drawn in rational practice. In this sphere the traveler colours her or his log uncertainly and always again and again, as the act of knowing comes to be embedded in a multiple way within the act of traveling. But she or he may always still find reference for her or his attempts through prior understanding that there is some domain of humans and human agencies within which a certain dynamic of movement holds. Hence, this traveler may always submit the changes of experience and the calls for response to how a human being always is.

Critical inquiry of international politics thus demands that one's ethical position in such work not rely on an idea of how the varied experiences of change and movement in one's life take shape. Rather, critique requires that one keep focus on the change and movement of relations themselves. Judgments regarding how one is to make sense of these appearances are of course inescapable. However, as a starting point, it is crucial that critical inquiry finds its principle in movement and not what might be judged as a consequences of such change. In this regard a critical approach toward international politics can be guided only by that which it experiences. For it is incumbent on such activity to frustrate all views as starting points into such inquiry. It remains a question, though, whether or not experience could actually provide such a guide.

Doubting World Politics

With the failure of an ethical response to world politics to overcome the confining tension between universality and particularity, it may seem that the project of critique in this respect is doomed to fall back toward radical doubt. Apparently, a critique of world politics taken to its full implications pushes one back toward a skeptical position, in which no frame of reference may be granted either practicability or possibility. And one's efforts, eroded through their own rigor, cause one to slide back to where Ashley and Walker leave one: perpetually asking "How?" and resisting the domination of any discipline whatsoever. In sum, one is left with the following question: Does taking up Kantian critique with respect to world politics beyond the final stifling dogma of Kant require that one give up on ever being able to make universally legitimate claims about world politics and that one quit any pretense to offering a viable theory of international relations at all? And the answer is: Yes.

Answering in the affirmative to the above question, however, it is not my intention to suggest that Ashley or Walker necessarily take that position themselves. One or both may each answer "yes" as well. But, regardless, I merely wish to indicate that the critical inquiries into international relations, international politics, world politics, or whatever other moniker may be here employed, that they respectively offer do not only provide striking rereadings of the discipline of international relations, which follow in the critical-Kantian enlightenment energy required in the face of Kant's own specific deficiencies. The positions Ashley and Walker stake out, in tune with a Foucauldian-Kant, also imply the need to view the activity of analyzing, interpreting, and practicing international or world politics as something altogether different from anything that could be captured by the referents "international" or "world." And, again, this is *not* to suggest that international life and politics are somehow unreal or consisting of mere illusions. It is merely to say that one can hope to gain strong critical purchase on these phenomenon only insofar as one's empirical sense and analysis are not already driven by universal categories of judgment unsubstantiated by human experience.

Kant employs the skeptical powers of critique to provide definition or, at least, an appropriate working definition of the universal limits of possible human experience. In this way, he invests in critique a containing function that must ultimately work against the impetus behind it. In addition, it is the case that any attempt to survey the globular limits of humans social and political life via critique neglects how such an enterprise is already prescribed uncritically from the start. What is shown, however, is that the boundaries of human experience and thought are established in the very interaction and confrontation between attempts to describe the human world and presentations of counterevidence to express the lack of universal appeal such descriptions hold. It is in the flux of dogma and doubt that humans apparently gain sense of what is possible and what is not. And this is a constantly altering situation.

Campbell himself admits that "engagement with the world is necessarily 'global' in its scope." In addition, he recognizes that "the world is characterized by a multiplicity of agents none of whom can singlehandedly bear the burden of global responsibility." And, on this basis, he recommends that "the way in which our ethical responsibility is to be acted upon has to be contested and negotiated."[114] In this way, Campbell supports the point that all views of the world must be evaluated with respect to one another and incessantly so. He recognizes, as do others, that social interaction produces a great many totalizing views to the world that automatically compete with one another. Campbell's hope is that they may do so in such a way that one is not necessarily privileged over others in any space or time. Yet, in the same stroke, it is important to also recognize that one is faced with a competition of totalizing claims to "the globe" only insofar as there are engagements with "the world." Fueling an agonistic competition of worldviews may serve to keep the limits of human experience and social/political possibility a question to a very large degree. However, what the skeptical aspect of critique also necessarily teaches one is that there is no basis on which to prefigure a world for the view of politics.

As recognized by Kant, a or the world may arise quite easily as a reference for political views through societal contact. But as in the context of Kant's writing, worldviews arise inevitably in relation to quests for meaning, certainty, and knowledge, in which these things are already given the possibility of a fixed final form. Hence, views to the world may be seen to function precisely in the service of quashing the sort of agonistic competition of global perspectives that Campbell desires. As a total perspective, a worldview competes for the description of a globe. To say, then, that we must keep the worldviews that emerge through the flux of experience in debate with respect to one another does little more than keep at bay the decision regarding which view or which amalgam shall dominate. For, supporting a competition of worldviews as a way to maintain a critical perspective on world politics retains the world as a legitimate domain where none in fact exists. And, as a result, it serves to continue to suppress the political activity that gives rise to world images. A world is presupposed as the given limits with respect to which theoretical and political engagements are to be globalized.

Critical inquiries into world politics do offer the scholar a positive position from which to conduct research. However, from this standing one must recognize that "the world" or "the international" and any representations of these things are first and foremost the consequences of *politics*. By "politics" I mean the interaction and engagement of humans with one another which constitutes the, as Kant frames it, asocial sociability of persons. And my contention is that it is the conflict of ideas and actions in inter-human encounters that produces the possibility of world politics. Experiencing the way in which one's views and actions are inhibited or even negated through contact and engagement with others produces the grounds under which a competition of views may seem necessary. And the most successful medium through which one's own views may survive is one that can claim global validity. Even where persons may decide that competition is undesirable, it is only through a general subscription to some sort of universal concept that the experience of conflict may be avoided. In this case, all, willingly or through coercion, may agree to a fundamental sense of how things are in order to enjoy respective differences, as in social contract theory. Hence, all politics may be viewed as essentially a world politics, as politics involves constant efforts to *world* in one sense or another. But, paradoxically, critical inquiry must also take the position that there is no world in world politics, understood in whatever manner. To assume the world as an object first negates the breadth of politics in the world that is one's object to know.

In taking up a critique of world politics, then, the only appropriate response to world politics is to always place the effects of *worlding* into doubt. The disciplinary guide for a critique of world politics could only be one that allowed the critic to place any claim to the world into doubt to begin with. For the function of such an effort must always be to bring focus to the moments of struggles, the experiences of limits in all manners, wherein the globe becomes a political device. As a political device, the globe effectively seeks to quell the moments of conflict that allow critique its freedom.

From this skeptical energy it may then be possible to engage political events and crises without the violence of the Enlightenment and the dogma traditionally and unfortunately secured within the discipline of international relations.

Surely violence in all its forms cannot be eradicated from politics. Politics, as presented here, is always to be a experience of conflict. However, with focus placed on politics first, the social interaction of human beings may be spared the responses that seek to force the very character of such conflicts into an atemporal sense of how human life actually is. In contrast, such a skeptical response may be able to keep alive a sense of how political events are always in the processes of establishing limits to the political. And it may then be possible to respond to politics (in 'the world') in such a way that both the specific dynamics of various experiences and the particular relations of responsibility may be appreciated.

Conclusion: Global Limits

As a study of Kant in international relations, this book describes three broad conclusions. First, contrary to what generations of scholarship would have us believe, his theory cannot be reduced to any one theory of international relations. And a deep understanding of how Kant comes to think problems of international politics demonstrates the fact that he must reject the analytic foundations on which modern international relations theory is built in any event. Second, in engaging questions of international politics, Kant ultimately fails to meet his own standards of critique. In this respect, the understanding of the world he builds suffers from a dogmatism not unlike that he first identifies in both realism and idealism. But, third, through an examination of Kant's failings, it is possible to reinvigorate his critical approach to international politics so as to finally overcome the anchor of dogma. I argue that it is possible to renew his project into a positive and productive Kantian approach to international politics However, this approach also leaves one in a position where one must quit the traditional aims of international relations as a discipline of inquiry. It asks scholars of international politics to reimagine what it means to speak of politics in the world at the most radical of levels.

One may then question the value of investigating Kant's thought with respect to international relations at all. One might decide that attention to Kant is best left to philosophers and that students of international politics ought not to worry so much about attaching his name to the theories of democratic peace that pervade current literature. But to do so would be, again, to privilege and presuppose a domain of something that one might call "international relations" prior to an examination of the grounds on which such a sphere may be legitimately thought. To suggest that Kant's thinking is in the end merely a peculiar sideshow to the central concerns of the discipline is to accept the validity and authority of the global view prior to critical practice. And it is, thus, to bring the value of the discipline itself into question.

The fact is, regardless of how one might feel about it, Kant's thought is at the core of the paradoxical shifts that constitute the conventional range of international relations theory. He persists across the field both as essential prophet and dreamer, as well as at numerous splits that may be negotiated between realism and idealism. Kant's thought *matters* to the discipline of international relations. Read accurately or not, his words provide in some cases the framework through which idealism may be given its most authoritative voice. And in other cases they provide a sounding board for globalization theorists trying to root their analyses of changing "realities" within a history of political thought. Conversely, while giving credence to realpolitik in certain aspects, Kant also provides the abstract utopianism against which realists are able to give their own accounts definition and substantial presence.

If his theory poses difficulty for the study of international relations, then, the task ought not to be a questioning of Kant in relation to an allegedly self-sufficient and self-grounding discipline. Rather, it is incumbent on those who support the central functions of the discipline to question its use of Kant as a theoretical ground. And this is probably equally recommendable with respect to others such as Thucydides, Machiavelli, Hobbes, or Rousseau. Furthermore, scholars of international relations need to take seriously the challenges that Kant's critical inquiry suggest. For, Kant's texts compose a core ground within international relations theory, posed positively, negatively, or a bit of both. And if it is the case that the discipline is unable to provide solid responses to these challenges, it is clearly unable to respond to at least one foundation on which it purports to rest. It would deligitimize itself.

I show here that Kant's philosophy ultimately brings at least two difficulties for consideration to bear on theories of international relations. The first of these is the claim that one need always be willing to rethink the manner in which the international is to be represented as a whole. Within his analyses, I argue, Kant insists that one must always be tentative in all judgments regarding what the world of international politics might be. The point here is that there are always possible others whose experiences may demonstrate practical differences to which one's own vision of the globe is inadequate. Second, through an examination of Kant's own shortcomings with respect to the force of his critique, one is asked to question the actual merit, to begin with, of using the global concept of "the international" as one's starting point in investigating politics in the world. Taking seriously the critical impetus in Kant's work from which the structure for his own idea of the international flowers, I contend that his theory finally suggests that "international relations" must be understood as a device in political struggles, through which the theory and practice of politics may be calmed and disciplined. "International relations" is thus to be viewed as a conceptual move in a politics that actually does not have the convenience of global bounds from which rational principles of politics may be approximated or determined.

In these manners, I maintain that Kantian theory finally suggests that the limits to international politics are indeed global. But they are not global in the sense that they must historically saturate an observable or universally applicable human sphere. Rather his work implies global limits in the sense that the politics and struggles between humans and communities are universally uncontainable in any final way. The limits in one's ability to accurately and properly conceive of the total realm of human politics are global in themselves, in that they are always present. There is no manner in which one could transcend these limits. Thus any judgments regarding the shape of politics in a global fashion are simply irresponsible to the experience of personal, social, and geographical limits that condition the political. To assert a final sphere in which politics is to be imagined is to disregard the primary political quality in any attempt to conceive conflict, confrontation, and differences from the start. For, to place global limits around all experiences of these sorts is to pretend to an unlimited position from which one may either see how all conflict is played out or how all difference may be resolved. And such a vantage point is simply unavailable.

If the discipline of international relations is to deal responsibly with its awkward relationship to Kant's thought, international relations theorists must begin to proffer substantial answers to these problems. Otherwise, there must be substantial work to show how it is that the discipline could function legitimately without a

Kantian or Kantian-like root at all. And, as indicated above, this is work that need not be limited to Kant. A study into Kant should exemplify the fact that such work must be conducted with each and every pillar of thought on which the discipline of international relations claims to stand or stand against.

Notes

Introduction

1. R. B. J. Walker, *Inside / Outside: International Relations as Political Theory* (Cambridge: Cambridge University Press, 1993), 6.

2. Ibid.

3. One should not overlook the fact, though, that Kant's articulations are not purely original in themselves. Certainly, modern theories of international relations draw a direct parallel to the philosophy of Kant. But Kant's own thinking in this regard is constructed through a rethinking and amalgamation of ideas put forth by other prominent philosophers, such as Plato, Augustine, Thomas Hobbes, David Hume, and Jean-Jacques Rousseau.

4. Jens Bartelson, *A Genealogy of Sovereignty* (Cambridge: Cambridge University Press, 1995), 5.

5. Nicholas Greenwood Onuf, *The Republican Legacy in International Thought* (Cambridge: Cambridge University Press, 1998).

6. Ibid., 3.

7. Ibid., 218.

8. Ibid., 218–219.

9. Bartelson, *A Genealogy of Sovereignty*, 13.

10. Andrew Linklater, *The Transformation of Political Community: Ethical Foundations of the Post-Westphalian Era* (Columbia: University of South Carolina Press, 1998).

11. Linklater, *The Transformation of Political Community*, 1–3.

12. Ibid., 2–3.

13. Ibid., 5.

14. Ibid.

15. Ibid., 24.

16. Ibid., 6.

17. Ibid., 7.

18. Ibid., 25.

19. Ibid., 7

20. Ibid., 192.

21. Ibid., 211.

22. For traditional analyses and representations of Kant's thought by theorists of international relations, see A. C. Armstrong, "Kant's Philosophy of Peace and War," *The Journal of Philosophy* 28, no. 8 (April 1931): 197–204; Ian Clark, *Reform and Resistance in the International Order* (Cambridge: Cambridge University Press, 1980); Carl Joachim Friedrich, *Inevitable Peace* (Cambridge, Mass.: Harvard University Press, 1948); W. B. Gallie, *Philosophers of Peace and War: Kant, Clausewitz, Marx, Engles and Tolstoy* (Cambridge: Cambridge University Press, 1978); F. H. Hinsley, *Power and Pursuit of Peace: Theory and Practice in the History of Relations Between States* (Cambridge: Cambridge University Press, 1963); and Kenneth N. Waltz, "Kant, Liberalism, and War," *American Political Science Review* 56 (June 1962): 331–340.

23. Cecilia Lynch, "Kant, the Republican Peace, and Moral Guidance in International Law," *Ethics and International Affairs* 8 (1994): 39.

Chapter One

1. The inspiration of any images associated with knackeries or glue–factories by the use of the term *rendering* is purely intentional.

2. Thomas Hobbes, *Leviathan*, ed. C. B. Macpherson (London: Penguin Books, 1968).

3. Ibid., 183–188.

4. Immanuel Kant, "Perpetual Peace: A Philosophical Sketch," in *Political Writings*, 2nd ed., ed. Hans Reiss, trans. H. B. Nisbet (Cambridge: Cambridge University Press, 1991), 93–130.

5. See in particular Kant, "Idea for a Universal History with a Cosmopolitan Purpose," in *Political Writings*, 41–53; and Kant, "On the Common Saying: 'This May Be True in Theory, But It Does Not Apply in Practice," in *Political Writings*, 61–92.

6. E. H. Carr, *The Twenty Years' Crisis, 1919–1939: An Introduction to the Study of International Relations* (New York: Harper & Row Publishers, 1964).

7. Kant, "Perpetual Peace," 93–96.

8. Ibid., 93.

9. Ibid., pp. 94–95.

10. Ibid., p. 95.

11. Ibid., p. 94.

12. Ibid., p. 96.

13. Ibid., p. 98.

14. See Jean-Jacques Rousseau, "Discourse on the Origin of Inequality" and "On the Social Contract," in *The Basic Political Writings*, ed. and trans. Donald A. Cress (Indianapolis and Cambridge: Hackett Publishing Company, 1987), 25–109; 137–227.

15. Kant, "Perpetual Peace," 98.

16. Ibid., 99–108.

17. Ibid., 99.

18. Ibid., 100.

19. Ibid., 102.

20. Ibid., 104.

21. Ibid., 106.

22. Ibid., 105.

23. Ibid.

24. Ibid., 123.

25. Hedley Bull, *The Anarchical Society: A Study of Order in World Politics* (New York: Columbia University Press, 1977), 262.

26. Ibid., 262–263.

27. Ibid., 263.

28. Thomas L. Carson, "*Perpetual Peace*: What Kant Should Have Said," *Social Theory and Practice* 14, no. 2 (Summer 1988): 173–214.

29. Friedrich, *Inevitable Peace*, 45.

30. Hinsley, *Power and the Pursuit of Peace*, 66.

31. Kant, "Perpetual Peace," 104.

32. Ibid.

33. Ibid.

34. Hinsley, *Power and the Pursuit of Peace*, 69.

35. Howard Williams, *Kant's Political Philosophy* (Oxford: Basil Blackwell, 1983), 259.

36. Kant, "Perpetual Peace," 103, 121.

37. Ibid., 121.

38. Ibid., 116.

39. Ibid., 120–121.

40. Ibid., 118.

41. Ibid., 121.

42. Ibid., 118.

43. Ibid., 108–115.

44. Ibid., 125.

45. Torbjörn L. Knutsen, *A History of International Relations Theory: An Introduction* (Manchester and New York: Manchester University Press, 1992).

46. F. Parkinson, *The Philosophy of International Relations: A Study in the History of Thought* (Beverly Hills and London: Sage Publications, 1977).

47. It is worthy to note here how often it is that scholars of international relations lump together such disparately situated writers as Thucydides, Machiavelli, Hobbes, and Morgenthau. It is regularly supposed in the discipline that these figures along with others are somehow linked at a theoretical level and subscribe to the same assumptions regarding international politics. Yet, it is seldom noted that each and every one of these writers is discussing a condition of politics and political institutions that is highly specific to his own social and historical context.

48. Parkinson, *The Philosophy of International Relations*, 65–66.

49. Knutsen, *A History of International Relations Theory*, 111.

50. Kant, "Perpetual Peace," 114.

51. Parkinson, *The Philosophy of International Relations*, 68–69.

52. Here I have in mind those recent theorists who tend to link Kant with theses suggesting that the spread of democracy will bring about increased international peace. The most notable character in this regard is Michael W. Doyle. Doyle and others are discussed further on.

53. A. C. Armstrong, "Kant's Philosophy of Peace and War."

54. Ibid., 198.

55. Ibid., 201.

56. Ibid., 203.

57. Ibid., 203–204.

58. Ibid., 201–202.

59. Hinsley, *Power and the Pursuit of Peace*, 69.

60. Friedrich, *Inevitable Peace*, 16–17.

61. Ibid., 27–28.

62. Patrick Riley, *Kant's Political Philosophy* (Totowa, New Jersey: Rowman and Littlefield, 1983), 134.

63. Charles R. Beitz, *Political Theory and International Relations* (Princeton: Princeton University Press, 1979), 144.

64. Clark, *Reform and Resistance*.

65. Ibid., 40–41.

66. Howard Williams, *International Relations in Political Theory* (Milton Keynes and Philadelphia: Open University Press, 1992), 88; and Howard Williams, *Kant's Political Philosophy*, 256, 259.

67. Jürg Martin Gabriel, *Worldviews and Theories of International Relations* (New York: St. Martin's Press, 1994), 54.

68. Ibid.

69. The difficulty that theorists of international relations have had in sorting out Kant's 'proper place' in the discipline is well demonstrated in Kenneth W. Thompson, "The Nineteenth Century," in *The Fathers of International Thought: The Legacy of Political Theory* (Baton Rouge: Louisiana State University Press, 1994), 103–112.

70. Charles Covell, *Kant, Liberalism and the Pursuit of Justice in the International Order* (Hamburg and Münster: LIT, 1994), 72–73.

71. Michael C. Williams, "Reason and Realpolitik: Kant's 'Critique of International Politics,'" *Canadian Journal of Political Science* 25, no. 1 (March 1992): 100.

72. Clark, *Reform and Resistance*, 41.

73. Waltz, "Kant, Liberalism, and War," 331.

74. Ibid., 339.

75. See Gallie, "Kant's View of Reason in Politics," *Philosophy: The Journal of the Royal Institute of Philosophy* 54, no. 207 (January 1979), 29; Gallie, *Philosophers of Peace and War*; and Gallie, "Wanted: A Philosophy of International Relations," *Political Studies* 27, no. 3 (September 1979): 484–492.

76. Gallie, "Kant's View of Reason," 20–21; Gallie, *Philosophers of Peace and War*, 33–34; and Gallie, "Wanted," 485.

77. Gallie, "Kant's View of Reason," 21.

78. Gallie, *Philosophers of Peace and War*, 35.

79. Gallie, "Kant's View of Reason," 25–27; Gallie, *Philosophers of Peace and War*, 29–33; and Gallie, "Wanted," 485–487.

80. Gallie, "Wanted," 486.

81. Gallie, "Kant's View of Reason in Politics," 32–33.

82. Andrew Hurrell, "Kant and the Kantian paradigm in international relations," *Review of International Studies* 16 (1990): 204.

83. Ibid.

84. Michael C. Williams, "Reason and Realpolitik," 118.

85. Bull, *The Anarchical Society*.

86. John Herz, *International Politics in the Atomic Age* (New York: Columbia University Press, 1959); Herz, "The Territorial State Revisited, Reflections on the Future of the Nation-state," *Polity* 1, no. 1, (1968): 11–34.

87. For writings which seek to connect Kant to so-called "peace-loving democracies hypotheses," see Bruce Bueno de Mesquia and David Lalman, *War and Reason* (New Haven: Yale University Press, 1992); Doyle, "Kant, Liberal Legacies, and Foreign Affairs, Part 1," *Philosophy and Public Affairs* 12, no. 3 (Summer 1983): 205–235; Doyle, "Kant, Liberal Legacies, and Foreign Affairs, Part 2," *Philosophy and Public Affairs* 12, no. 4 (Fall 1983): 323–353; Doyle, "Liberalism and International Relations," in *Kant and Political Philosophy: The Contemporary Legacy*, ed. Ronald Beiner and William James Booth (New Haven and London: Yale University Press, 1993), 173–203; Doyle, "Liberalism and World Politics," *American Political Science Review* 80, no. 4 (December 1986): 1151–1169; Francis Fukuyama, *The End of*

History and the Last Man (New York: Basic Books, 1992); Charles Kegley, Jr., "The Neo-Idealist Moment in Internationalist Studies? Realist Myths and New International Realities," *International Studies Quarterly* 37, no. 2 (June 1993): 131–146; Christopher Layne, "Kant or Cant: The Myth of the Democratic Peace," *International Security* 19, no. 2 (Fall 1994): 5–49; Jack Levy, "The Causes of War: A Review of Theories of Evidence," in *Behavior, Society and Nuclear War*, vol. 1, ed. Philip E. Tetlock, et al. (Oxford: Oxford University Press, 1989), 209–333; Levy, "Domestic Politics and War," *Journal of Interdisciplinary History* 18, no. 4 (Spring 1988): 653–673; T. Clifton Moran and Valerie Schwebach, "Take Two Democracies and Call Me in the Morning: A Prescription for Peace?," *International Interactions* 17, no. 4(1992): 305–320; John Mueller, *Retreat From Doomsday: The Obsolescence of Major War* (New York: Basic Books, 1988); John M. Owen, "How Liberalism Produces Democratic Peace," *International Security* 19, no. 2 (Fall 1994): 87–125; Bruce Russett and William Antholis, "Do Democracies Fight Each Other? Evidence from the Peloponnesian War," *Journal of Peace Research* 29, no. 4 (November 1992): 415–434; Russett, *Grasping the Democratic Peace: Principles for a Post-Cold War World* (Princeton: Princeton University Press, 1993); Georg Sørensen, *Democracy and Democratization: Processes and Prospects in a Changing World* (Boulder, Colo.: Westview Press, 1993); Sørensen, "Kant and Processes of Democratization: Consequences of Neorealist Thought," *Journal of Peace Research* 29, no. 4 (1992): 397–414; David E. Spiro, "The Insignificance of the Liberal Peace," *International Security* 19, no. 2 (Fall 1994): 50–81; Harvey Starr, "Democracy and War: Choice, Learning and Security Communities," *Journal of Peace Research* 29, no. 2 (May 1992): 207–213; and Erich Weede, "Some Simple Calculations on Democracy and War Involvement," *Journal of Peace Research* 29, no. 4 (November 1992): 377–383.

88. This suggestion, that one may legitimately identify modern western democratic states with what Kant understands as a republican rule, is highly contested and ought not to be overlooked. I engage this problem directly in the following chapter, where I argue that this association is quite dubious and ill-founded.

89. Doyle, "Kant, Liberal Legacies, and Foreign Affairs, Part 1"; and Doyle, "Kant, Liberal Legacies, and Foreign Affairs, Part 2."

90. Doyle, "Kant, Liberal Legacies, and Foreign Affairs, Part 1," 206–207.

91. Ibid., 207–208.

92. Ibid., 225.

93. For example, see Ibid., 213.

94. Doyle, "Kant, Liberal Legacies, and Foreign Affairs, Part 2," 349.

95. Ibid., 349–351.

96. Doyle, "Kant, Liberal Legacies, and Foreign Affairs, Part 1," 206.

97. Ibid.

98. Ibid., 217.

99. Spiro, "The Insignificance of the Liberal Peace."

100. Layne, "Kant or Cant."

101. Kegley, Jr., "The Neoidealist Moment in International Studies?"

102. Diana T. Meyers, "Kant's Liberal Alliance: A Permanent Peace?," in *Political Realism and International Morality: Ethics in the Nuclear Age*, ed. Kenneth Kipnis and Meyers (Boulder and London: Westview Press, 1987), 212–219.

103. Russett and Antholis, "Do Democracies Fight Each Other?"; Bueno de Mesquita and Lalman, *War and Reason*; Morgan and Schwebach, "Take Two Democracies"; and Weede, "Some Simple Calculations."

104. Waltz, *Man, the State and War: A Theoretical Analysis* (New York: Columbia University Press, 1954).

105. Bueno de Mesquita and Lalman, *War and Reason*; and Starr, "Democracy and War."

106. Layne, "Kant or Cant."

107. Gabriel L. Negretto, "Kant and the Illusion of Collective Security," *Journal of International Affairs* 46, no. 2 (Winter 1993): 501–523.

108. Ibid., 522.

109. Ibid., 521.

110. Ibid., 523.

111. Levy, "Domestic Politics and War."

112. Ibid., 658–662.

113. Russett, *Grasping the Democratic Peace*, 31.

114. Doyle, "Kant, Liberal Legacies, and Foreign Affairs," 213.

115. Beitz, *Political Theory and International Relations*.

116. Sørensen, "Kant and Processes of Democratization," 401.

117. Ibid., 402–408.

118. While concluding that Kant's theory is essentially sound, Sørensen warns that a proliferation of basically liberal states around the world is itself no guarantee for perpetual peace. His point is that the "new" democra-

cies that have recently emerged, largely from the former colonised and communist states, do not inherently add to the prospects of a pacific order just because they are democratic in form. Ibid., 412.

119. John J. Mearsheimer, "Back to the Future: Instability in Europe After the Cold War," *International Security* 15, no. 1 (Summer 1990): 5–57.

120. Wade L. Huntley, "Kant's Third Image: Systemic Sources of the Liberal Peace," *International Studies Quarterly* 40, no. 1 (1996): 45–76.

121. Ibid., 51–52.

122. I do not mean to give the impression here that the readings typically given to Kant's writing in the field of international relations are actually more or less accurate. There are in fact serious problems with the ways in which Kant is taken up in the discipline. However, there are clearly elements in *Perpetual Peace* that have inevitably lead theorists of international relations to crude approximations of broader themes in Kant's thought. In light of this, I will discuss Kant's commitment to rational autonomy in his political theory in some detail in the following chapter.

123. Leslie A. Mulholland, "Kant on War and International Law," *Kant-Studien* 78, no. 1 (1987): 28–29.

124. Ibid., 40–41.

125. Daniele Archibugi, "Models of international organization in perpetual peace projects," *Review of International Studies* 18 (1992): 295–317.

126. Ibid., 315.

127. Ibid., 316.

128. Fernando R. Tesón, "The Kantian Theory of International Law," *Columbia Law Review* 92, no. 1 (January 1992): 53–102.

129. Ibid., 54.

130. Ibid., 53.

131. Ibid., 56.

132. Ibid., 101–102.

133. Lynch, "Kant, the Republican Peace, and Moral Guidance," 46.

134. Tesón, "The Kantian Theory of International Law," 81, 92–93.

135. Lynch, "Kant, the Republican Peace, and Moral Guidance," 54–55.

136. Chris Brown, *International Relations Theory: New Normative Approaches* (New York: Columbia University Press, 1992), 14.

137. Ibid.

138. Linklater, *Men and Citizens in the Theory of International Relations*, 2nd ed. (London: Macmillan, 1990), 205–206.

139. Stanley Hoffmann, *Duties Beyond Borders: On the Limits and Possibilities of Ethical International Politics* (Syracuse, N.Y.: Syracuse University Press, 1981), 198–99.

140. Ibid., 205.

141. Ibid., 225–228.

142. Ibid., 231.

143. Tesón, "The Kantian Theory of International Law," 99–100.

144. Ibid., 100.

145. Hans Saner, *Kant's Political Thought: Its Origins and Development*, trans. E. B. Ashton (Chicago and London: The University of Chicago Press, 1973).

146. Ibid., 307.

147. Bartelson, "The Trial of Judgment: A Note on Kant and the Paradoxes of Internationalism," *International Studies Quarterly* 39 (1995): 255–279.

148. Bartelson's work on Kant's theory is of particular interest in this regard. I have not spent time discussing his writing in this chapter, as Bartelson's article is a very recent addition to these debates that diverts from the mainstream in a highly dramatic way. Although I find points of contention with it, I understand Bartelson's work is most close to my own position. In producing a direct critical evaluation of Kant's possible contribution to thinking international politics, I make note of the relative successes of Bartelson's reading in chapter 3.

149. Owen, "How Liberalism Produces Democratic Peace"; and Payne, "Kant or Cant."

150. Hoffmann, "The Crisis of Liberal Internationalism," *Foreign Policy* 98 (Spring 1995): 175–176.

151. Ido Oren, "The Subjectivity of the 'Democratic' Peace: Changing U.S. Perceptions of Imperial Germany," *International Security* 20, no. 2 (Fall 1995): 147–184.

152. Ibid., 147, 178.

153. Neta C. Crawford, "A security regime among democracies: cooperation among Iroquois nations," *International Organization* 48, no. 3 (Summer 1994): 345–385.

154. Ibid., 380.

155. Ibid., 347.

156. Ibid., 384.

157. Carol R. Ember, Melvin Ember, and Russett, "Peace Between Participatory Polities: A Cross-Cultural Test of the 'Democracies Rarely Fight Each Other' Hypothesis," *World Politics* 44 (July 1992): 579; and Russett, *Grasping the Democratic Peace: Principles for a Post-Cold War World* (Princeton: Princeton University Press, 1993): 100.

158. Crawford, "A security regime among democracies," 381.

Chapter Two

1. See Ronald Beiner and William James Booth, eds., *Kant & Political Philosophy: The Contemporary Legacy*; Ernst Cassirer, *Kant's Life and Thought*, trans. James Haden (New Haven: Yale University Press, 1981); Ruth E. Chadwick, ed., *Immanuel Kant, Critical Assessments: Volume III, Kant's Moral and Political Philosophy* (London: Routledge, 1992); Andrew Cutrofello, *Discipline and Critique: Kant, Poststructuralism and the Problem of Resistance* (Albany: State University of New York Press, 1994); Eduard Gerresheim, ed., *Immanuel Kant 1724/1974: Kant as a Political Thinker* (Bonn and Bad Godesberge: Inter Nationes, 1974); Dieter Henrich, *Aesthetic Judgement and the Moral Image of the World* (Stanford, Calif.: Stanford University Press, 1992); Dick Howard, *The Politics of Critique* (Minneapolis: University of Minnesota Press, 1988); Kimberly Hutchings, *Kant, Critique and Politics* (London and New York: Routledge, 1996); Riley, *Kant's Political Philosophy*; Allen D. Rosen, *Kant's Theory of Justice* (Ithaca, New York: Cornell University Press, 1993); Saner, *Kant's Political Thought*; Susan Meld Shell, *The Embodiment of Reason: Kant on Spirit, Generation, and Community* (Chicago and London: The University of Chicago Press, 1996); Shell, *The Rights of Reason: A Study of Kant's Philosophy and Politics* (Toronto: University of Toronto Press, 1980); Howard Williams, ed., *Essays on Kant's Political Philosophy* (Chicago: University of Chicago Press, 1992); and Howard Williams, *Kant's Political Philosophy*.

2. I certainly do not wish to suggest here that this is an entirely original thought or position. For example, Saner, in his *Kant's Political Thought*, certainly aims to show how Kant's political theory may be seen to arise from his earlier philosophical work. Howard Williams claims that there is a connection between Kant's Critical works and his political philosophy in his *Kant's Political Philosophy*. Also, in Michael C. Williams, "Reason and Realpolitik," there is a direct effort to illustrate a significant connection with Kant's interest in critique and what he develops as a theory pertaining to international politics. However, I am suggesting a much deeper debt in Kant's political thought to his other work in philosophy than these writers affirm.

And I believe that the extent to which I do find a radical source for Kant's ideas about international politics in his larger philosophical efforts, through this chapter and chapter 3, is unprecedented.

3. Kant, "Idea for a Universal History," 46.

4. Kant, *Religion Within the Limits of Reason Alone*, trans. Theodore M. Greene and Hoyt H. Hudson (New York: Harper and Row Publishers, 1960), 92.

5. Readers should make particular note of the fact that Kant recognizes only adult men as full members of political life. He sets off women with others he considers to be essentially "passive" members of civil community, not fit to vote and thus not deserving of citizenship. He writes:

> Fitness to vote is the necessary qualification which every citizen must possess. To be fit to vote, a person must have an independent position among the people. He must therefore be not just a part of the commonwealth, but a member of it, i.e., he must by his own free will actively participate in a community of other people. But this latter quality makes it necessary to distinguish between the *active* and the *passive* citizen, although the latter concept seems to contradict the definition of the concept of a citizen altogether. The following examples may serve to overcome this difficulty. Apprentices to merchants or tradesmen, servants who are not employed by the state, minors (*naturaliter vel civiliter*), women in general and all those who are obliged to depend for their living (i.e., for food and protection) on the offices of others (excluding the state)—all of these people have no civil personality, and their existence is, so to speak, purely inherent. The woodcutter whom I employ on my premises; the blacksmith in India who goes from house to house with his hammer, anvil and bellows to do work with iron, as opposed to the European carpenter or smith who can put the products of his work up for public sale; the domestic tutor as opposed to the academic, the tithe-holder as opposed to the farmer; and so on—they are all mere auxiliaries to the commonwealth, so that they do not possess civil independence. (Kant, "The Metaphysics of Morals," in *Political Writings*, 139–140).

At the very least, I do not wish this point to be ignored. I recognize the gendered quality of Kant's writings as significant and warranting investigation. Unfortunately, as is evidenced once more in this book, he has been subject to very little interpretation in this regard. In chapter 3, I raise the point of his sexism as a particularly damning aspect in his analysis of human reason and, thus, politics. However, my central task in this work is to respond to how Kant is taken up within the mainstream of international relations theory. The focus of my discussions remains on the traditional center of the discipline, where issues of gender are primarily suppressed to begin with. So, I myself have not engaged in a sustained feminist critique of Kant along the way. Such very interesting and provocative work, I have left to further projects.

For examples of recent efforts to engage Kant's theory on issues of gender, see Sarah Kofman, "The Economy of Respect: Kant and Respect for Women," trans. Nicola Fisher, *Social Research: An International Quarterly of the Social Sciences* 49, no. 2 (Summer 1982): 383–404; Susan Mendus, "Kant: 'An Honest but Narrow-Minded Bourgeois'?," in *Essays on Kant's Political Philosophy*, 166–190; Robin May Schott, ed., *Feminist Interpretations of Immanuel Kant* (University Park: The Pennsylvania State University Press, 1997); Shell, *The Embodiment of Reason*; and Shell, "Kant's Political Cosmology: Freedom and Desire in the 'Remarks' Concerning *Observations on the Feeling of the Beautiful and the Sublime*," in *Essays on Kant's Political Philosophy*, pp. 81–119.

In her *The Embodiment of Reason*, Shell provides a particularly innovative and provocative reading of gender dynamics through the entire course of Kant's philosophical development. She provides a unique argument suggesting questions of sexual difference at the very roots of his thought.

6. Kant, "Conjectures on the Beginning of Human History," in *Political Writings*, 228; Kant, "The Metaphysics of Morals," 157, 164–168; and Kant, "Perpetual Peace," 96, 102, 104, 121.

7. Kant, "On the Common Saying," 83n.; and Kant, "Perpetual Peace," 96, 113.

8. See: Kant, *Conflict of the Faculties*, trans. Mary J. Gregor (Lincoln: University of Nebraska Press, 1979); Kant, "Idea for a Universal History"; and Kant, "Perpetual Peace."

9. Kant, "Perpetual Peace," 102.

10. Kant, "Idea for a Universal History," 41.

11. Ibid., 45.

12. Kant, *Critique of Pure Reason*, trans. Norman Kemp Smith (London: Macmillan Education, 1929).

13. Ibid. (A19/B33), 65.

14. Ibid.

15. Ibid. (A20/B34), 65–66.

16. Ibid. (B16), 53.

17. Ibid. (A20/B34), 66.

18. Ibid. (A31/B46), 74–75.

19. Ibid. (A21/B35), 66–67.

20. Kant, *Anthropology from a Pragmatic Point of View*, trans. Victor Lyle Dowdell (Carbondale and Edwardsville: Southern Illinois University Press, 1978) (§4), 17.

21. Kant, *Pure Reason* (A34/B51), 77.

22. Ibid. (A36/B52), 78.

23. Ibid. (A362), 341.

24. Kant, *Anthropology* (§7), 24–28.

25. Kant, *Pure Reason* (A363), 342.

26. Kant, *Critique of Judgment*, trans. J. H. Bernard (New York: Hafner Press, 1951).

27. Ibid. (§73), 241–242.

28. Ibid., p. 242.

29. Kant, *Religion*, 28–29.

30. Ibid., 29–30.

31. Kant, *Anthropology* (§89), 241–246.

32. Kant, *Religion*, 23–24.

33. Ibid., 27–32.

34. Ibid., 31.

35. Kant, *Religion*, 46; and Kant, "Grounding for the Metaphysics of Morals," in *Ethical Philosophy*, trans. James W. Ellington (Indianapolis and Cambridge: Hackett, 1983), 19–20.

36. Kant, *Judgment* (§73), 240.

37. Kant makes this point at length in Ibid.

38. Henry E. Allison, *Kant's Transcendental Idealism: An Interpretation and Defense* (New Haven and London: Yale University Press, 1983). See especially "Part I," 1–61.

39. Kant, *Pure Reason* (A79/B105), 113.

40. Ibid. (A77/B103), 111.

41. Ibid. (A69/B94), 106.

42. Kant, *Judgment* (§IV), 15.

43. Kant, *Pure Reason* (A302/B359), 303.

44. Ibid. (A300/B357), 301.

45. Ibid. (A306/B362), 305.

46. In this manner, Kant understands reason to operate by means of syllogism, where (1) a rule serves as the major premise through the understanding, (2) something known is subsumed within the condition of the rule through judgment, serving as the minor premise, and (3) what follows as knowledge, the conclusion, is determined through the predicate of the rule, a priori through reason. Ibid. (A304/B360), 304.

47. Kant, *Anthropology* (§41), 91.

48. Kant, *Pure Reason* (A642/B670), 532.

49. Ibid. (A405/B432–A567/B595), 384–484.

50. Ibid. (A302/B359), 303.

51. Ibid. (A307/B364), 306.

52. Ibid. (A586/B614), 497.

53. Ibid. (A590/B618–A630/B658), 492–524.

54. Ibid. (A492/B520), 440.

55. Ibid. (B274–275, A347/B405–A348/B406, A354–356, A367–368), 244, 332, 336–338, 344–445.

56. Ibid. (A492/B521), 440.

57. Paul Guyer, *Kant and the Claims of Knowledge* (Cambridge: Cambridge University Press, 1987), 323–324.

58. Allison, *Kant's Theory of Freedom* (Cambridge: Cambridge University Press, 1990).

59. Michael C. Williams, "Reason and Realpolitik."

60. Karl Jaspers, *Philosophy and the World*, trans. E. B. Ashton (Chicago: Henry Regnery Company, 1963).

61. Michael C. Williams, "Reason and Realpolitik," 118.

62. Kant, *Pure Reason* (A293/B349–A298/B355), 297–300.

63. Ibid. (A675/B703–A679/B707), 553–555.

64. Ibid. (A682/B710–A686/B714), 557–559.

65. Ibid. (A681/B709), 556.

66. Ibid. (A692/B720), 563.

67. Ibid. (A738/B766), 593.

68. Lynch, "Kant, the Republican Peace, and Moral Guidance."

69. Ibid., 42.

70. Kant, "Idea for a Universal History," 41–42.

71. Kant, *Pure Reason* (A495/B523), 442.

72. Gallie, "Kant's View of Reason," 29.

73. Kant, "Idea for a Universal History," 42.

74. Kant, *Pure Reason* (A495/B523), 464–465.

75. Kant, *Critique of Practical Reason*, 3rd ed., trans. Lewis White Beck (New York: Macmillan, 1993), 55.

76. Kant, "Idea for a Universal History," 42.

77. Kant, *Conflict*, 149.

78. Kant, *Pure Reason* (A58/B83), 97.

79. Kant, "Perpetual Peace," 108–109.

80. Ibid., p. 141.

81. Ibid., p. 143.

82. Kant, "Conjectures on the Beginning of Human History," 221.

83. Ibid.

84. Kant, "Idea for a Universal History," 42.

85. Kant, *Pure Reason* (A556/B584), 478.

86. Ibid. (A803/B831), 634.

87. Ibid. (A556/B584), 478.

88. Ibid. (A553/B581), 476.

89. Kant, "Grounding," 8.

90. Kant, "Idea for a Universal History," 43.

91. Ibid.

92. Kant, *Pure Reason* (A114), 140; and Kant, *Anthropology* (§89), 246–247.

93. Kant, *Pure Reason* (A802/B831), 633.

94. Kant, *Practical Reason*, 3–4.

95. Kant, *Pure Reason* (A802/B831), 634.

96. Kant, *Practical Reason*, 49.

97. Ibid., 33.

98. Ibid., 19.

99. Ibid., 116.

100. Kant, "Conjectures on the Beginning of Human History," 223–226.

101. Ibid., 227.

102. Kant, *Conflict of the Faculties*, 159.

103. Kant, "Idea for a Universal History," 41.

104. Kant, "Grounding," 52.

105. Kant, "Perpetual Peace," 106.

106. Kant, "The Metaphysics of Morals," 137.

107. Kant, "On the Common Saying," 91.

108. Kant, "The Metaphysics of Morals," 137.

109. Kant, *Anthropology* (§89), 238.

110. For recent discussions of the relation between morality and politics in Kant's writings, see Sharon Anderson-Gold, "Kant's Ethical Commonwealth: The Highest Good as a Social Goal," *International Philosophical Quarterly* 26, no. 1 (March 1986): 22–32; Brown, *International Relations Theory*; Chadwick, *Immanuel Kant, Critical Assessments: Volume III*; Steven M. Delue, "Kant's Politics as Expression of the Need for His Aesthetics," *Political Theory* 13, no. 3 (August 1985): 409–429; Thomas Donaldson, "Kant's Global Rationalism," in *Traditions of International Ethics*, ed. Terry Nardin and David R. Mapel (Cambridge: Cambridge University Press, 1992), 136–157; Jean Bethke Elshtain, "Kant, Politics, Persons: The Implications of His Moral Philosophy," *Polity: The Journal of the Northeastern Political Science Association* 14, no. 2 (Winter 1981): 203–221; Riley, "The 'Elements' of Kant's Practical Philosophy: The *Groundwork* After 200 Years (1785–1985)," *Political Theory* 14, no. 4 (November 1986): 552–583; and Tom Sorell, "Self, Society and Kantian Impersonality," *The Monist: An International Quarterly Journal of General Philosophical Inquiry* 74, no. 1 (January 1991): 30–42.

111. For recent discussions of how Kant's political theory may be read historically into Hobbes's theory, see Craig L. Carr, "Kant's Theory of Political Authority," *History of Political Thought* 10, no. 4 (Winter 1989): 719–731; Philip J. Kain, "Kant's Political Theory and Philosophy of History," *Clio: A Journal of Literature, History and the Philosophy of History* 18, no. 4 (Summer 1989): 235–245; and Gorazd Korosec, "Hobbes and the Theory of Social

Contract as the Context for Kant's Political Philosophy," *Filozofski Vestnik* 13, no. 2 (1992): 97–113.

112. Kant, "Perpetual Peace," 111.

113. Kant, "Metaphysics of Morals, " 174.

114. Kant, "On the Common Saying," 90.

115. Kant, "Conjectures on the Beginning of Human History," 226.

116. Kant, "Idea for a Universal History," 46.

117. Wolfgang Kersting, "Kant's Concept of the State," in Howard Williams, *Essays on Kant's Political Philosophy*, 148.

118. Hobbes, "Chap. IV, Of Speech," and "Chap. V, Of Reason, and Science," *Leviathan*, 100–119.

119. These points emerge across Hobbes, "Of Man," *Leviathan*, 81–222.

120. For a discussion of the importance of this theme, see R. B. J. Walker, *Inside/Outside: International Relations as Political Theory* (Cambridge: Cambridge University Press, 1993).

121. Gallie, "Kant's View," 32–33.

122. Kant, "Grounding," 9.

123. Kant, *Judgment*, 282.

124. Kant, "Metaphysics of Morals," 137.

125. Kant, "Idea for a Universal History," 45–46.

126. Ibid., 46.

127. Kant, "Perpetual Peace," 93.

128. Kant, *Judgment* (§83), 282.

129. Kant, "An Answer to the Question: 'What is Enlightenment?,' " in *Political Writings*, 59.

130. Kant, "Metaphysics of Morals," 140–142.

131. Kant, "Idea for a Universal History," 45.

132. Kant, "On the Common Saying," 74.

133. Ibid., 74–75.

134. Ibid., 73.

135. Kant, "Metaphysics of Morals," 133.

136. Ibid., 132–133.

137. Kant, "Perpetual Peace," 99.

138. Arguments against the notion that Kant somehow promotes democratic reform are indeed rare to the discipline of international relations. Lynch provides one of the few attempts to reject this notion in her: "Kant, the Republican Peace, and Moral Guidance in International Law." However, such arguments are not as novel amongst political theorists. For examples of support for my position here, see Riley, *Kant's Political Philosophy*, 101–102; Rosen, *Kant's Theory of Justice*, 34; and Howard Williams, *Kant's Political Philosophy*, 172–174.

139. This claim is made in Archibugi, "Models of international organization," 311.

140. Kant, "Perpetual Peace," 101.

141. John MacMillan, "A Kantian Protest Against the Peculiar Discourse of Inter-State Peace," *Millennium: Journal of International Studies* 24, no. 3 (1994): 549–562.

142. Guyer, *Kant and the Experience of Freedom: Essays on Aesthetics and Morality* (Cambridge: Cambridge University Press, 1993), 22–23.

143. Kant, "Metaphysics of Morals," 163.

144. Kant, "Perpetual Peace," 104.

145. Ibid., 100.

146. Kant, *Conflict*, 159.

147. Kant, "On the Common Saying," 79.

148. Ibid.

149. Kant, *Pure Reason* (A316/B373), 312.

150. Kant, "On the Common Saying," 80–81.

151. Kant, "Perpetual Peace," 116.

152. Kant, "Grounding," 3.

153. Ibid., 29.

154. Ibid., 29–30.

155. Ibid., 30.

156. Ibid.

157. Kant, "Metaphysics of Morals," 132–134.

158. Kant, *Conflict*, 167.

159. Ibid., 169.

160. Kant, "Metaphysics of Morals," 143–145.

161. Kant, *Conflict*, 153.

162. Henrich, "On the Meaning of Rational Action in the State," in *Kant and Political Philosophy*, 111. Aspects of this argument are also supported by Ferenc Fehér, "Practical Reason in the Revolution: Kant's Dialogue with the French Revolution," *Social Research* 56, no. 1 (Spring 1989): 161–185.

163. Kant, "Metaphysics of Morals," 156–159.

164. See: Michel Foucault, "Kant on Enlightenment and Revolution," *Economy and Society* 15, no. 1 (February 1986): 88–96.

165. Howard Williams, *Kant's Political Philosophy*, 211.

166. Kant, "Metaphysics of Morals," 146.

167. Kant, "On the Common Saying," 81.

168. Ibid.

169. Kant, "Grounding," 36.

170. Kant, "Idea for a Universal History," 42.

171. Ibid., 47.

172. Kant, "Perpetual Peace," 96.

173. Kant, "Conjectures," 231.

174. Kant, "Idea for a Universal History," 47.

175. Kant, "Metaphysics of Morals," 137.

176. Kant, *Conflict*, 165–167.

177. Kant, "Perpetual Peace," 102.

178. Ibid., 107–108.

179. Kant, "Idea for a Universal History," 50–51; and Kant, "Perpetual Peace," 95, 114.

180. For recent discussions of Kant's idea of international right and contemporary international law, see: Lynch, "Kant, the Republican Peace, and Moral Guidance in International Law"; Mulholland, "Kant on War and International Justice"; Téson, "The Kantian Theory of International Law."

181. Kant, "On the Common Saying," 91–92.

182. Kant, "Metaphysics of Morals," 171.

183. Kant, "Perpetual Peace, " 102.

184. Kant, *Anthropology* (§89), 236–237.

185. Kant, "Perpetual Peace," 104.

186. Ibid.

187. Ibid., 93.

188. Ibid., 93–94.

189. Kant, "The Metaphysics of Morals," 165.

190. Kant, "On the Common Saying," 92.

191. George Modelski, "Is World Politics Evolutionary Thinking?," *International Organization* 44, no. 1 (Winter 1990): 1–24.

192. Negretto, "Kant and the Illusion of Collective Security."

193. Kant, *Judgment* (§83), 283.

194. Ibid. (§28), 102.

195. Ibid. (§25), 86.

196. Ibid. (§27), 96.

197. Kant, *Pure Reason* (A816/B844), 642.

198. Kant, *Opus Postumum*, ed. Eckart Förster, trans. Förster and Michael Rosen (Cambridge: Cambridge University Press, 1993), 210.

199. See especially Kant, *Conflict*; Kant, "Idea for a Universal History"; Kant, "Perpetual Peace"; and Kant, "What Is Enlightenment?"

200. Kant, "Idea for a Universal History," 44.

201. Ibid.

202. Kant, "What Is Enlightenment?," 58.

203. Ibid., 54.

204. John Christian Laursen, *The Politics of Skepticism in the Ancients, Montaigne, Hume, and Kant* (Leiden: E. J. Brill, 1992), 210.

205. Kant, "Idea for a Universal History," 42–43.

206. Kant, "What Is Enlightenment?," 58.

207. Kant, *Anthropology*, (§43), 95.

208. Kant, *Pure Reason*, (A752/B780), 602.

209. Onora O'Neill, *Constructions of Reason: Explorations of Kant's Practical Philosophy* (Cambridge: Cambridge University Press, 1989), 56.

210. Kant, *Anthropology*, (§53), 117.

211. Kant, "Metaphysics of Morals," 171.

212. Kant, *Anthropology*, (§89), 249.

213. This point is made with greater detail, with particular respect to Kant's theory of action, in O'Neill, *Faces of Hunger: An Essay on Poverty, Justice and Development* (London: Allen & Unwin, 1986), 132.

214. Kant, *Lectures on Ethics*, trans. Louis Infield (Indianapolis and Cambridge: Hackett, 1963), 193–194.

Chapter Three

1. Bartelson, "The Trial of Judgment."

2. By "internationalism" I take Bartelson to be referring mostly to the general spirit evident in the work of those international relations scholars who support a peace-loving democracies hypothesis. However, he is also broadly addressing approaches to international relations that simply wish to promote inter-state and world politics that somehow manage to overcome the traditionally understood condition of anarchy or war between communities on the planet.

3. Here, Bartelson has in mind the sort of position put forward, for example, in Waltz, *Theory of International Politics* (Reading, MA.: Addison-Wesley, 1979).

4. Here, Bartelson has in mind the sort of position put forward, for example, in Bull, *The Anarchical Society*; Bull and Adam Watson, eds., *The Expansion of International Society* (Oxford: Oxford University Press, 1984); and Watson, *The Evolution of International Society* (London: Routledge, 1992).

5. Bartelson, "The Trial of Judgment," 260.

6. See Hannah Arendt, *Lectures on Kant's Political Philosophy*, ed. Ronald Beiner (Chicago: University of Chicago Press, 1982); Jean-François Lyotard, *The Differend: Phrases in Dispute*, trans. Georges Van Den Abbeele (Minneapolis: University of Minnesota Press, 1988); and Lyotard and J.-L. Thebaud, *Just Gaming*, trans. W. Godzich (Minneapolis: University of Minnesota Press, 1985).

7. Bartelson, "The Trial of Judgment," 276.

8. Kant recognizes the right of each rational person to have a say in the development of a universal human reason (Kant, *Pure Reason* [A752/B780], 602). This is made most pointedly evident in his simultaneous com-

mitments to both the essential equality of all rational human beings and to right as the foundation of moral political theory and action. In his Definitive Articles of "Perpetual Peace," for example, Kant clearly weds his analysis to the notion that the inevitable international politics he anticipates must be founded in a primary respect for the equal freedom of individual human beings and their equal mutual claims to the entire earth's surface as a final communal space (Kant, "Perpetual Peace," 99–106). In addition, just as he understands the moral state to be founded on a rule in which the respective wills of each person within their communal relations may be reconciled in accordance with a universal law of freedom (Kant, "Metaphysics of Morals," 132–133), Kant universalizes this notion on a cosmopolitan level. He demands that the will toward perpetual peace be developed in constant recognition of the inescapable relations Kant understands that all humans at all points of the planet ultimately have with one another (Kant, "Metaphysics of Morals, 172–173).

9. Kant, "Perpetual Peace," 129.

10. Kant, "Idea For a Universal History," 45–46.

11. Kant, "Perpetual Peace," 113–114.

12. Ibid., 130.

13. This spirit is most succinctly expressed by in Kant, "What Is Enlightenment?," 59–60.

14. Arendt, *Lectures on Kant's Political Philosophy*, 7.

15. Riley, "Hannah Arendt on Kant, Truth and Politics," in *Essays on Kant's Political Philosophy*, ed. Howard Williams, 305–332.

16. Ibid., p. 305.

17. Riley, *Kant's Political Philosophy*, 98.

18. Rosen, *Kant's Theory of Justice*.

19. Kant, *Pure Reason* (B141), 159.

20. Ibid. (A69/B94), 105–106.

21. Kant, *Judgment* (§IV), 15.

22. Ibid. (§II), 12.

23. Ibid.

24. Kant, *Pure Reason* (A533/B561), 464.

25. Ibid. (A556/B584), 478.

26. Ibid. (A533/B561), 464–465.

27. Ibid. (A534/B562), 465.

28. Ibid. (A643/B671), 532–533.

29. Bartelson, "The Trial of Judgment," 270.

30. Kant, *Judgment* (§IV), 15.

31. Ibid. (§69), 232.

32. Ibid. (§IV), 15–16.

33. Ibid., 16.

34. Bartelson, "The Trial of Judgment," 270–272.

35. Kant, *Judgement* (§IV), 17.

36. Kant, *Practical Reason*, 44.

37. Kant, *Judgment* (§82), 276.

38. Ibid., 276–277.

39. Ibid., 278–279.

40. Ibid. (§83), 279.

41. Ibid. (§84), 286.

42. Ibid. (§83), 279.

43. Kant, *Pure Reason* (A316/B373), 312.

44. Ibid. (A800/B828), 632.

45. Kant, *Judgment* (§83), 280.

46. Kant, *Pure Reason* (A813/B841), 640–641; and Kant, "On the Common Saying," 64–68.

47. Kant, *Judgment* (§83), 279.

48. Ibid., 281.

49. Ibid., 282.

50. Hutchings, "The Possibility of Judgement: Moralizing and Theorizing in International Relations," *Review of International Studies* 18 (1992): 51–62.

51. Bartelson, "The Trial of Judgment," 270–271.

52. Kant, *Judgment* (§20–21), 74–76.

53. Arendt, *Lectures on Kant's Political Philosophy*, 40.

54. Kant, *Judgment* (§40), 136.

55. Arendt, *Lectures on Kant's Political Philosophy*, 43.

56. Kant, *Pure Reason* (A260/B316), 276.

57. Kant, *Judgment* (§72), 236–237.

58. Kant, "Metaphysics of Morals," 137; and Kant, "Perpetual Peace," 106.

59. Kant, *Pure Reason* (A418/B446, A507/B535), 392, 449.

60. Ibid., (A495/B523–A496/B524), 442.

61. Ibid., (A507/B535), 449.

62. Ibid., (A504/B532–A506/B534), 447–448.

63. Kant, "Metaphysics of Morals," 172.

64. It is important to note here that, for Kant, "the world" is more properly referred to as "nature" when viewed in its dynamic state. Kant, *Pure Reason*, (A418/B446), 392.

65. Like other Enlightenment writers, Kant tends to contrast what he sees as the rationality of European cultures with what he projects as a barbaric innocence in the people of non-European races. And he is more than willing to use this alleged difference to make his arguments about the connection between rationality and civil culture. For example, he writes:

> Living carelessly (without foresight or care) does not give much credit to a man's understanding; it is like the Carib who sells his sleeping-mat in the morning, and in the evening is perplexed because he does not know where he will sleep during the night .(Kant, *Anthropology* [§35], 78)

Kant does not necessarily see anything wrong with the "careless" life he exemplifies in the non-European. His point is merely that not much is going to come from it, except perhaps an ignorant joy. And the suggestion then is that the Carib will ultimately be better off once he is admitted into the kind of republican society and culture Kant sees as the necessary goal of all societies.

66. Kant, "Metaphysics of Morals," 172–173.

67. Ibid., 173.

68. Ibid.

69. Ibid., 173–175.

70. Kant, *Pure Reason*, (A483/B511), 434–435.

71. Ibid. (A505/B533, A522/B550–A523/B551), 448, 458.

72. Kant, *Judgment* (§91), 319.

73. Kant, *Pure Reason* (A775/B803), 616.

74. Ibid. (A759/B787), 606.

75. I am here referring to the distinction Kant makes between mathematics and philosophy. In his introduction to *Pure Reason* Kant takes the position that mathematics is an area of human knowledge than can progress independent of experience (Kant, *Pure Reason*, [A4/B8], 46–47). He goes on to explain that all mathematical propositions are a priori synthetic, (Ibid., [B14–15], 52). In light of this position, I am arguing that Kant proposes to view the empirical limits of human life as inscribed within a specifically mathematical determination, prior to what experience may avail.

76. Ibid. (A759/B787), 606.

77. Ibid. (B14), 52.

78. Ibid. (B40), 70.

79. Charles Parsons, "Kant's Philosophy of Arithmetic," in *Kant's Philosophy of Mathematics: Modern Essays*, ed. Carl J. Posy (Dordrecht: Luwer Academic Publishers, 1992), 49.

80. Kant, *Pure Reason* (A87/B120), 122.

81. Ibid., (A163/B204), 199.

82. Béatrice Longuenesse, *Kant and the Capacity to Judge: Sensibility and Discursivity in the Transcendental Analytic of the Critique of Pure Reason*, trans. Charles T. Wolfe (Princeton: Princeton University Press, 1998), 274–275.

83. Rudolf A. Makkreel, *Imagination and Interpretation in Kant: The Hermeneutical Import of the Critique of Judgment* (Chicago and London: The University of Chicago Press, 1990), 63.

84. Kant's commitment to geometrical principles are, without doubt, quite genuine. However, it is also of biographical interest, in this regard, to note the fact that Kant himself never traveled much farther than a few kilometers beyond his native home-city of Königsberg in East Prussia (now Kalingrad). From this narrow point on the globe, Kant dared to think the conditions of the entire species of human beings.

85. Guyer, *Kant and the Claims of Knowledge*, 361–362.

86. Kant, "Appendix. A Translation of the Introduction to Kant's 'Physische Geographie,'" trans. J. A. May, in May, *Kant's Concept of Geography and Its relation to Recent Geographical Thought* (Toronto: University of Toronto Press, 1970), 255–264.

87. Ibid., 256.

88. Kant, *Pure Reason* (A760/B788), 606.

89. Ibid. (A758/B786), 605.

90. May, *Kant's Concept of Geography*, 132–133.

91. Kant, *Education*, trans. Annette Churton (Ann Arbor: University of Michigan Press, 1960), 78–79.

92. Ibid., 77–79.

93. Kant, "Physische Geographie," 257–258.

94. Kant, *Anthropology*, 5.

95. Ibid., 4–5.

96. Kant, *Pure Reason* (A48/B65), 86.

97. Kant, "Physische Geographie," 257.

98. Ibid.

99. Ibid., 261–262.

100. Kant, *Pure Reason* (A760/B788), 606–607.

101. Ibid. (A762/B790), 607–608.

102. Ibid., 608.

103. Ibid. (A761/B789), 607.

104. Arendt, *Lectures on Kant's Political Philosophy*, 43.

105. The relationship between judgments of taste and Kant's concern for politics is discussed with some thoroughness in Beiner, *Political Judgment* (Chicago: The University of Chicago Press, 1983); and Booth, *Interpreting the World: Kant's Philosophy of History and Politics*.

106. Kant, *Judgment* (§1), 38.

107. Howard Caygill, *A Kant Dictionary* (Oxford and Cambridge, Mass.: Blackwell Publishers, 1995), 321.

108. Kant, *Judgment* (§VI), 23.

109. Ibid., 24.

110. Ibid.

111. Kant, *Pure Reason* (B161), 171.

112. Kant, *Judgment* (§2), 38.

113. Ibid. (§3), 39.

114. Ibid. (§5), 43.

115. Ibid. (§7), 46–48.

116. Ibid. (§29), 107.

117. Ibid. (§41), 138–140.

118. Ibid. (§42), 140–145.

119. Ibid., 141.

120. Ibid., 143.

121. Ibid., 141–142.

122. Ibid., 142–143.

123. Ibid. (§18), 73–74.

124. This is an issue of particular motivation in Arendt's reading. See her *Lectures on Kant's Political Philosophy*, 66–77.

125. Kant, *Judgment* (§40), 135–136.

126. Ibid., 138.

127. It is interesting to note here that Kant deems taste as "a faculty of the social judgment of external objects within the imagination" (Kant, *Anthropology*, [§67], 43). He understands taste to always be a matter of judgments one would wish to express communally.

128. Kant, *Judgment* (§17), 73.

129. Ibid. (§18), 73n.

130. Ibid. (§59), 198.

131. Ibid., 199.

132. Ibid.

133. Makkreel, *Imagination and Interpretation in Kant*, 163.

134. Bernard Yack, "The Problem with Kantian Liberalism," in *Kant & Political Philosophy*, eds. Beiner and Booth, 224–225.

135. Guyer, *Kant and the Experience of Freedom*, 11–12.

136. Kant, *Pure Reason* (532/B560–A535/B563), 464–465.

137. Kant, *Practical Reason*, 3–4.

138. Kant, "Conjectures on the Beginning of Human History," 226.

139. Kant, *Anthropology* (§89), 216.

140. Ibid. (§48, §89), 105, 216–225.

141. Kant, *Pure Reason* (A578/B606), 491–492.

142. Ibid. (A644/B672), 533.

143. Ibid. (A662/B690–A663/B691), 544–545.

144. Ibid. (Aix, Bxxv), 8, 26–27.

145. Longuenesse, *Kant and the Capacity to Judge*, 320.

146. Kant, *Pure Reason*, (A712/B740–A738/B766), 576–592.

147. Caygill, "Violence, Civility and the Predicaments of Philosophy," in *The Political Subject of Violence*, eds. David Campbell and Michael Dillon (Manchester and New York: Manchester University Press, 1993), 56.

148. Kant, *Pure Reason* (A260/B316), 276.

149. Ibid.

150. Ibid. (A263/B319–A268/B324), 278–281.

151. Caygill, "Violence, civility and the predicaments of philosophy," 59.

152. The writings of Russell, Carnap, Schlick and Reichenbach are of particular importance here.

153. For an account of the central Euclidean tenets to which Kant adheres, see Stephen Barker, "Kant's View of Geometry: A Partial Defense," in *Kant's Philosophy of Mathematics*, ed. Posy, 224. For a summary of the standard complaints against Kant's position, see Michael Friedman, *Kant and the Exact Sciences* (Cambridge, Mass. and London: Harvard University Press, 1992), 55–56.

154. Caygill, *Art of Judgement* (Oxford and Cambridge, Mass.: Basil Blackwell, 1989), 370–371.

155. Gilles Deleuze, *Difference and Repetition*, trans. Paul Patton (London: The Athlone Press, 1994), 136.

156. Ibid., 136–137.

157. It is, unfortunately, quite difficult to definitively assess Deleuze's analysis on this point. His tendency throughout this text is to discuss Kant's philosophy at great detail while rarely ever providing direct references to Kant's texts.

158. William E. Connolly, "A Critique of Pure Politics," *Philosophy & Social Criticism* 23, no. 5 (1997): 1–26.

159. Gordon E. Michalson, Jr., *Fallen Freedom: Kant on Radical Evil and Moral Regeneration* (Cambridge: Cambridge University Press, 1990).

160. Ibid., 6.

161. Kant, *Religion*, 32.

162. Connolly, "A Critique of Pure Politics," 5.

163. Kant, *Religion*, 40–41.

164. Ibid., 42.

165. Michalson, *Fallen Freedom*, 102.

166. Ibid., 106.

167. Connolly, "A Critique of Pure Politics," 7.

168. Deleuze, *Kant's Critical Philosophy: The Doctrine of the Faculties*, trans. Hugh Tomlinson and Barbara Habberjam (Minneapolis: University of Minnesota Press, 1984), 36–37.

169. Michalson, *Fallen Freedom*, 28.

170. Connolly, "A Critique of Pure Politics," 10.

171. Guyer, *Kant and the Experience of Freedom*, 280–281.

172. Philip Kitcher, "Kant and the Foundations of Mathematics," in *Kant's Philosophy of Mathematics*, ed. Posy, 128.

173. This point is loosely derived from a point of analysis of Kant's theory of geometry in Anthony Winterbourne, *The Ideal and the Real: An Outline of Kant's Theory of Space, Time and Mathematical Construction* (Dordrecht: Kluwer Academic Publishers, 1988), 68.

174. Deleuze, *Difference and Repetition*, 161.

175. Ibid., 161–162.

176. Kant, *Pure Reason* (A74/B100–A76/B101), 109–110.

177. Deleuze, *Difference and Repetition*, 162.

178. Bartelson, "The Trial of Judgment," 276.

179. Makkreel, *Imagination and Interpretation in Kant*, 127–128.

180. Richard K. Ashley, "Living on Border Lines: Man, Poststructuralism, and War," in *International/Intertextual Relations*, eds. Der Derian and Shapiro, 259–321.

181. Ibid., 268.

182. Ibid.

183. Ibid., 269.

184. Ibid., 296–297,

185. Ibid., 311–312.

186. Hobbes, "Of Man," *Leviathan*, 81–222. See especially, chaps. VI, XIII, and XVI.

187. Ibid., 185–186.

188. Arendt, *Lectures on Kant's Political Philosophy*, 58–59.

189. Kant, "Metaphysics of Morals," 140, 161.

190. Shell, *The Embodiment of Reason*, 155.

191. For a direct glimpse at Kant's views on extraterrestrial life, see Kant, *Universal Natural History and Theory of the Heavens, or An Essay on the Constitution and Mechanical Origins of the Entire World Edifice treated according to Newtonian Principles*, trans. Stanley L. Jaki (Edinburgh: Scottish Academic Press, 1981); and Kant, *Judgment* (§91), 319.

192. Kant, *Pure Reason* (A735/B763), 591.

Chapter Four

1. The title for this chapter is largely inspired by a subsection, entitled "From international relations to world politics," in Walker's, *Inside / Outside: International Relations as Political Theory*, 99 and by Walker's "From International Relations to World Politics," in *The State in Transition: Reimagining Political Space*, ed. Joseph A. Camilleri, Anthony P. Jarvis, and Albert J. Paolini (Boulder and London: Lynne Rienner Publishers, 1995), 21–38. In both texts he proposes the need to push conceptual focus from that of international relations to one of world politics. In brief, Walker's point is that there is much that occurs within the domain of politics on a world-wide scale that simply may not be captured by a vision dominated by the politics of inter-state relations. Walker stresses the idea that a primary view to international relations itself serves greatly to limit one's ability to even perceive those political events and relations that exceed, cut through, or transcend the geopolitical organization of the world into sovereign territorial units. I delve into this issue with some greater detail further in this chapter. However, for the moment, I wish to simply indicate here that, while I greatly appreciate Walker's sentiments on this point, I also think that in the context of my study of the relationship between Kant's critical project and the study of international politics it is important to push Walker's move one step further. As I argue over the length of this chapter, to engage in a truly critical approach to international politics requires that one give up all pretense to even holding the world as an object of reflection. A critique of world politics

demands that one understand how it is that world politics is itself a product of political struggles and never separable from such.

2. Realists generally understand humans to always rationalize their respective actions and goals via selfish ends. Idealists believe that human agents will ultimately see the logic of peace via the rational character each shares.

3. Kant refers to skeptics as "a species of nomads, despising all settled modes of life (Kant, *Pure Reason* (Aix), 8." He views a commitment to skepticism as ultimately giving no possibility of peace, meaning, or knowledge. Yet, skepticism remains a central aspect of the mature critique Kant wishes to promote. And, depending on how skepticism is read, it is possible to argue that skepticism is really the heart of critique. For a broader discussion of this particular point, see Laursen, "Skepticism and Intellectual Freedom: The Philosophical Foundations of Kant's Politics of Publicity," in *The Politics of Skepticism in the Ancients, Montaigne, Hume, and Kant* (Leiden: E. J. Brill, 1992), 193–212. Also, for a discussion of how skepticism may be understood as central component of Kant's transcendental deduction, see Stephen Engstrom, "The Transcendental Deduction and Skepticism," *Journal of the History of Philosophy* 32, no. 3 (July 1994): 359–380.

4. This complex of points is exhibited in Jürgen Habermas, *Knowledge and Human Interests*, trans. Jeremy J. Shapiro (Boston: Beacon Press, 1968).

5. See, for example, Habermas, *Communication and the Evolution of Society*, trans. Thomas McCarthy (Boston: Beacon Press, 1979); and Habermas, *The Theory of Communicative Action*, trans. Thomas McCarthy (Boston: Beacon Press, 1984).

6. Habermas, "The Unity of Reason in the Diversity of Its Voices," trans. William Mark Hohengarten, in *What Is Enlightenment?: Eighteenth-Century Answers and Twentieth-Century Questions*, ed. James Schmidt (Berkeley: University of California Press, 1996), 400.

7. Arendt, *Lectures on Kant's Political Philosophy*, 72.

8. Hutchings provides a very helpful discussion on issues closely related to this point in Hutchings, *Kant, Critique and Politics*, 94–100.

9. Arendt, *Lectures on Kant's Political Philosophy*, 75.

10. Arendt revises the categorical imperative to read: "Always act on the maxim through which this original compact can be actualized into a general law," (Ibid). And on this point she is appealing to Kant's concept of the same in Kant *Judgment*, (§41).

11. A helpful discussion of the different responses offered respectively by Foucault and Habermas to Kant's concern for the question of enlightenment appears in Lewis Hinchman, "Autonomy, Individuality, and Self-Determination," in *What Is Enlightenment?*, ed. Schmidt, 488–516.

12. Foucault, "What Is Enlightenment?," in *The Foucault Reader*, ed. Paul Rabinow (New York: Pantheon Books, 1984), 39.

13. I am indebted to James Tully for identifying this point.

14. Foucault, "What Is Enlightenment?," 47–48.

15. Foucault, "What Is Critique?," in *What Is Enlightenment?*, ed. Schmidt, 386.

16. Ibid., 387.

17. Foucault, "What Is Enlightenment?," 42.

18. Ibid., 42–43.

19. Ibid., 45.

20. This is a point to be found throughout the writings by Foucault. With respect to the specific issue of Kant and enlightenment, though, see Ibid., 50.

21. Cutrofello, *Discipline and Critique*, 128.

22. Ibid., 78–83.

23. Cutrofello's point here is that Kant mistakenly reads the implications of his own formulation of the categorical imperative. Cutrofello writes:

> The problem is that Kant gives us no room to maneuver at this point. Having demonstrated that we cannot universalize a maxim that recommends indiscriminate lying, he concludes that we must adopt the maxim that recommends indiscriminate truth-telling. He has left himself no room to change his maxims as his moral experience broadens. However, is this the fault of the categorical imperative? Or is it Kant's fault for assuming that we can tell a priori which specific maxims must be universalized? Put otherwise, we could say that Kant errs by hastily affirming the "CI consistency" of a maxim simply on the basis of having demonstrated the "CI inconsistency" of its symmetrical opposite. That is, he has decided that we can will a world in which everyone always lies. Yet he gives us no reason to think that our choices must be limited to this either/or set of options.
>
> At issue here is a question of the narrowness and broadness of maxims. Assuming that we cannot universalize the broad maxim that sanctions indiscriminate lying, why are we then prohibited from considering whether a somewhat narrower maxim—one that sanctions lying under certain specific circumstances—might be CI-consistent? When is a maxim too narrowly constructed, and when is it too broadly constructed? (Ibid., 89–90)

24. Ibid., 91–95.

25. Ibid., 95–98.

26. Ibid., 85.

27. Ibid.

28. This view appears in Ashley, "Living on Border Lines." This is a rather loaded summary of Walker's position, though, drawing on several aspects of his analyses. Perhaps the most important point here is that he understands international relations as a discourse founded largely on the same sort of Euclidean and Newtonian assumptions that fuel Kant's primary commitments. Walker understands sovereignty to offer a spatial and temporal ordering principle, which allows, through such categories as identity/difference and inside/outside to provide the literal frame of references from which the sovereign voice, as discussed by Ashley, to produce an 'enlightened' knowledge. In this regard, I recommend looking at Walker, "The Territorial State and the Theme of Gulliver," *Inside / Outside*; and Walker, "Security, Sovereignty, and the Challenge of World Politics," *Alternatives: Social Transformation and Humane Governance* 15 (1990): 3–27.

29. Hutchings also offers commentary on the strong connection between Foucault's vision of Kantian enlightenment and the works of Ashley and Walker in Hutchings "The Dissident Work of Thought," *Kant, Critique and Politics*, 158–166. Her discussion is, however, focused most clearly on the joint writings of Ashley and Walker and much less so on their respective individual works.

30. It is interesting to note on this point that Walker prefers to "treat 'international relations' as an *object* of enquiry, as one constitutive aspect of contemporary world politics" (Walker, "Gender and Critique in the Theory of International Relations," in *Gendered States: Feminist (Re)Visions of International Relations Theory*, ed. V. Spike Peterson [Boulder and London: Lynne Rienner Publishers, 1992], 198n).

31. Ashley is quite explicit on this point, aligning himself with little qualification, to Foucault's refusal of the "blackmail" of the Enlightenment. See Ashley, "Geopolitics, supplementary, criticism: A reply to Professors Roy and Walker," *Alternatives: Social Transformation and Humane Governance* 13 (1988): 94; and Ashley, "The Geopolitics of Geopolitical Space: Toward a Critical Social Theory of International Politics," *Alternatives: Social Transformation and Humane Governance* 12 (1987): 409. Ashley also generally champions the enlightenment attitude Foucault derives from his reading of Kant as the appropriate interpretation of and response to modern structures and truths. See, for example Ashley, "Living on Border Lines," 260, 311; and Ashley, "Untying the Sovereign State: A Double Reading of the Anarchy Problematique," *Millennium: Journal of International Studies* 17, no. 2 (1988): 228.

While addressing Foucault and Kant far less directly by name on this issue, Walker repeatedly solicits support for Foucault's turn to the question of "How?" in his critical stand. A particularly telling example of this attitude may be found in Walker, *Inside / Outside*, 182.

32. Walker, *Inside / Outside*, 5.

33. Ashley, "Living on Border Lines," 311.

34. Here I have in mind Kant's fundamental desire to answer: "What can I know?," "What ought I to do?," and "What may I hope?," in Kant *Pure Reason*, (A805/B833), 635.

35. To be sure, Walker does not necessarily draw from Kant's work in any direct way on this point. In addition to Foucault, he finds more immediate encouragement in the writings of contemporary philosophers, such as Jacques Derrida and Julia Kristeva, who, themselves, address issues and problems raised by Kant.

36. Walker, *Inside / Outside*, p. 25.

37. Ibid., 88–92; and Walker, *One World, Many Worlds: Struggles for a Just World Peace* (Boulder: Lynne Rienner Publishers, 1988), 11–32.

38. Kant, *Pure Reason*, (A396/B454–A460/B488), 396–421.

39. Ibid., (A462/B490–A567/B595), 422–484.

40. Ashley, "The Geopolitics of Geopolitical Space," 403–434.

41. Ibid., 404.

42. Ibid., 403.

43. Ashley, "The achievements of post-structuralism," in *International Theory: Positivism and Beyond*, ed. Steve Smith, Ken Booth, and Marysia Zalewski (Cambridge: Cambridge University Press, 1996), 240–253.

44. Walker, "Realism, Change, and International Political Theory," *International Studies Quarterly* 31 (1987): 69–70.

45. Walker, "Social Movements/World Politics," *Millennium: Journal of International Studies* 23, no. 3 (1994): 696.

46. Walker, "Security, Sovereignty, and the Challenge of World Politics," *Alternatives: Social Transformation and Humane Governance* 15 (1990): 15.

47. Thus, Walker reads the phenomenon of international politics as, for example: a conflict between stasis and change or being and becoming, where stasis and being are determined as the condition of peace and stability alleged to be found within sovereign states and where change or becoming are representative of the contingency between states; a distinction between economics and the relations between states, where the former is viewed as a

'lower' form of the international to the privileged status of the latter; a separation between identity and difference, where the terms provide for an "us" and a "them"; a delineation between public and private, where the paradoxical association between "universalist aspirations" and "particularist practice" haunts democratic theory and practice; an opposition between ethics and international relations is struck, where norms are viewed as belonging to a realm different in kind from what in 'reality' happens in the world; and representations of presence in contrast to absence, where the definite outline of a sovereign state is given substance inside through the simultaneous demarcation of a nonpolitical but 'natural' terrain outside. See Walker, "Realism, Change, and International Political Theory," 67, 69, 83; Walker, "On the Spatiotemporal Conditions of Democratic Practice," *Alternatives: Social Transformation and Humane Governance* 16 (1991): 248; Walker, "Ethics, Modernity, Community," *Inside / Outside*, 50–80; and Walker, "International Relations and the Concept of the Political," in *International Theory Today*, Ken Booth and Steve Smith (Cambridge: Polity Press, 1995), 308–309.

48. This is indeed the most pervasive conclusion upon which the majority of Walker's work rests. The most sustained exposition of this position is to be found throughout Walker, *Inside / Outside*.

49. Walker discusses at some length in Walker "Security, Sovereignty, and the Challenge of World Politics," how it is that he understands the presupposition of sovereignty to elegantly reconcile the conflict between such things as community and anarchy or universality and particularity. See also, for example, Walker, "On the Spatiotemporal Conditions of Democratic Peace," 255; and Walker, "State Sovereignty and the Articulation of Political Space/ Time."

50. Ashley, "Untying the Sovereign State," 232–233.

51. Ibid., 242, 249–250.

52. Walker, "Security, Sovereignty, and the Challenge of World Politics," 13.

53. Ashley, "Living on Border Lines."

54. Ashley, "The Geopolitics of Geopolitical Space," 406.

55. Walker, *Inside / Outside*, 176.

56. In general, Walker views the principle of state sovereignty to function as a fixing limit to time and space. For a more recent summation of his views on this accord see Walker, "International Relations and the Concept of the Political." This is also a stand that Ashley and Walker take together in Ashley and Walker, "Reading Dissidence/Writing the Discipline: Crisis in the Question of Sovereignty in International Studies," *International Studies Quarterly* 34 (1990): 387.

57. Ashley and Walker, "Speaking the Language of Exile: Dissident Thought in International Studies," *International Studies Quarterly* 34: (1990): 261.

58. Ashley and Walker, "Reading Dissidence/Writing the Discipline," 376.

59. This effort is particularly evident in Walker, "Realism, Change, and International Political Theory," and Ashley, "Untying the Sovereign State."

60. Walker, *Inside / Outside*, 25.

61. The most dramatic example of this work is in Ashley's attempts to outline a genealogical approach to the study of geopolitics. See Ashley, "The Geopolitics of Geopolitical Space."

62. Ashley, "Untying the Sovereign State," 252–253.

63. See Walker, "From International Relations to World Politics."

64. Walker, *Inside / Outside*, 103.

65. Walker himself admits to the inherent danger and potential contradictions within an employment of "world politics" to overcome "international relations." Walker, "Gender and Critique in the Theory of International Relations," 181–182.

66. Walker, "Security, Sovereignty, and the Challenge of World Politics," 7.

67. Walker, *Inside / Outside*, 169.

68. Walker, "Social Movements/World Politics," 700.

69. Ibid., 699.

70. The extreme difficulty that Walker understands this critical position to place one in is strikingly articulated in the following passage:

> Whether in relation to culture, class or gender, to the demands of security or the possibilities of equity, a critique of modern theories of international relations, and thus of the principle of state sovereignty that has set the conditions under which those theories could be articulated, must lead to very difficult questions about principles and aspirations that presuppose a nice tidy world of Cartesian coordinates, at least as a regulative position. How is it possible to articulate a plausible account of identity, democracy, community, responsibility or security without assuming the presence of a territorial space, a sharp line between here and there, the celebratory teleologies of modern political life within the great universalising particular, the modern state? How is it possible to engage with aspirations for emancipation knowing that so many of those aspirations have

> merely affirmed a parochial particularity masquerading as universal? How is it possible to engage with others without relapsing into the rituals of identity and non-identity, affirmation and denial, the great battle between the righteous and the barbarian that is so deeply inscribed in the constitutive discourses of modern politics? (Walker, *Inside / Outside*, 182)

71. Ashley, "Untying the Sovereign State," 260.

72. Ashley and Walker, "Reading Dissidence/Writing the Discipline," 398.

73. Walker, *Inside / Outside*, 183.

74. Ashley and Walker, "Speaking the Language of Exile," 265.

75. Walker, "The *Prince* and the 'Pauper': Tradition, Modernity and Practice in the Theory of International Relations," in *International / Intertextual Relations*, ed. Der Derian and Shapiro, 25–48.

76. Walker, "On the Possibilities of World Order Discourse," *Alternatives: Social Transformation and Humane Governance* 19 (1994): 245.

77. Significant elements of this section and the one that follows it appear together in a substantially revised and much extended version within Franke, "Refusing an Ethical Approach to World Politics in Favour of Political Ethics," *European Journal of International Relations*, 6:3 (September 2000). Permission to draw from this material here was provided by Sage Publications Ltd.

78. A rich example of this point may be found in Walker, "On the Possibilities of World Order Discourse."

79. Campbell, "Political Excess and the Limits of Imagination," *Millennium: Journal of International Studies* 23, no. 2 (1994): 372–373; Campbell, "Political Prosaics, Transversal Politics, and the Anarchical World," in *Challenging Boundaries: Global Flows, Territorial Identities*, ed. Michael J. Shapiro and Hayward R. Alker (Minneapolis and London: University of Minnesota Press, 1996), 20; and Campbell, "The Politics of Radical Interdependence: A Rejoinder to Daniel Warner," *Millennium: Journal of International Studies* 25, no. 1 (1996): 140–141.

80. Campbell, *Writing Security: United States Foreign Policy and the Politics of Identity* (Minneapolis: University of Minnesota Press, 1992), 11.

81. For a deeper expression of Campbell's point in this specific instance, see Campbell, *Politics Without Principle: Sovereignty, Ethics, and the Politics of Identity* (Boulder: Lynne Rienner Publishers, 1992).

82. Ibid., 8; and Campbell, "Political Excess and the Limits of Imagination," *Millennium: Journal of International Studies* 23, no. 2 (1994): 365.

83. Dillon, *Politics of Security: Towards a Political Philosophy of Continental Thought* (London and New York: Routledge, 1996), 8; and Dillon, "Sovereignty and Governmentality: From the Problematics of the "New World Order" to the Ethical Problematic of the World Order," *Alternatives: Social Transformation and Humane Governance* 20 (1995): 351.

84. Campbell and Dillon, "The end of philosophy and the end of international relations," in *The Political Subject of Violence*, ed. Campbell and Dillon (Manchester and New York: Manchester University Press, 1993), 19.

85. Ibid., *passim*.

86. Jim George provides a helpful review of how the discipline of international relations is *ethically* organized on this point in George "Realist 'Ethics,' International Relations, and Post-modernism: Thinking Beyond the Egoism-Anarchy Thematic," *Millennium: Journal of International Studies* 24, no. 2 (1995): 195–223. In this article, George also offers a strong support for the work of Campbell, Dillon, and Warner as generally representative of a "postmodern" alternative within studies of international relations.

87. The most complex articulation of Campbell's point here is to be found in Campbell, *Writing Security*. See also, for example Campbell, *Politics Without Principle*, 24.

88. Campbell identifies this approach as a principle in Campbell, "The Deterritorialization of Responsibility," 477. As articulated there, however, this principle is associated more directly with issues of responsibility in international politics. The whole question of responsibility does indeed bring out the fuller aspect of the principle of critical approach Campbell proposes, and will be discussed further in this section.

It is the radical interdependence that, according to Campbell, disallows humans to avoid an ethical situation. Campbell, "The Politics of Radical Interdependence," 131.

89. Warner, *An Ethic of Responsibility in International Relations*.

90. The primary texts of Levinas from which Campbell works include Emmanuel Levinas, *The Levinas Reader*, ed. Sean Hand (Oxford: Basil Blackwell, 1989); Levinas, *Otherwise than Being or Beyond Essence*, trans. Alphonso Linguis (The Hague: Martinus Nijhoff Publishers, 1981); Levinas, *Totality and Infinity*, trans. Linguis (Pittsburgh: Duquesne University Press, 1969); and Levinas and Richard Kearney, "Dialogue with Emmanuel Levinas," in *Face to Face with Levinas*, ed. Richard A. Cohen (Albany: SUNY Press, 1986).

91. Campbell, "Ethical Engagement and the Practice of Foreign Policy," in Campbell, *Politics Without Principle*.

92. Campbell, "The Deterritorialization of Theory," 460–461.

93. Ibid., 460.

94. In short, understanding that no relation of responsibility occurs only in a totalised self/other dyad, Levinas also recognises the persistence of what he terms "the third person" in any relation. And it is this observing "neighbor," who forces the recognition that the other one encounters in a face-to-face relation, as in the case of oneself, is just one among many possible others. Hence, the question of justice arises, in which one must compare others against one another in an effort to anticipate what responsibilities are due whom. And Levinas' general guide on this point is that one is primarily responsible to the other who is closest, one "who is not necessarily kin, but who can be (Levinas, "Ethics and Politics," *The Levinas Reader*, 294.)"

95. Derrida's text which are most relevant to Campbell's discussion here include Jacques Derrida, "Afterword: Toward an Ethic of Discussion," in *Limited Inc.* (Evanston: Northwestern University Press, 1988); Derrida, "Force of Law: The 'Mystical Foundations of Authority,' " in *Deconstruction and the Possibility of Justice*, ed. Drucilla Cornell, Michel Rosenfeld, and David Gray Carlson (New York: Routledge, 1992); Derrida, *The Other Heading: Reflections on Today's Europe*, trans. Pascale-Anne Brault and Michael B. Nass (Bloomington: Indiana University Press, 1992); and Derrida and Kearney, "Dialogue with Jacques Derrida," in *Dialogues with Contemporary Continental Thinkers*, ed. Kearney.

96. Campbell, "The Deterritorialization of Responsibility," 468.

97. The state and its authority, for Derrida, could never be a self-founding entity. Its limits are made possible only in the differences struck between the political structure and its others. Moreover, the state's significance is always deferred to prior and future historical events (Ibid., 469–471*)*. In other words, Derridean deconstruction seeks to show that no political structure contains itself. Rather, its 'presence' is made imaginable only in references to those things which are absent. Hence, Derrida offers a way of understanding the state as always a question itself. For, if accepted, deconstruction may reveal that the institutions, nations, and borders fought for and over in such a place as the Balkans of recent years are based on ungrounded violence themselves (Ibid., p. 470).

98. Campbell takes to heart that the *undecidability* that deconstruction proports to introduce with respect to identities, locations, and relations keeps the ethical dimension of political decisions in view. His reasoning here, following Derrida, is that without facing the undecidability of one's situation with others the political and ethical aspects of that situation are removed. If one were only to make claim to a metric or canon of knowledge in the face of decisions, one's actions would amount more to the marshaling of policy. And, in this analysis, as with the state, policy cannot found itself. Rather, its certitude could arise only through a potential or actual contest of different views and impressions. (Campbell provides another good example of his reasoning

on these points in Campbell, "Violent Performances: Identity, Sovereignty, Responsibility," in *The Return of Culture and Identity in IR Theory*, ed. Yosef Lapid and Friedrich Kratochwil [Boulder and London: Lynne Rienner Publishers, 1996], 163–180.) Hence, to deploy policy in the ordering of communities and borders is to again perpetrate a violence on these issues. On the other hand, Campbell agrees with Derrida, to understand decisions as themselves always made in the condition of undecidability is to immediately bring to bear the responsibility one has to others at all times (Campbell, "The Deterritorialization of Responsibility," 471–477). Furthermore, it is to maintain a responsibility to deciding how one ought to respond to the various others called up within all relations to the other.

99. Campbell, "The Deterritorialization of Responsibility," 477–478; and Campbell, "The Politics of Radical Interdependence," 140–141.

But this is surely Campbell's point, that an approach to international politics must be difficult, no less so because he understands one's facing of the international as always political itself. He thus writes that:

> The critical challenge for an ethico-politics of responsibility is to foster a range of practices which constantly keep ethics and the interhuman in tension with morality and its effacement. Our limitless responsibility has to be in a relationship of perpetual agonism with the countless efforts to contain or diminish it. (Campbell, "The Politics of Radical Interdependence," 135)

And, following Ashley's call in particular, Campbell presses to overcome the antinomy set between anarchy and community, in favor of a sense of what he views as the *an-archical* character of human social life, where there are indeed principles along which people function with one another but no one principle that may in itself legitimately ground the commerce of all (Campbell, "Political Prosaics, Transversal Politics, and the Anarchical World"; and Campbell, *Politics Without Principle*, 91–92).

100. Warner, "Levinas, Buber and the Concept of Otherness in International Relations: A Reply to David Campbell," *Millennium: Journal of International Studies* 25, no. 1 (1996): 112–119.

101. Ibid., 123–125. His point in this respect is that acts of supplementation do not move to the heart of the concrete issues of ethics sufficiently but, rather, elevate the discussion to mere theory.

102. Campbell, "The Politics of Radical Interdependence," 130–135, 137–141.

103. Warner, "Levinas, Buber and the Concept of Otherness in International Relations," 125.

104. Warner himself simply introduces Buber's writing as an example of how responsibility *may* be thought of truly in terms of a response toward

other persons and things, as opposed to something directed back towards the individual (Warner, *An Ethic of Responsibility in International Relations*, 20). Campbell turns first to Levinas for the reason that he believes Levinas to provide the "best expression" of an-archical ethics (Campbell, *Politics Without Principle*, 92). Further, Campbell submits that "Levinas's thought is appealing for rethinking the question of responsibility, especially with respect to situations like the Balkan crisis, because it maintains that there is no circumstance under which we could declare that it was not our concern" (Campbell, "The Deterritorialization of Responsibility," 462). Together, Campbell and Dillon suggest that "with Levinas's rendering of ethics and subjectivity in mind, it is possible to overcome the allure of the idea of an ethics removed from subjectivity" (Campbell and Dillon, "The Political and the Ethical," in *The Political Subject of Violence*, ed. Campbell and Dillon, 171). Through his supportive discussion of recent turns to Levinas in rethinking international ethics, Jim George not only suggests that "some very basic themes drawn from Levinas's perspective might illustrate the nature and direction of this reframing enterprise" (George, "Realist 'Ethics,' International Relations, and Postmodernism," 209) but also goes so far as to claim that "via Levinas, . . . it becomes possible to begin to think outside of the egoism-anarchy thematic and reconstruct a notion of responsibility which insists that 'my freedom is anteceded by an obligation to the other,' and a general ethics which redefines subjectivity as 'heteronomous responsibility in contrast of autonomous freedom,' " (Ibid., 210–211). (The phrases in subquotation marks are quoted from Campbell, "The Deterritorialization of Responsibility," 463.) In addition, while claiming that Levinas' thought holds "importance in building a better IR," Molloy shows how a Levinasian framework allows a reading of one's relationship to one's others in terms of obligation (Patricia Molloy, "Face-to-Face with the Dead Man: Ethical Responsibility, State-Sanctioned Killing, and Empathetic Impossibility," *Alternatives: Social Transformation and Humane Governance* 22, no. 4 [1997]: 469).

105. Molloy, "Face-to-Face with the Dead Man."

106. Campbell, "The Deterritorialization of Responsibility," 477.

107. Warner, "Levinas, Buber and the Concept of Otherness in International Relations," 126.

108. Campbell, "The Politics of Radical Interdependence," 140.

109. Campbell, "The Deterritorialization of Responsibility," 478.

110. Caygill, "Violence, Civility and the Predicaments of Philosophy," 59.

111. I am indebted to Siba N'Zatioula Grovogui for drawing this connection.

112. Kant is careful here, however, to limit this right to resort only. He suggests that any rights to be treated as a guest in foreign lands does not

follow naturally. Claiming rights to friendly treatment outside of one's own state would need to be grounded in subsequent social agreements (Kant, "Perpetual Peace," 105–106).

113. Ibid., 106.

114. Campbell, *Politics Without Principle*, 99.

Bibliography

Allison, Henry E. *Kant's Transcendental Idealism: An Interpretation and Defense*. New Haven and New York: Yale University Press, 1983.

———. *Kant's Theory of Freedom*. Cambridge: Cambridge University Press, 1990.

Anderson-Gold, Sharon. "Kant's Ethical Commonwealth: The Highest Good as a Social Goal." *International Philosophical Quarterly* 26, no. 1 (March 1986): 22–32.

Archibuigi, Daniele. "Models of International Organization in Perpetual Peace Projects." *Review of International Studies* 18 (1992): 295–317.

Arendt, Hannah. *Lectures on Kant's Political Philosophy*. Edited by Ronald Beiner. (Chicago: University of Chicago Press, 1982).

Armstrong, A. C. "Kant's Philosophy of Peace and War." *The Journal of Philosophy* 28, no. 8 (April 1931): 197–204.

Ashley, Richard K. "The Achievements of Post-Structuralism." In *International theory: positivism and beyond*, edited by Steve Smith, Ken Booth, and Marysia Zalewski, 240–253. Cambridge: Cambridge University Press, 1996.

———. "The Geopolitics of Geopolitical Space: Toward a Critical Social Theory of International Politics." *Alternatives: Social Transformation and Humane Governance* 12 (1987): 403–434.

———. "Geopolitics, Supplementary Criticism: A Reply to Professors Roy and Walker." *Alternatives: Social Transformation and Humane Governance* 13 (1988): 88–102.

———. "Living on Border Lines: Man, Poststructuralism, and War." In *International/Intertextual Relations: Postmodern Readings of World Politics*, edited by James Der Derian and Michael J. Shapiro, 259–321. Lexington, Mass.: Lexington Books, 1989.

———. "Untying the Sovereign State: A Double Reading of the Anarchy Problematique." *Millennium: Journal of International Studies* 17, no. 2 (1988): 227–262.

Ashley, Richard K. and R. B. J. Walker. "Reading Dissidence/Writing the Discipline: Crisis in the Question of Sovereignty in International Studies." *International Studies Quarterly* 34 (1990): 367–416.

———. "Speaking the Language of Exile: Dissident Thought in International Studies." *International Studies Quarterly* 34 (1990): 259–268.

Barker, Stephen. "Kant's View of Geometry: A Partial Defense." In *Kant's Philosophy of Mathematics: Modern Essays*, edited by Carl J. Posy, 221–243. Dordrecht: Kluwer Academic Publishers, 1992.

Bartelson, Jens. *A Genealogy of Sovereignty*. Cambridge: Cambridge University Press, 1995.

———. "The Trial of Judgment: A Note on Kant and the Paradoxes of Internationalism." *International Studies Quarterly* 39 (1995): 255–279.

Beiner, Ronald. *Political Judgment*. Chicago: University of Chicago Press, 1983.

Beiner, Ronald and William James Booth, eds. *Kant & Political Philosophy: The Contemporary Legacy*. New Haven and London: Yale University Press, 1993.

Beitz, Charles R. *Political Theory and International Relations*. Princeton: Princeton University Press, 1979.

Bohman, James and Matthias Lutz-Bachman, eds. *Perpetual Peace: Essays on Kant's Cosmopolitan Ideal*. Cambridge, Mass. and London: The MIT Press, 1997.

Booth, William James. *Interpreting the World: Kant's Philosophy of History and Politics*. Toronto: University of Toronto Press, 1986.

Brown, Chris. *International Relations Theory: New Normative Approaches*. New York: Columbia University Press, 1992.

Bueno de Mesquia, Bruce and David Lalman. *War and Reason*. New Haven: Yale University Press, 1992.

Bull, Hedley. *The Anarchical Society: A Study of Order in World Politics*. New York: Columbia University Press, 1977.

Campbell, David. "The Deterritorialization of Responsibility: Levinas, Derrida, and Ethics After the End of Philosophy." *Alternatives: Social Transformation and Humane Governance* 19 (1994): 455–484.

———. "Political Excess and the Limits of Imagination." *Millennium: Journal of International Studies* 23, no. 2 (1994): 365–375.

———. "Political Prosaics, Transversal Politics, and the Anarchical World." In *Challenging Boundaries: Global Flows, Territorial Identities*, edited by Michael J. Shapiro and Hayward R. Alker, 7–31. Minneapolis and London: University of Minnesota Press, 1996.

———. "The Politics of Radical Interdependence: A Rejoinder to Daniel Warner." *Millennium: Journal of International Studies* 25, no. 1 (1996): 129–141.

———. *Politics Without Principle: Sovereignty, Ethics, and The Narratives of the Gulf War*. Boulder: Lynne Rienner Publishers, 1993.

———. *Writing Security: United States Foreign Policy and the Politics of Identity*. Minneapolis: University of Minnesota Press, 1992.

Campbell, David and Michael Dillon. "The End of Philosophy and the End of International Relations." In *The Political Subject of Violence*, edited by David Campbell and Michael Dillon, 1–47. Manchester and New York: Manchester University Press, 1993.

———. "The Political and the Ethical." In *The Political Subject of Violence*, edited by David Campbell and Michael Dillon, 161–178. Manchester and New York: Manchester University Press, 1993.

Carr, Craig L. "Kant's Theory of Political Authority." *History of Political Thought* 10, no. 4 (Winter 1989): 710–731.

Carr, E. H. *The Twenty Years' Crisis, 1919–1939: An Introduction to the Study of International Relations*. New York: Harper and Row Publishers, 1964.

Carson, Thomas L. "*Perpetual Peace*: What Kant Should Have Said." *Social Theory and Practice* 14, no. 2 (Summer 1988): 173–214.

Cassirer, Ernst. *Kant's Life and Thought*. Translated by James Haden. New Haven: Yale University Press, 1981.

Caygill, Howard. *Art of Judgement*. Oxford and Cambridge, Mass.: Basil Blackwell, 1989.

———. *A Kant Dictionary*. Oxford and Cambridge, Mass.: Blackwell Publishers, 1995.

———. "Violence, Civility and the Predicaments of Philosophy." In *The political Subject of Violence*, edited by David Campbell and Michael

Dillon, 48–72. Manchester and New York: Manchester University Press, 1993.

Chadwick, Ruth E., ed. *Immanuel Kant, Critical Assessments: Volume III, Kant's Moral and Political Philosophy*. London: Routledge, 1992.

Clark, Ian. *Reform and Resistance in the International Order*. Cambridge: Cambridge University Press, 1980.

Connolly, William E. "A Critique of Pure Politics." *Philosophy & Social Criticism* 23, no. 5 (1997): 1–26.

Covell, Charles. *Kant, Liberalism and the Pursuit of Justice in the International Order*. Hamburg and Münster: LIT, 1994.

Crawford, Neta C. "A Security Regime Among Democracies: Cooperation Among Iroquois Nations." *International Organization* 48, no. 3 (Summer 1994): 345–385.

Cutrofello, Andrew. *Discipline and Critique: Kant, Poststructuralism and the Problem of Resistance*. Albany: State University of New York Press, 1994.

Delue, Steven M. "Kant's Politics as Expression of the Need for His Aesthetics." *Political Theory* 13, no. 3 (August 1985): 409–429.

Deleuze, Gilles. *Difference and Repetition*. Translated by Paul Patton. London: The Athlone Press, 1994.

———. *Kant's Critical Philosophy: The Doctrine of the Faculties*. Translated by Hugh Tomlinson and Barbara Habberjam. Minneapolis: University of Minnesota Press, 1984.

Dillon, Michael. *Politics of Security: Towards a Political Philosophy of Continental Thought*. London and New York: Routledge, 1996.

———. "Sovereignty and Governmentality: From the Problematics of the 'New World Order' to the Ethical Problematic of the World Order." *Alternatives: Social Transformation and Humane Governance* 20 (1995): 323–368.

Donaldson, Thomas. "Kant's Global Rationalism." In *Traditions of International Ethics*, edited by Terry Nardin and David R. Mapels, 136–157. Cambridge: Cambridge University Press, 1992.

Doyle, Michael W. "Kant, Liberal Legacies, and Foreign Affairs, Part 1." *Philosophy and Public Affairs* 12, no. 3 (Summer 1983): 205–235.

———. "Kant, Liberal Legacies, and Foreign Affairs, Part 2." *Philosophy and Public Affairs* 12, no. 4 (Fall 1983): 323–353.

———. "Liberalism and International Relations." In *Kant and Political Philosophy: The Contemporary Legacy*, edited by Ronald Beiner and William James Booth, 173–203. New Haven and London: Yale University Press, 1993.

———. "Liberalism and World Politics." *American Political Science Review* 80, no. 4 (December 1986): 1151–1169.

Elshtain, Jean Bethke. "Kant, Politics, Persons: The Implications of His Moral Philosophy." *Polity* 14, no. 2 (Winter 1981): 203–221.

Engstrom, Stephen. "The Transcendental Deduction and Skepticism." *Journal of the History of Philosophy* 32, no. 3 (July 1994): 359–380.

Fehér, Ferenc. "Practical Reason in the Revolution: Kant's Dialogue with the French Revolution." *Social Research* 56, no. 1 (Spring 1989): 161–185.

Foucault, Michel. "Kant on Enlightenment and Revolution." *Economy and Society* 15, no. 1 (February 1986): 88–96.

———. "What Is Critique?" In *What Is Enlightenment?: Eighteenth-Century Answers and Twentieth-Century Questions*, edited by James Schmidt, 382–398. Berkeley: University of California Press, 1996.

———. "What Is Enlightenment?" In *The Foucault Reader*, edited by Paul Rabinow, 32–50. New York: Pantheon Books, 1984.

Franke, Mark F. N. "Immanuel Kant and the (Im)Possibility of International Relations Theory." *Alternatives: Social Transformation and Humane Governance* 20, no. 3 (July–Sept. 1995): 279–322.

———. "Refusing and Ethical Approach to World Politics in Favour of Political Ethics." *European Journal of International Relations* 6, no. 3 (September 2000): 307–333.

Friedman, Michael. *Kant and the Exact Sciences*. Cambridge, Mass. and London: Harvard University Press, 1992.

Friedrich, Carl Joachim. *Inevitable Peace*. Cambridge, Mass.: Harvard University Press, 1948.

Fukuyama, Francis. *The End of History and the Last Man*. New York: Basic Books, 1992.

Gabriel, Jürg Martin. *Worldviews and Theories of International Relations*. New York: St. Martin's Press, 1994.

Gallie, W. B. "Kant's View of Reason in Politics." *Philosophy: The Journal of the Royal Institute of Philosophy* 54, no. 207 (January 1979): 19–33.

———. "Wanted: A Philosophy of International Relations." *Political Studies* 27, no. 3 (September 1979): 484–492.

———. *Philosophers of Peace and War: Clausewitz, Marx, Engles and Tolstoy*. Cambridge: Cambridge University Press, 1978.

George, Jim. "Realist 'Ethics,' International Relations, and Postmodernism: Thinking Beyond the Egoism-Anarchy Thematic." *Millennium: Journal of International Studies* 24, no. 2 (1995): 195–223.

Gerresheim, Eduard, ed. *Immanuel Kant 1724/1974: Kant as a Political Thinker*. Bonn and Bad Godesberge: Inter Nationes, 1974.

Guyer, Paul. *Kant and the Claims of Knowledge*. Cambridge: Cambridge University Press, 1987.

———. *Kant and the Claims of Taste*, 2nd ed. Cambridge: Cambridge University Press, 1997.

———. *Kant and the Experience of Freedom: Essays on Aesthetics and Morality*. Cambridge: Cambridge University Press, 1993.

Habermas, Jürgen. *Communication and the Evolution of Society*. Translated by Thomas McCarthy. Boston: Beacon Press, 1979.

———. *Knowledge and Human Interests*. Translated by Jeremy J. Shapiro. Boston: Beacon Press, 1968.

———. *The Theory of Communicative Action*. Translated by Thomas McCarthy. Boston: Beacon Press, 1984.

———. "The Unity of Reason in the Diversity of Its Voices." Translated by William Mark Hohengarten. In *What Is Enlightenment?: Eighteenth-Century Answers and Twentieth-Century Questions*, edited by James Schmidt, 399–425. Berkeley: University of California Press, 1996.

Henrich, Dieter. *Aesthetic Judgement and the Moral Image of the World*. Stanford, Calif.: Stanford University Press, 1992.

———. "On the Meaning of Rational Action in the State." In *Kant & Political Philosophy: The Contemporary Legacy*, edited by Ronald Beiner and William James Booth, 97–116. New Haven and London: Yale University Press, 1993.

Herz, John. *International Politics in the Atomic Age*. New York: Columbia University Press, 1959.

———. "The Territorial State Revisited, Reflections on the Future of the Nation-state." *Polity* 1, no. 1 (1968): 11–34.

Hinchman, Lewis. "Autonomy, Individuality, and Self-Determination." In *What Is Enlightenment?: Eighteenth-Century Answers and Twentieth-Century Questions*, edited by James Schmidt, 488–516. Berkeley: University of California Press, 1996.

Hinsley, F. H. *Power and Pursuit of Peace: Theory and Practice in the History of Relations Between States*. Cambridge: Cambridge University Press, 1963.

Hobbes, Thomas. *Leviathan*. Edited by C. B. Macpherson. London: Penguin Books, 1968.

Hoffmann, Stanley. "The Crisis of Liberal Internationalism." *Foreign Policy* 98 (Spring 1995): 159–177.

———. *Duties Beyond Borders: On the Limits and Possibilities of International Politics*. Syracuse, N.Y.: Syracuse University Press, 1981.

Howard, Dick. *The Politics of Critique*. Minneapolis: University of Minnesota Press, 1988.

Huntley, Wade L. "Kant's Third Image: Systemic Sources of the Liberal Peace." *International Studies Quarterly* 40, no. 1 (1996): 45–76.

Hurrell, Andrew. "Kant and the Kantian Paradigm in International Relations." *Review of International Studies* 16 (1990): 183–205.

Hutchings, Kimberly. *Kant, Critique and Politics*. London and New York: Routledge, 1996.

———. "The Possibility of Judgement: Moralizing and Theorizing in International relations." *Review of International Studies* 18 (1992): 51–62.

Jaspers, Karl. *Philosophy and the World*. Translated by E. B. Ashton. Chicago: Henry Regnery Company, 1963.

Kain, Philip J. "Kant's Political Theory and Philosophy of History." *Clio* 18, no. 4 (Summer 1989): 325–345.

Kant, Immanuel. "An Answer to the Question: 'What Is Enlightenment?'" In *Political Writings*, 2nd ed., translated by H. B. Nisbet and edited by Hans Reiss, 54–60. Cambridge: Cambridge University Press, 1991.

———. *Anthropology from a Pragmatic Point of View*. Translated by Victor Lyle Dowdell. Carbondale and Edwardsville: Southern Illinois University Press, 1978.

———. *Conflict of the Faculties*. Translated by Mary J. Gregor. Lincoln: University of Nebraska Press, 1979.

———. "Conjectures on the Beginning of Human History." In *Political Writings*, 2nd ed., translated by H. B. Nisbet and edited by Hans Reiss, 221–234. Cambridge: Cambridge University Press, 1991.

———. *Critique of Judgment*. Translated by J. H. Bernard. New York: Hafner Press, 1951.

———. *Critique of Practical Reason*, 3rd ed. Translated by Lewis White Beck. 3rd ed. New York: Macmillan, 1993.

———. *Critique of Pure Reason*. Translated by Norman Kemp Smith. London: Macmillan Education, 1929.

———. *Education*. Translated by Annette Churton. Ann Arbor: University of Michigan Press, 1960.

———. "Grounding for the Metaphysics of Morals." In *Ethical Philosophy*, translated by James W. Ellington. Indianapolis and Cambridge: Hackett Press, 1983.

———. "Idea for a Universal History with a Cosmopolitan Purpose." In *Political Writings*, 2nd ed., translated by H. B. Nisbet and edited by Hans Reiss, 41–53. Cambridge: Cambridge University Press, 1991.

———. *Lectures on Ethics*. Translated by Louis Infield. Indianapolis and Cambridge: Hackett Press, 1963.

———. "The Metaphysics of Morals." In *Political Writings*, 2nd ed., translated by H. B. Nisbet and edited by Hans Reiss, 131–175. Cambridge: Cambridge University Press, 1991.

———. "On the Common Saying: 'This May Be True in Theory, But It Does Not Apply in Practice." In *Political Writings*, 2nd ed., translated by H. B. Nisbet and edited by Hans Reiss, 61–92. Cambridge: Cambridge University Press, 1991.

———. *Opus Postumum*. Edited by Eckart Förster. Translated by Förster and Michael Rosen. Cambridge: Cambridge University Press, 1993.

———. "Perpetual Peace: A Philosophical Sketch." In *Political Writings*, 2nd ed., translated by H. B. Nisbet and edited by Hans Reiss, 93–130. Cambridge: Cambridge University Press, 1991.

———. *Religion Within the Limits of Reason Alone*. Translated by Theodore M. Greene and Hoyt H. Hudson. New York: Harper and Row Publishers, 1960.

———. "A Translation of the Introduction to Kant's 'Physische Geographie,' " translated by J. A. May. In *Kant's Concept of Geography and Its Relation to Recent Geographical Thought*, edited by J. A. May, 255–264. Toronto: University of Toronto Press, 1970.

———. *Universal Natural History and Theory of the Heavens, or An Essay on the Constitution and Mechanical Origins of the Entire World Edifice Treated according to Newtonian Principles*. Translated by Stanley L. Jaki. Edinburgh: Scottish Academic Press, 1981.

Kegley, Jr., Charles. "The Neo-Idealist Moment in Internationalist Studies? Realist Myths and New International Realities." *International Studies Quarterly* 37, no. 2 (June 1993) 131–146.

Kersting, Wolfgang. "Kant's Concept of the State." In *Essays on Kant's Political Philosophy*, edited by Howard Williams, 143–165. Chicago: University of Chicago Press, 1992.

Kitcher, Philip. "Kant and the Foundations of Mathematics." In *Kant's Philosophy of Mathematics: Modern Essays*, edited by Carl J. Posy, 109–131. Dordrecht: Kluwer Academic Publishers, 1992.

Knutsen, Torbjörn L. *A History of International Relations Theory: An Introduction*. Manchester and New York: Manchester University Press, 1992.

Kofman, Sarah. "The Economy of Respect: Kant and Respect for Women." Translated by Nicola Fisher. *Social Research: An International Quarterly of the Social Sciences* 49, no. 2 (Summer 1982): 383–404.

Korosec, Gorazd. "Hobbes and the Theory of the Social Contract as the Context for Kant's Political Philosophy." *Filozofski Vestnik* 13, no. 2 (1992): 97–113.

Laursen, John Christian. *The Politics of Skepticism in the Ancients, Montaigne, Hume, and Kant*. Leiden: E. J. Brill, 1992.

Layne, Christopher. "Kant or Cant: The Myth of Democratic Peace." *International Security* 19, no. 2 (Fall 1994): 5–49.

Levy, Jack. "The Causes of War: A Review of Theories of Evidence." In *Behavior, Society and Nuclear War*, Vol. 1, edited by Philip E. Tetlock et al., 209–333. Vol. 1 Oxford: Oxford University Press, 1989.

———. "Domestic Politics and War." *Journal of Interdisciplinary History* 18, no. 4 (Spring 1988): 653–673.

Linklater, Andrew. *Men and Citizens in the Theory of International Relations*, 2nd ed. London: Macmillan, 1990.

———. *The Transformation of Political Community: Ethical Foundations of the Post-Westphalian Era*. Columbia: University of South Carolina Press, 1998.

Longuenesse, Béatrice. *Kant and the Capacity to Judge: Sensibility and Discursivity in the Transcendental Analytic of the "Critique of Pure Reason."* Translated by Charles T. Wolfe. Princeton: Princeton University Press, 1998.

Lynch, Cecilia. "Kant, the Republican Peace, and Moral Guidance in International Law." *Ethics and International Affairs* 8 (1994): 39–58.

MacMillan, John. "A Kantian Protest Against the Peculiar Discourse of Inter-State Peace." *Millennium: Journal of International Studies* 24, no. 3 (1994): 549–562.

Makkreel, Rudolf A. *Imagination and Interpretation in Kant: The Hermeneutical Import of the "Critique of Judgment."* Chicago and London: The University of Chicago Press, 1990.

May, J. A. *Kant's Concept of Geography and Its Relation to Recent Geographical Thought*. Toronto: University of Toronto Press, 1970.

Mearsheimer, John J. "Back to the Future: Instability in Europe After the Cold War." *International Security* 15, no. 1 (Summer 1990): 5–57.

Melnick, Arthur. *Space, Time, and Thought in Kant*. Dordrecht: Kluwer Academic Publishers, 1989.

Mendus, Susan. "Kant: 'An Honest but Narrow-Minded Bourgeois'?" In *Essays on Kant's Political Philosophy*, edited by Howard Williams, 166–190. Chicago: University of Chicago Press, 1992.

Meyers, Diana T. "Kant's Liberal Alliance: Permanent Peace?" In *Political Realism and International Morality: Ethics in the Nuclear Age*, edited by Kenneth Kipnis and Diana T. Meyers, 212–219. Boulder and London: Westview Press, 1987.

Michalson, Gordon E. *Fallen Freedom: Kant on Radical Evil and Moral Regeneration*. Cambridge: Cambridge University Press, 1990.

Modelski, George. "Is World Politics Evolutionary Thinking?" *International Organization* 44, no. 1 (Winter 1990): 1–24.

Molloy, Patricia. "Face-to-Face with the Dead Man: Ethical Responsibility, State-Sanctioned Killing, and Empathetic Impossibility." *Alternatives: Social Transformation and Humane Governance* 22, no. 4 (1997): 467–492.

Moran, Clifton and Valerie Schwebach. "Take Two Democracies and Call Me in the Morning: A Prescription For Peace?" *International Interactions* 17, no. 4 (1992): 305–320.

Mueller, John. *Retreat From Doomsday: The Obsolescence of Major War*. New York: Basic Books, 1988.

Mulholland, Leslie A. "Kant on War and International Law." *Kant-Studien* 78, no. 1 (1987): 25–41.

Negretto, Gabriel L. "Kant and the Illusion of Collective Security." *Journal of International Affairs* 46, no. 2 (Winter 1993): 501–523.

O'Neill, Onora. *Constructions of Reason: Explorations of Kant's Practical Philosophy*. Cambridge: Cambridge University Press, 1989.

———. *Faces of Hunger: An Essay on Poverty, Justice and Development*. London: Allen and Unwin, 1986.

Onuf, Nicholas Greenwood. *The Republican Legacy in International Thought*. Cambridge: Cambridge University Press, 1998.

Oren, Ido. "The Subjectivity of the 'Democratic' Peace: Changing U.S. Perceptions of Imperial Germany." *International Security* 20, no. 2 (Fall 1995): 147–184.

Owen, John M. "How Liberalism Produces Democratic Peace," *International Security* 19, no. 2 (Fall 1994): 87–125.

Parkinson, F. *The Philosophy of International Relations: A Study in the History of Thought*. Beverly Hills and London: Sage Publications, 1977.

Parsons, Charles. "Kant's Philosophy of Arithmetic." In *Kant's Philosophy of Mathematics: Modern Essays*, edited by Carl J. Posey, 43–79. Dordrecht: Kluwer Academic Publishers, 1992.

Riley, Patrick. "The 'Elements' of Kant's Practical Philosophy: The *Groundwork* After 200 Years (1785–1985)." *Political Theory* 14, no. 4 (November 1986): 552–583.

———. "Hannah Arendt on Kant, Truth and Politics." In *Essays on Kant's Political Philosophy*, edited by Howard Williams, 305–323. Chicago: University of Chicago Press, 1992.

———. *Kant's Political Philosophy*. Totowa, New Jersey: Rowman and Littlefield, 1983.

Rosen, Allen D. *Kant's Theory of Justice*. Ithaca, New York: Cornell University Press, 1993.

Rousseau, Jean-Jacques. *The Basic Political Writings*. Edited and translated by Donald A. Cress. Indianapolis and Cambridge: Hackett Publishing Company, 1987.

Russett, Bruce. *Grasping Democratic Peace: Principles for a Post-Cold War World*. Princeton: Princeton University Press, 1993.

Russett, Bruce and William Antholis. "Do Democracies Fight Each Other? Evidence from the Peloponnesian War." *Journal of Peace Research* 29, no. 4 (November 1992): 415–434.

Saner, Hans. *Kant's Political Thought: Its Origins and Development*. Translated by E. B. Ashton. Chicago and London: The University of Chicago Press, 1973.

Schott, Robin May, ed. *Feminist Interpretations of Immanuel Kant*. University Park, PA.: The Pennsylvania State University Press, 1997.

Shell, Susan Meld. *The Embodiment of Reason: Kant on Spirit, Generation, and Community*. Chicago and London: The University of Chicago Press, 1996.

———. *The Rights of Reason: A Study of Kant's Philosophy and Politics*. Toronto: University of Toronto Press, 1980.

Sorell, Tom. "Self, Society and Kantian Impersonality." *The Monist* 74, no. 1 (January 1991): 30–42.

Sørensen, Georg. *Democracy and Democratization: Processes and Prospects in a Changing World*. Boulder, Colo.: Westview Press, 1993.

———. "Kant and Processes of Democratization: Consequences of Neorealist Thought." *Journal of Peace Research*, 29, no. 4 (1992): 397–414.

Spiro, David E. "The Insignificance of the Liberal Peace." *International Security* 19, no. 2 (Fall 1994): 50–81.

Starr, Harvey. "Democracy and War: Choice, Learning and Security Communities." *Journal of Peace Research* 29, no. 2 (May 1992): 207–213.

Tesón, Fernando R. "The Kantian Theory of International Law." *Columbia Law Review* 92, no. 1 (January 1992) 53–102.

Thompson, Kenneth W. *The Fathers of International Thought: The Legacy of Political Theory*. Baton Rouge: Louisiana State University Press, 1994.

Walker, R. B. J. "From International Relations to World Politics." In *The State in Transition: Reimagining Political Space*, edited by A Camilleri et al., 21–38. Boulder and London: Lynne Rienner Publishers, 1995.

———. "Gender and Critique in the Theory of International Relations." In V. Spike Peterson, ed., *Gendered States: Feminist (Re)Visions of International Relations Theory*, edited by V. Spike Peterson, 179–202. Boulder and London: Lynne Rienner Publishers, 1992.

———. *Inside/Outside: International Relations as Political Theory*. Cambridge: Cambridge University Press, 1993.

———. "International Relations and the Concept of the Political." In *International Theory Today*, edited by Ken Booth and Steve Smith, 306–327. Cambridge: Polity Press, 1995.

———. *One World, Many Worlds: Struggles for a Just World Peace*. Boulder: Lynne Rienner Publishers, 1988.

———. "On the Possibilities of World Order Discourse." *Alternatives: Social Transformation and Humane Governance* 19 (1994): 237–245.

———. "On the Spatiotemporal Conditions of Democratic Practice." *Alternatives: Social Transformation and Humane Governance* 15 (1991): 243–262.

———. "The *Prince* and the 'Pauper': Tradition, Modernity and Practice in the Theory of International Relations." In *International/Intertextual Relations: Postmodern Readings of World Politics*, edited by James Der Derian and Michael J. Shapiro, 25–48. Lexington, Mass.: Lexington Books, 1989.

———. "Realism, Change, and International Political Theory." *International Studies Quarterly* 31 (1987): 65–86.

———. "Security, Sovereignty, and the Challenge of World Politics." *Alternatives: Social Transformation and Humane Governance* 15 (1990): 3–27.

———. "Social Movements/World Politics." *Millennium: Journal of International Studies* 23, no. 3 (1994): 669–700.

Waltz, Kenneth N. "Kant, Liberalism, and War." *American Political Science Review* 56 (June 1962): 331--340.

———. *Man, the State and War: A Theoretical Analysis*. New York: Columbia University Press, 1954.

Warner, Daniel. *An Ethic of Responsibility in International Relations*. Boulder and London: Lynne Rienner Publishers, 1991.

———. "Levinas, Buber and the Concept of Otherness in International Relations: A Reply to David Campbell." *Millennium: Journal of International Studies* 25, no. 1 (1996): 111–128.

Weede, Erich. "Some Simple Calculations on Democracy and War Involvement." *Journal of Peace Research* 29, no. 4 (November 1992): 377–383.

Williams, Howard, ed. *Essays on Kant's Political Philosophy*. Chicago: University of Chicago Press, 1992.

———. *International Relations in Political Theory*. Milton Keynes and Philadelphia: Open University Press, 1992.

———. *Kant's Political Philosophy*. Oxford: Basil Blackwell, 1983.

Williams, Michael C. "Reason and Realpolitik: Kant's 'Critique of International Politics.'" *Canadian Journal of Political Science* 25, no. 1 (March 1992): 99–119.

Winterbourne, Anthony. *The Ideal and the Real: An Outline of Kant's Theory of Space, Time, and Mathematical Construction*. Dordrecht: Kluwer Academic Publishers, 1988.

Yack, Bernard. "The Problems with Kantian Liberalism." In Ronald Beiner and William James Booth, eds., *Kant & Political Philosophy: The Contemporary Legacy*, edited by Ronald Beiner and William James Booth, 224–244. New Haven and London: Yale University Press, 1993.

SUNY series in Global Politics
James N. Rosenau, Editor

List of Titles

American Patriotism in a Global Society—Betty Jean Craige

The Political Discourse of Anarchy: A Disciplinary History of International Relations—Brian C. Schmidt

From Pirates to Drug Lords: The Post–Cold War Caribbean Security Environment—Michael C. Desch, Jorge I. Dominguez, and Andres Serbin (eds.)

Collective Conflict Management and Changing World Politics—Joseph Lepgold and Thomas G. Weiss (eds.)

Zones of Peace in the Third World: South America and West Africa in Comparative Perspective—Arie M. Kacowicz

Private Authority and International Affairs—A. Claire Cutler, Virginia Haufler, and Tony Porter (eds.)

Harmonizing Europe: Nation-States within the Common Market—Francesco G. Duina

Economic Interdependence in Ukrainian-Russian Relations—Paul J. D'Anieri

Leapfrogging Development?: The Political Economy of Telecommunications Restructuring—J. P. Singh

States, Firms, and Power: Successful Sanctions in United States Foreign Policy—George E. Shambaugh

Approaches to Global Governance Theory—Martin Hewson and Timothy J. Sinclair (eds.)

After Authority: War, Peace, and Global Politics in the 21st Century—Ronnie D. Lipschutz

Pondering Postinternationalism: A Paradigm for the Twenty-First Century?—Heidi H. Hobbs (ed.)

Beyond Boundaries?: Disciplines, Paradigms, and Theoretical Integration in International Studies—Rudra Sil and Eileen M. Doherty (eds.)

Why Movements Matter: The West German Peace Movement and U. S. Arms Control Policy—Steve Breyman

International Relations—Still an American Social Science?: Toward Diversity in International Thought—Robert M. A. Crawford and Darryl S. L. Jarvis (eds.)

Which Lessons Matter? American Foreign Policy Decision Making in the Middle East, 1979–1987—Christopher Hemmer (ed.)

Hierarchy Amidst Anarchy: Transaction Costs and Institutional Choice—Katja Weber

Counter-Hegemony and Foreign Policy: The Dialectics of Marginalized and Global Forces in Jamaica—Randolph B. Persaud

Money and Power in Europe: The Political Economy of European Monetary Cooperation—Matthias Kaelberer

Index